"THE STORIES THAT COME OUT OF CRIMINAL COURT ARE UNFAILINGLY FASCINATING and Heilbroner tells scores of them. . . . His conclusions about why the system doesn't work . . . [are] important, and they're firmly buttressed by the evidence he gives." —*Newsweek*

DAVID HEILBRONER

ROUGH JUSTICE

"VIVID . . . AN ENORMOUSLY VALUABLE PORTRAIT . . . A chronicle of his personal transformation as well as a trip through what has become the courthouse of the absurd. . . . A comprehensive portrayal of court life, a fine primer on the way individual prosecutors make decisions, it is richly detailed. . . . Taken as a whole, the psychiatric interviews and records, the conversations with colleagues, witnesses, victims and cops, the off-the-record bench conferences with judges make *Rough Justice* sparkle."
—*The New York Times Book Review*

"ENGROSSING . . . A memorable and reflective portrayal, nicely leavened with humor, of one humane man's struggle with an overwhelming moral dilemma." —*Kirkus Reviews*

"Countless war stories, some illuminating, some tragic, and some out-and-out hilarious." —*San Diego Tribune*

QUANTITY SALES

Most Dell books are available at special quantity discounts when purchased in bulk by corporations, organizations, or groups. Special imprints, messages, and excerpts can be produced to meet your needs. For more information, write to: Dell Publishing, 666 Fifth Avenue, New York, NY 10103. Attention: Director, Diversified Sales.

Please specify how you intend to use the books (e.g., promotion, resale, etc.).

INDIVIDUAL SALES

Are there any Dell books you want but cannot find in your local stores? If so, you can order them directly from us. You can get any Dell book currently in print. For a complete up-to-date listing of our books and information on how to order, write to: Dell Readers Service, Box DR, 666 Fifth Avenue, New York, NY 10103.

David Heilbroner

ROUGH JUSTICE

A DELL BOOK

Published by
Dell Publishing
a division of
Bantam Doubleday Dell Publishing Group, Inc.
666 Fifth Avenue
New York, New York 10103

ISBN: 0-440-21030-5

Reprinted by arrangement with Pantheon Books, New York, New York

Printed in the United States of America

Published simultaneously in Canada

September 1991

10 9 8 7 6 5 4 3 2 1

RAD

Contents

Preface and Acknowledgments

Rough Justice is a work of nonfiction that began as a journal I kept sporadically during my three-year tenure in the Manhattan DA's office and was then reworked into its present form in the year following my departure. Since the book is both a portrait of the New York City criminal justice system and a personal account of my experience as a prosecutor, it contains a mixture of factual reporting and subjective impression.

In an effort to protect the privacy of the individuals mentioned, I have changed the names, physical descriptions, and identifying characteristics of all but a few celebrities (e.g., Robert M. Morgenthau and Andy Warhol). With the same end in mind, I have altered details of certain "signature crimes," as well as most of the crime-scene locations. All of the conversation and testimony took place in my presence and has been re-created from my own notes and recollections. Otherwise, every event recorded is true and based upon my own direct observation. If some incidents seem curious or bizarre, the reader can have the satisfaction of knowing that they are true.

Writing this book has been one of the most enjoyable traumas of my life. The trauma was entirely self-inflicted; the joy came in large part from the assistance, patience, and support of friends and family who helped at every stage. Joel Harrison, Ali Miller, Ray Gordon, Ellinor Mitchell, Joe Wilson, Jim Barondess, John Pfeiffer, Miriam Davidson, David Lasagna, Liz and Bernie Davis, my parents, and Judge Walter Jay Skinner are among those who read early drafts and offered useful criticism. Mark Avnet, Yvette Colon, Mark Shelley, and the members of Sea Studios provided shelter, peace, and quiet that made writing all the more pleasurable. Finally, Kate Davis lived with this project from its inception, and helped in every aspect. My deep thanks to them all.

These remarks would not be complete without further thanks to Irene Skolnick, David Rakoff, and my editor, Susan Rabiner, for their material contributions to the text, and to Akiko Takano for her hard work and goodwill.

To Kate,
the Honorable Walter Jay Skinner,
and all honest cops.

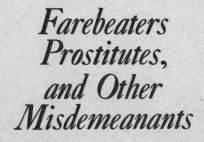

PART I

Farebeaters Prostitutes, and Other Misdemeanants

ONE

ECAB

Monday morning I arrived at 100 Centre Street, the massive gray New York City Criminal Justice Building, coffee and doughnut in one hand, Penal Code and ECAB manual under my arm. The South Entrance Hall lobby, with its plain granite walls and echoey green-gray floor, was still dark. Police barricades stood in a semicircle just inside the revolving doors at the entrance and behind the barricades a skinny man with thick glasses arranged newspapers at his concession stand. Near the center of the lobby a few prostitutes, looking the worse for wear after a night that began on the streets and ended in the pens, waited at a line of pay phones beside an abandoned information desk. White-shirted court officers hovered in the shadows; lawyers with their clients ambled out of night court. At this hour, a quarter to eight, the denizens of 100 Centre Street —judges, court officers, clerks, stenographers, police officers, prison guards, defense lawyers, and prosecutors— all stretched and yawned at the simultaneous close of one day and beginning of another.

To the far right of the entrance, a flight of stairs with a tarnished brass railing curved up to a second-floor walkway that led, among other places, to ECAB. As I walked across the lobby toward the stairs, a court officer asked, "DA?" I nodded; he waved me by. I climbed the staircase and headed down a dimly lit corridor, past a sign warning, DEFENSE LAWYERS NOT PERMITTED BEYOND THIS POINT.

It was mid-September. The DA's five-week training course had ended, my fingerprints and photographs were filed, security clearance had come through, and my law books stood lined up and unthumbed on the shelves of an office that I shared with three other assistant district attorneys. A few days ago, my first official assignment appeared in the monthly roster: like every prosecutor, I would begin my career drafting misdemeanor complaints in a place we called "eekab." It was the acronym for Early Case Assessment Bureau, the complaint room, the heart of the DA's office.

Just outside ECAB I was brought up short by about a dozen police officers in full uniform sleeping on the floor. Scattered along the corridor they looked like blue whales washed up on shore, and they were snoring loudly. I climbed over their blue legs and heavily booted feet and continued on into a vestibule lit by a couple of fluorescent bulbs and covered with plastic wood paneling. This was the officers' waiting room. More cops—some uniformed, with hats pulled over their eyes, others in plain clothes—slouched in orange seats affixed to the floor around the periphery. There were no windows, the doorways had no doors, and, mysteriously, a few footprints dusted the walls.

One officer mumbled, "Mornin', Counselor," as I walked through, still balancing my coffee and doughnut, on my way into the complaint room: a complex of rooms, or rather cubicles, arranged along an L-shaped hallway. Cubicles were occupied first come, first served, so I went looking for a vacant spot. To the right and left, ADAs with their neckties loosened yawned as they finished writing up the last cases of the midnight-to-eight shift. Coffee cups lay crumpled on the floor. Someone announced happily that the relief troops had arrived.

At the end of the hallway I found a free cubicle outfitted with the usual spartan DA accommodations: a few chairs, a beige metal desk, and a telephone. Like the other cubicles, it also looked generally abused. A pile of form complaints had spilled off the desk, and in a corner a folding lamp that looked like a crippled ostrich lay in a heap gathering dust. Sheets of corkboard had been glued to the dividers separating our "offices"—to help muffle the noise of half a dozen simultaneous interviews—but the cork had started to disintegrate and shed onto the floor.

When I sat down, I noticed that the desk was bolted to the floor and the phone bolted to the desk. I later learned that there had been a rash of thefts from ECAB in which bags, wallets, and even telephones had been taken, hence the security measures. Rumor had it that some of the officers themselves were responsible. After a few sips of coffee, I went to see the supervisor about picking up a case.

The supervisor's office was just another cubicle with a bolted-down desk facing into the hallway, but it had the distinction of being the closest to the police waiting area. I stood at the doorway and watched a woman in a plain gray suit question a police officer. In a clinical, almost bored manner she asked, "How many knife wounds did the victim receive?"

"At least three to the right arm," said the officer, "and maybe a couple to her side. There was so much blood it was hard to tell."

"Do you think she might go out of the picture?"

"Nah," the officer laughed. "They just stitched her up in the ER and I gave her a ride home."

Hearing this, the supervisor looked up at me over the officer's shoulder. "You one of the rookies?" she asked. I explained that this was my first day.

"Welcome to ECAB." She brightened a little. "Last night was really busy, as you can see from the cops in the hallway out there. A couple of drug sweeps on the Lower East Side, so you better get down to it." She started to turn back to the officer, then added, "Oh yeah, start with the 'in' cases first, then move on to the DATs."

Cases came to ECAB in the form of an officer's blue or

yellow arrest report stapled to a ragged manila envelope. On a table in a corner of the supervisor's office the reports lay stacked in three wire baskets labeled Felonies, Misdemeanors, and Desk Appearance Tickets. DATs are misdemeanor cases in which the defendant receives a summons to appear in court. "In" cases are misdemeanors in which defendants are brought downtown immediately upon arrest and locked in a holding cell.

I pulled an envelope off the top of the "in" misdemeanors and read the charges listed by the officer: Assault in the Third Degree and Harassment. The victim was Mrs. Dorothy Regis and the arresting officer Theodore Rostow of TPD, the transit police. A pink note stapled to the report read: "Priority case—complainant in Witness Aid Services Unit."

Since almost all complaints were drafted on the basis of an officer's testimony, crime victims rarely came to the complaint room. In my first case, however, I would meet the victim face-to-face. It seemed a good omen. Instinctively I wanted to begin by speaking with Mrs. Regis, but protocol required that I interview the officer first. Learning the officer's opinion of the case beforehand was supposed to help us speed "civilians" through the complaint room and prepare us for dealing with distraught victims.

Arrest report in hand, I went to the police waiting room and announced, "Officer Rostow." Hearing no response, I went to the hallway and called louder, "Officer Rostow!" One of the prostrate blue figures stirred.

"Rostow?" I asked.

"Yeah, here I come."

Officer Rostow pulled himself up and arranged the nightstick and memo book that stuck out from his utility belt. He had been sleeping on his gun.

"Come on, Officer," I urged, "we've got a complaint downstairs, but I have to talk to you first."

Back inside my cubicle, Rostow wiped his face on his sleeve and straightened his bulletproof vest. With all the police accoutrements attached to his uniform—mace, revolver, rounds of ammunition, speed loaders, back-up pistol, flashlight, nightstick, memo book—he barely fitted between the arms of the folding chair bolted to the floor opposite my desk.

I began the interview with an introduction recommended to us in a lecture. "Good morning, Officer. I'm an assistant district attorney and I want to speak to you about the arrest you made last night. Would you please tell me the facts of the assault?"

"Well, Counselor," he said, "it all started when this guy —the perp—cuts in front of the old lady."

"Excuse me, Officer," I interrupted, "the what?"

"The perp," he said.

"You mean the defendant . . . the perpetrator?"

"Yeah." Rostow leaned back in the chair and looked me up and down suspiciously. "Say, you must be one of the new rookies." I admitted that I was, feeling my inexperience nearly tattooed on my face. "You know, Counselor," he continued, "I always wanted to go to law school. Ever since I saw *The Paper Chase*. Do they really grill you like that in the classroom?"

"Sometimes they do," I said. "But it really isn't all that bad."

"You know, I was thinking of applying to law school and doing personal-injury work. After a few years here, you'll be going to one of those big-bucks Wall Street places, right?"

"I don't know, Officer," I said. "So far, I like it here. Anyway, Mrs. Regis is downstairs and I'm sure you both wouldn't mind getting out of here. So let's talk about the case."

"Don't hurry on my account, Mr. DA. I can use the overtime." I hoped he was kidding.

"Officer," I said a bit more sternly, "why don't you tell me about what happened?"

"Okay, Counselor. Like I was saying, this mope cuts in front of the complainant in the subway. Well, she gets pretty ticked at him, you know, yelling and so on. So, anyways, as she goes through the turnstile, the mope boots her one in the rear end. At that point I step in and ask what the commotion's about, you know, just trying to keep the peace and get everybody to calm down. To be honest, I didn't expect to make a collar, but Mrs. Regis insists that 'this man kicked me and I want to press charges!' " Rostow imitated a whining voice. "So, anyway, she came downtown with me, even though she didn't have to. I told her I would see the DA on my own but she said she wanted to speak to you in person."

"Now, Officer, let me get this straight. Did the defendant actually cut in front of the complainant? I mean, if he *did* cut in front of her, how could he kick her as she was going through the turnstile?"

"Well, Counselor, that's not too clear. The lady, Mrs. Regis, told me that the guy . . ."

"No, no, Officer, I just want to know what you personally observed."

"Counselor, like I said, it's not too clear. I only came over because I heard some kind of dispute going on near the turnstile. When I got there, the two was already going at each other."

"Wait a minute, Officer, you didn't actually see any of the assault take place?"

"To tell the truth, Counselor, no. I just went by what people were saying at the time. Let me tell you, there was getting to be a pretty good-sized crowd for that time of the morning."

"Oh," I said, grasping at a possible lead, "so there were witnesses?"

"Oh, yeah, plenty of 'em."

"Now that's more like it. Did you get some of their names?"

"Well, people were willing to talk, all right, but I didn't take names. I mean, between me and you," he leaned forward and lowered his voice, "this case is never going anywhere."

I sent Rostow to the Witness Aid Services Unit to bring

Mrs. Regis upstairs for an interview. Certainly, I thought, she could help straighten out the facts.

In a moment Rostow, still looking half asleep, returned with an elderly black woman. I rose, shook her hand, and asked her to please have a seat. She looked testily around my cubicle and then sat down in a huff.

Now that I was confronted with a victim—a civilian—the excitement of starting work quickened into nervousness. My entire prosecutorial experience consisted of a month-long lecture course in which the subject of interviewing was treated almost as an afterthought, yet here I sat in my cubicle, wearing a suit and tie like an expert, a "knowledgeable professional" cloaked with the power of the state. I hoped it would not be too obvious to Mrs. Regis that hers was my first case.

"Good morning, Mrs. Regis," I said, and repeated the stock opening for civilians. "I am an assistant district attorney. I'm here to interview you in order to decide what charges to bring against the man who kicked you. Would you please tell me what happened to you on the subway?"

"I already told the police officer all about what happened," she snapped. "What's the matter, don't you believe me? Of course you don't."

"Well, I'm sure it's annoying to have to tell the same story over and over, but I need to hear the facts from you so I can figure out how serious a crime was committed."

"Serious? Damn right it was serious. 'Course you don't care. I've been sitting downstairs since four o'clock this morning!"

I glanced for the first time at a tiny space in the arrest report labeled "Time of Occurrence." Rostow had written 2:30 A.M. Had Mrs. Regis really been waiting for more than four hours just to tell me she was kicked in the behind on the subway? The assault was not particularly serious, at least compared to the supervisor's stabbing case, but Mrs. Regis had a right to be annoyed at a four-hour wait. No one, apparently, had seen the "priority" notice.

"Ma'am," I said, "I want to apologize to you for the long

wait. I've heard it's been a very busy night, and you've been more than patient, but you're going to have to go over the facts one more time with me. I can promise you, though, that I'm the last person you'll have to tell the story to."

"Well, if I was the mayor and I got kicked in the subway, you think I'd have to wait all night long?" she scowled. "But, hell, you don't care nothin' about what happens to poor old black people."

Rostow started to fall asleep in the corner, his pistol resting on the arm of his chair and pointing into the corridor. I took a bite of doughnut, finished my coffee in one gulp, and pressed on.

"Now, Mrs. Regis," I tried a firmer tone, "I admit that if you were the mayor you'd probably not have to wait as long as you did, but I can tell you that it doesn't matter to me one way or the other whether you're black or white or rich or poor. Only, you've got to help me or there's nothing I can do for you. So would you please just tell me what happened to you on the subway last night?"

As she related a rather heated version of the crime, in which the defendant kicked her "as hard as he could" after they had both gone through the turnstile, I perused the arrest report further. By Rostow's estimation, the defendant stood six feet three inches tall and weighed over two hundred pounds. It seemed likely that had he really kicked this cranky old woman in earnest, she would have landed in the hospital, or at least received a bruise large enough to keep her limping for days. Instead, she looked all too energetic.

"How badly were you hurt, ma'am?" I interjected as she paused in describing the powerful kick dealt by "that man."

"I told you already, dammit, I was hurt bad. How'd you like someone to come up behind you and do that?" She kicked her foot against my desk with a loud clang. Rostow woke up for a moment.

"Did you go to the hospital or get any medical attention?" I asked.

" 'Course I didn't go to no hospital. Didn't this policeman even tell you that?" I was beginning to feel like kicking Mrs. Regis myself, but I also felt reasonably certain that her tale made out an Assault and a Harassment, so I drew the interview to a close. She was hardly the sweet-natured woman I had hoped to meet, but that made no difference: she was a crime victim, a member of the public whom I had come to the DA's office to protect.

Officer Rostow and Mrs. Regis waited quietly while I drafted a two-count complaint. Complaint-writing had been reduced by the DA's office to a foolproof method, one that ensured every charge met the strictures of the law. This effort, now handed down from year to year, culminated in the xeroxed, looseleaf ECAB manual—the rookie DA's survival kit. Turning to "Assault, 3rd Degree" and "Harassment," I copied the wording for the appropriate transgressions out of the manual, inserting the defendant's name where the manual said "defendant's name," and the time and place where it asked for "time and place," and then added a skeleton version of the crime itself.

I read the draft back to Mrs. Regis to ensure its accuracy. The formal language of the ECAB manual, however, somehow failed to capture the full flavor of the subway incident:

Deponent Mrs. Dorothy Regis of an address known to the District Attorney's Office, being duly sworn, deposes and says that on September 30, 1985, at approximately 2:30 A.M., at the downtown entrance to the IRT subway at 42nd Street, she observed defendant, with intent to cause physical injury to another, cause physical injury to deponent, to wit contusions to deponent's buttocks, by kicking deponent in the buttocks at the above-stated location.

Deponent further states that she observed defendant, with intent to harass, annoy and alarm deponent, kick deponent in the buttocks at the above-stated location.

"Who's this deponent?" she asked.

"Anyone who swears to a complaint is a deponent," I explained. "In this case, you are. Now, before I send this off to be typed, is there anything else you want to tell me?"

She was pleased, she said, about the word "contusions" and added that she hoped this criminal would get put away for a long time. I agreed that he should be punished but said that I doubted very much whether he would actually serve a prison sentence.

With these words making an obviously sour last impression, I shook Mrs. Regis's hand and asked her to wait in Witness Aid for the complaint to be typed. "After you sign it," I said, "you can go home." Escorted by Officer Rostow, she walked down the hall without the slightest trace of a limp and disappeared around the corner.

As I finished writing a summary of the case, I thought of a number of questions I had overlooked. What was Mrs. Regis doing in the subway at two-thirty in the morning, and why was she willing to go to the trouble of having a stranger arrested for what amounted to little more than a minor affront? Had she seen the man before? Was she a little crazy? I should have pressed her harder. And I never asked Rostow what the defendant himself had to say about the case. For all I knew, Mrs. Regis had started the whole thing.

More unsettling still was the dawning realization that in this and probably every other case, I was at the mercy of a police officer's judgment. In Mrs. Regis's assault there might have been a dozen witnesses at the scene, but because Rostow thought the case wasn't going anywhere I had only her version to go by. Without more evidence it seemed impossible to make any judicious, or at least informed, decision about guilt or innocence. Nevertheless, I was pleased to have treated Mrs. Regis politely and hoped she left ECAB knowing that someone in the halls of justice was willing to act on her complaint, even if she had been made to wait longer than the mayor would have.

But the hallway full of sleeping officers, each bringing an equally pressing matter, left no time for mulling things over. I went back to the supervisor's office and picked up another case. That was the last I saw of Officer Rostow and Mrs. Regis, and I never learned what became of the case.

I quickly discovered that ECAB operated like a legal assembly line. We moved cases in bulk, saving a close look at the facts for another prosecutor on another day. In our cubicles, we copied complaints out of the manual, copied the names and telephone numbers of police officers and witnesses into grids on our write-ups, called D.A. Data Sheets, and compressed the facts of each crime into barely more than a sketch. In training we were told that, for the purpose of an ECAB write-up, no case requires more than three sentences to summarize. The Watergate scandal would be reduced to: *Nixon campaign workers break into Watergate Hotel complex. Presidential aides involved. President attempts cover up upon learning of crime.* The routine was simple: Interview the cops, get the gist of the case on paper, copy a complaint out of the manual, and hurry on to the next arrest. Keep cases moving.

During my first few days I wrote up the most basic offenses. A large number were farebeats—not paying the subway fare, classified under the Penal Code as a Theft of Services. For these cases, we used a multiple-choice form complaint listing the four most common practices: manipulating or vaulting a turnstile, going through an exit gate, presenting a phony pass, and using a slug. After each interview, I copied the defendant's name at the top of the form and circled the appropriate modus operandi.

Apart from the "m.o.," there wasn't much to talk about: either the officer saw the defendant enter the subway without paying or he didn't. The only fact worth knowing was whether defendants had any money on them. If a kid with two hundred dollars in his pocket slipped through an exit gate, a judge would be more likely to impose a heavy fine or even a jail sentence than if the same kid had only two cents. At first, my summaries read: *Farebeat. Manipulating a turnstile. D. had $37 on him.* Eventually, they were reduced to: *Farebeat. $37.*

In addition to generating a steady stream of petty crimes, the subway was also a regular source of creative criminal activity. One day I picked up an arrest report charging Criminal Tampering and Criminal Mischief, along with the classic Theft of Services. I called the officer into my cubicle. He was a tough young foot patrolman from Harlem.

"Well, Counselor," he began, "this is really a bizarre one. You know about stuff 'n' suck?" I told him I'd missed that lecture at law school and asked him to tell me about it.

"Okay. Up in the three-four precinct we've got a lot of kids who are into token-sucking, and they're always hitting up the same fuckin' turnstiles. Every morning they're in the subway ten, maybe twenty, times and then they come back for more at night. And what they do is, they slip a folded piece of paper into the token slot so the token won't go through into the token box. After a passenger loses a token and walks away, the kids come back, suck it out of the slot, and sell it for a buck on the street."

"What do they use to suck the token out with?" I asked.

"What do you mean, Counselor? They put their mouth on the token slot and suck. That's why it's called stuff 'n' suck."

"So, Officer, what did the defendant actually do?"

"Okay, the way I got it was from the token booth clerk, a Mrs. Hillary Grimes," the officer said, checking his memo book. "She said that our boy Junior Eames here was sucking two or three tokens at about twenty-two hundred hours last night. So she calls the precinct and says, 'Hey, somebody's sucking tokens at 125th and Broadway, send an officer over.' Anyway, no one shows up, and, ten minutes later, Junior's screwing around with the turnstiles again and sucking a few more tokens. Again she calls the three-four and still nobody comes. Well, the kid does the same thing one more time and Mrs. Grimes's had it.

"You know about Krazy Glue, that it bonds skin instantly? Okay? Well, Mrs. Grimes takes the stuff and smears it all over the token slot. So, the next time little Junior comes along to suck a token, he gets bonded to the turnstile by his lips and teeth." The officer smirked.

"So, Officer," I asked, "how did you come on the scene?"

"Okay. The three-four got a call about some guy glued to the turnstile, and I was in the area on foot patrol, so I went over to investigate, figuring it was a lot of nonsense. When I got downstairs, though, there was Junior with his face stuck to the slot. Anyway, I've had trouble with Krazy Glue before, you know, people getting their skin bonded to stuff, and I knew the only way to get the perp free without ripping his mouth was to call EMS.

"They sent some people over within ten minutes who injected a saline solution between Junior's lips and the metal. Saline dissolves the glue. Anyway, the minute he got free, I arrested him. Okay, Counselor? So the first thing Junior says to me after I put the cuffs on him is, 'Listen, man, I wasn't sucking tokens.'"

Street kids had to be desperate, I thought, to spend hours sucking a few tokens, but according to the police department it was a common practice costing the city a small fortune each year. Still, Mrs. Grimes's "solution" seemed harsh. Maybe the officer should have arrested them both.

By the end of my first week in ECAB I had drafted more than a hundred complaints, interviewed as many police officers and spoken with half a dozen victims, though none as cranky as Mrs. Regis. In the morning, the waiting room was filled to capacity with snoring cops. At the end of the shift, I squeezed past a new band of officers bringing new arrests. The notion of a crime wave took on new, more immediate meaning.

There were shoplifters, farebeaters, and con men. Auto boosters breaking into cars on ill-lit side streets with slim-jims and slaphammers. Senegalese street vendors selling imitation Rolex watches on Fifth Avenue for twenty-five dollars. The vendors, who were arrested by the dozen for Fraudulent Accosting (a questionable charge since, as one judge aptly stated, anyone who thinks he can buy a real Rolex for a few bucks deserves whatever piece of junk he gets), spoke only Wolof, an African language, and were arraigned en masse by a special interpreter. There were battered wives, cuckolded husbands, common-law families, and pregnant teenagers. Runners and steerers who sold drugs under brand names. Hookers with fifty condoms in their purses and bankrolls in their crotches. Pickpocket teams paid by the week and recruited from the School of Fourteen Bells. Perps, mopes, skels, token-suckers, and trolls dealing in crack, coke, dust, smoke, black tar, hash, sense, smack, meth, acid, spikes, hypos, cricket lighters, glass pipes, shooting galleries, and crack houses. Kung-Fu stars, chuka sticks, numchucks, brass knuckles, handcuffs, sawed-off shotguns, Saturday-night specials, .38s, .45s, .357s, Uzis, bayonets, switchblades, butterfly knives, swords, and dirk knives. Imitation pistols and defendants posing as cops. An endless variety of strange and desperate criminal activity, the clamor and din of the streets.

TWO

An Unsentimental Education

Like many rookies, I came to the DA's office from the ivory tower. My father is a professor and a writer; my mother plays the piano and writes children's books. The only brush with crime I can remember happened when I was eight years old: a street kid swiped a dollar bill from my hand as I waited in line at a corner candy store. Although I was a little upset, I knew my parents would give me another dollar.

A few rookies starting work with me were from wealthy, famous families; others were barely managing to pay off student loans. But with the exception of one rookie I met who had been a police officer, the workings of the office were foreign to us all. We tumbled out of law school classrooms and libraries and landed in Criminal Court.

Enrique Sils was probably responsible for my joining the DA's office. I was clerking for a federal judge in Boston, the year after I graduated from law school. An undercover FBI agent had targeted Sils as a counterfeiter and arranged for a buy at two A.M. in the parking lot of a Kentucky Fried Chicken. During the transaction the agent revealed his identity; a shoot-out followed, and Sils tried to outrun the cops in his Jaguar. Sils in handcuffs standing before the judge, an agent playing a videotape of Sils's confession, the cops' cynical humor: the dark world of criminal law seemed far more alluring than the well-lit offices of corporate law firms, and I felt a vicarious charge brushing up against people who dared to cross the line of criminality. But as a lawyer, I had to choose between sides of the courtroom.

I respected criminal defense lawyers but never seriously considered becoming one. Friends at Legal Aid had told me war stories about helping child molesters and heroin sellers beat their cases. Someone has to stand up for those people's constitutional rights, I thought, but it doesn't have to be me.

From what I saw in federal court, prosecutors operated under an entirely different set of rules. They had the power to dismiss weak cases, lower the charges for deserving defendants, and lean on the truly heinous. Unlike defense lawyers, who must represent anyone who walks through the door, prosecutors can choose cases they believe are worth fighting for. I recognized that many people who commit crimes are themselves the victims of social injustices: racial discrimination, poverty, and inadequate educational and employment opportunities, to name only a few. But a gunpoint robber's unfortunate past makes no difference to a traumatized or wounded victim. Some sort of punishment must be meted out.

There remained one aspect of prosecuting, however, that I could not rationalize as easily. Law books are full of cases in which judges try to balance society's interests against a defendant's civil rights but in the end are frustrated by a police officer's illegal search, wanton brutalization of a defendant, or perjury. Having to protect police misconduct in order to win a case, no matter how serious the crime, seemed even more repugnant than defending sleazy drug dealers. I didn't want to rack up convictions like notches on a gun belt.

Growing up in Manhattan, I had seen the New York County District Attorney's Office—the Manhattan DA—cited as perhaps the most competent and honest state prosecutor's office in the country. The office had a reputation for giving its members wide leeway in exercising discretion, and faced with a deluge of crime there was reputed to be no time for pursuing dubious charges. It promised to be one of the few places where I could satisfy my curiosity about the shadowy dealings of police officers and criminals while doing what I considered the "right thing."

Not that getting in was a sure thing: two thousand people were vying for fifty slots. In response to my application I received a terse form letter asking that I "please be on time for my interview." I arrived at 100 Centre Street half an hour early.

For a few minutes, I stood outside and watched burnt-out junkies with swollen hands, police officers, and lawyers wander in and out of the south entryway. "Listen," said a bedraggled man to a shish-kebab vendor, "I just got out of Riker's. Can you help me out?" Compared to the trim federal courthouse in Boston, Manhattan Criminal Court, with its square, sooty façade, broken revolving doors, and tarnished brass railings, looked woebegone.

That morning I was interviewed by a panel of three senior assistant district attorneys. They were all clean-cut men in starched white shirts and they all had "just-the-facts-ma'am" demeanors. They glanced at my résumé—summers at large law firms, a federal clerkship, studies in environmental law—and asked whether I felt I could prosecute college students for drug sales, grill defendants at three A.M., and establish a rapport with drug-addict witnesses. The senior member of the panel, a man with a waxed mustache and drooping eyelids, asked why I wanted to handle shoplifting cases after working in the scholarly atmosphere of a judge's chambers. "You aren't going to be litigating big white-collar corruption cases, you know. You're going to be dealing with street crimes and street people." I explained my hope of using discretion to prosecute only the truly guilty, even for shoplifts.

The man with the drooping eyelids seemed a little nonplussed by my answer, and as I shook his hand to leave, I felt reasonably sure I would never see 100 Centre Street again. Three interviews later I found myself sitting across from a cigar-smoking Robert M. Morgenthau, the district attorney of New York County. After a few perfunctory questions, he said offhandedly, "I think you'll fit in here. That's my way of making you an offer."

August 26 began like most summer days in Manhattan: miserably hot and muggy, pollution hanging in the air. Undeterred by the weather or the prospect of waiting on an inferno of a subway platform, I put on my suit, elbowed into a train, and by nine A.M. arrived at One Hogan Place, ready to begin the DA's training course for its fledgling prosecutors.

During my interviews I had picked up some sense of the office's physical layout. With its libraries, rooms for three hundred ADAs, and specialized bureaus, the DA's office takes up the top four floors of One Hogan Place (itself a corner of 100 Centre Street) and three floors of neighboring 80 Centre Street. Throughout both buildings a maze of beige institutional hallways intersect and dead-end in thick metal doors. Art deco doorknobs—among the few decorative features breaking the monotony of the decor—bear the inscription NEW YORK COUNTY DISTRICT ATTORNEY. Occasional hand-stenciled signs taped to the doors announce: SEX CRIMES UNIT: AUTHORIZED PERSON-NEL ONLY; HOMICIDE UNIT; FRAUDS; or NO WITNESSES BEYOND THIS POINT.

As I walked into One Hogan Place that morning, a question from one of my interviews returned to me: "Are you sure you want to work for law enforcement?" The question now sounded a little ominous: I had some feeling for the building, but only the sketchiest idea of what exactly I would be doing.

The elevator to the DA's office was crowded with well-scrubbed, carefully dressed young men and women. We all got out on the ninth floor and proceeded to the grand jury room. Inside, rows of folding wooden seats, staggered as in an amphitheater, looked down over a desk and black-board. Sunlight poured through two large windows at the rear and streaked across the oak-paneled walls. This was the first part of the office I had seen that didn't have a harsh, institutional atmosphere. In a reassuring way, it resembled the Georgian college classrooms where I attended lectures on the English poets.

Waiting for our official introduction, I took a seat near the center aisle, talked with a few of my new colleagues, and watched the room fill up. Most members of the class appeared to be in their mid-twenties, and the great majority were white. Unlike in college or law school, there was no visible radical contingent, no one in jeans and Chairman Mao T-shirts. The men, who accounted for about half of the group, seemed especially conservatively groomed and dressed. They wore rep ties and had very short hair. I was one of the few with a beard. We were all full of nervous, gregarious talk. A few rookies, sitting together in the row behind me, had worked as summer interns in the office and were comparing opinions about "trial bureaus" and people called "bureau chiefs." A woman to my right had singlehandedly tried jury cases as a law student in legal defense clinics. Most everyone had taken the bar examination only two months ago—I had sat for the exam a year earlier—and they were all anxiously awaiting word on who had passed. The most popular subject of discussion, however, was how to afford an apartment on an ADA's salary.

School began as Harold Gardner, director of training, walked to a podium at the front of the room and welcomed us on behalf of the office and last year's rookies. In Levi's, an open-collared shirt, a bushy brown beard, and large, round eyeglasses, Gardner looked like a sixties intellectual more at home with Marx and Weber than with the Penal Code. He told us that after taking a year's leave of absence to play the guitar on a farm in Vermont, he had returned to the office as a legislative liaison and instructor. Gardner was hardly the tough-talking prosecutor I had envisioned as our mentor, but for that same reason he was a welcome surprise.

"This is the only law office in New York City," he said, "where you enter as a partner." Applause and cheers filled the room. "After taking your oath of office tomorrow afternoon, you will all be assistant district attorneys. Only Mr. Morgenthau is *The DA*. Everyone else is, more or less, an equal." More applause. "Now, I want to remind you, right from the start, that you have been hired to do justice, to exercise discretion—not just win cases and seek the maximum penalty.

"For example, what about a lady caught shoplifting meat from a supermarket to feed her family?" Every member of our class knew a variation on this theme from criminal law courses, but as Gardner continued it became clear that we were not being asked to philosophize about economic injustice or the need for a rule of law in civilized society: we were dealing with the practical. "Under the New York Criminal Procedure Law," he said, "a number of options are open to you. You have the power to dismiss the case, lower the charge, or seek a plea to the top count. Under these circumstances, of course, leniency should be shown."

Someone in the rear called out, "Hang her!"

"You could plea-bargain the case," Gardner moved on, unfazed, "and offer the defendant a small fine or even time served. A lot will depend on her rap sheet and her attitude in court. But you are going to have to learn to make these judgments, judgments that will determine whether a person goes to prison."

For two hours that morning Gardner gave us a tour through the Byzantine complexities of the Penal Code and the Criminal Procedure Law, books that constituted the mainstays of our profession, and he delved into legal niceties that reminded me all too vividly of bar review courses. We all took a few notes and shifted in our seats.

At the close of his lecture, Gardner returned to a subject of more immediate concern. "Very soon you will be working closely with police officers on a daily basis, and a common response of new ADAs is to start talking like cops and, worse, thinking about criminal cases like cops. Obviously, you will want to get along well with the police since in most cases they will be your principal witnesses, but you should try to keep a healthy mental distance. Your job is to do justice, not clean up the streets. And"—he paused —"you will wield an amount of power over people's lives entirely disproportionate to your age and experience. Don't let it go to your heads." Class broke for the morning.

For seven hours a day during the following weeks, we attended lectures and acted out courtroom scenes. Hardened detectives told us war stories and judges hypothesized ethical dilemmas. For evening study, we were assigned the entire New York Penal Code, Criminal Procedure Law, and ECAB manual, as well as volumes of case law. I dutifully read through the definitions of every crime in the Code, and promptly forgot most of them: there were seven different types of Disorderly Conduct, nine species of Loitering, endless subdivisions of the Robbery statute, and a number of crimes I had never heard of, like Jostling, Clipping a Dog's Ears Without Anesthetic, Fortune-Telling, and Uttering a Forged Instrument. The Criminal Procedure Law was an even more complex, and apparently random, agglomeration of deadlines, rules, and abstractions. The philosophy of the program seemed to be that we should encounter every aspect of criminal law at least once.

In addition to giving us a panoramic view of criminal law, the lectures also exposed us to a range of prosecutors throughout the office. Gardner's judicious approach hardly typified the prevailing attitude. In a lecture devoted to cross-examination, one senior prosecutor spoke with glee about how to grill a defendant on the witness stand and "really make him sweat." "Make the most out of having him admit every crime he ever committed," he said. Rubbing his hands, he added, "It works every time." He seemed to consider any sentence below the maximum tantamount to a loss and to take positive pride in the callousness that the job, in his opinion, required. At the end of his lecture he told a joke that I hoped revealed more about him than about prosecuting.

"A man has a heart attack and goes to the hospital. A heart surgeon examines the patient and announces that in order to survive he needs a new heart immediately. 'Fortunately,' says the doctor, 'two patients have just arrived and are willing to donate their hearts, so you actually have a choice of donors. One man is twenty-two years old and has been training to become an Olympic athlete. The other is a fifty-year-old prosecutor who drinks and smokes too much and almost never gets any exercise. Which will it be?' 'Well,' said the patient, 'I want the prosecutor's heart. He's probably never used it.' "

After a few weeks of classroom work we were given a break—a visit to a recently renovated part of 100 Centre Street used to hold prisoners currently on trial, better known as the Tombs. The cells had built-in radios, clean beds, and views of the Empire State Building. In a brightly lit common room were a Ping-Pong table and a large color television set. At the end of the tour, I asked our group leader if we could visit Riker's Island, a notoriously run-down facility where convicted defendants served their sentences. "Why on earth do you want to go there?" she asked. "It's depressing."

During the lecture series, I became friendly with a rookie named Jim Bronson. Jim was from a well-to-do Virginia family, and despite his genteel southern manner, he had a sharp wit that spared no one. We often sat together in the grand jury classroom and traded jokes about our lecturers. Jim nicknamed the academically inclined Harold Gardner "Noodles," while I referred to certain hardened ADAs as "career persecutors." Over lunch breaks, we left One Hogan Place and drank cheap red wine in Little Italy. It helped us sleep through the increasingly abstract afternoon law lectures in the overheated grand jury room. We had both hoped to get right into court, interview witnesses, meet cops, and argue points of law. Instead, we faced a month of study. We consoled ourselves with the thought that this would be the last opportunity to contemplate and debate in the safety of the classroom.

When training finally concluded, Gardner distributed sealed envelopes containing our permanent assignments. Jim, who had been a summer intern at the office, gave me the inside line. Most rookies went to general trial bureaus staffed by about forty ADAs, a deputy chief, and a chief. The bureaus—numbered 10, 20, 30, 40, 50, and 60 to correspond with courtroom numbers—accounted for the bulk of the office and handled every type of street crime from farebeat to homicide. A few rookies went to specialized bureaus—Appeals, Narcotics, Rackets, or Frauds— but these were rumored to be second-choice assignments. Appeals, though scholarly, was too far removed from trial courtrooms and flesh-and-blood witnesses. Narcotics cases tended to be too repetitive. And of the remaining two bureaus it was said simply that "Rackets is a fraud and Frauds is a racket."

Jim and I were both assigned to Trial Bureau 20, which he said was a stroke of luck. The bureau was located in the large, recently renovated 80 Centre Street offices and had carpeted hallways, frosted glass doors, and its own small law library. The room I shared with three other rookies, though equipped with the usual beat-up metal desks, filing cabinets, and telephones, had a large window that overlooked the courthouses in Foley Square. Conditions across the street were considerably more cramped and dark.

The real virtue of Bureau 20, however, lay in its relaxed internal procedures. Certain chiefs ran their bureaus with almost military rigidity. They called rookies at home to see if they were malingering and docked others half a day of vacation if they left before five. Our chief in 20 was

Mitchel Nelin, a remote but gentle man who welcomed us with a beer party and a low-key introduction. "Your time is your own," he said, "so long as you get the work done." As chief, Nelin devoted most of his time to senior ADAs handling felonies, but he nevertheless made certain that we were not drawn too quickly into the maelstrom that was 100 Centre Street. During our first week he gave us no assignments other than to tour the complaint room and arraignment court and to attend ongoing trials of note.

Of all the ADAs I met in Bureau 20, however, John Patton, our card-playing, chain-smoking deputy chief, made the deepest impression. With his blue-eyed good looks and jocular style, he came across more like a sports coach than a trial adviser. But as we all learned, Patton—with twenty years of trial experience and a ninety-percent win record—was a reliable source of sage advice. "I don't know what you're all so worried about," he said between drags on a cigarette at our first meeting. "For the first year nobody cares about what you do. You're only dealing with misdemeanors." It was a phrase I used to comfort myself in some of the more traumatic moments I would face, a sort of rookie's mantra.

Working under the direction of Nelin and Patton eased some of the load, but all the advantages in the world could not have made the job easy. By tradition, each incoming class of fifty rookies takes over the Sisyphean task of prosecuting the hundred thousand-plus misdemeanor arrests made every year in Manhattan, crimes for which defendants face no more than a thousand-dollar fine or one year in jail. The months ahead would also be spent rotating through the "institutional assignments": complaint room, arraignment court, and Criminal Court calendar.

Both the complaint room and the arraignment court had recently begun operating twenty-four hours a day, seven days a week—the direct result of a lawsuit brought by the Legal Aid Society charging that defendants frequently waited up to three days in the pens before seeing a judge. A federal judge found the situation constitutionally unacceptable and issued orders to the DA's office and the New York City Police Department to speed things up. Our class would be the first to have the honor of drafting complaints for shoplifting at four A.M. on Thanksgiving or arraigning junkies on Christmas Eve. In our "spare time" —about one week out of every month—we would manage our individual caseloads, soon to exceed a hundred and fifty apiece. For the foreseeable future we would be awash in petty crime. I began to understand why Harold Gardner had welcomed us on behalf of former rookies.

In all, eight rookies went to Bureau 20, and I shared an office with three: Arnold Weinberg, who came from Harvard Law School and had traveled in the Far East during the summer; Annette Holt, a woman who, in her fifties, left a career in publishing to go to law school; and Alex Barnette, a California woman whose enthusiasm for the job, even during some of the darkest moments we faced that year, seemed unbounded. Jim Bronson worked down the hall from me and shared an office with the others. Apart from Annette, I was, at twenty-eight, the oldest rookie in Bureau 20 and one of the few who were married.

Camaraderie and morale among our class in Bureau 20 ran high—in spite, or perhaps because, of the overwhelming workload. There were no partnerships or promotions to compete for and no ranking system to cause resentment. We were a team. Regrouping after hours at Forlini's, an Italian restaurant and bar decorated in plush red leather, we traded courtroom anecdotes and gloated about how lousy life must be for our law school classmates who were working eighty hours a week in corporate sweatshops.

Over a beer one evening I met Scott Pryor, a rookie from the midwest who shared an office down the hall with Jim. Scott said he was already worried about becoming too hardened by the job. He told me about a law school friend of his, one year ahead of us, who worked in the office. "Before he came here," Scott said, "the guy was practically a Marxist. He used to talk about private property as a

THREE

The Paper Trail

The first words I spoke in court on behalf of the DA's office were during a session of the almost terminally overburdened Criminal Court calendar, conducted in a room known as All-Purpose Court Part 2: "Your Honor, the People are filing a copy of a laboratory report with the Court and serving a copy on defense counsel." I handed our report to the clerk and a copy to the Legal Aid lawyer. "Two weeks for motions," said His Honor. The clerk called the next case. It was hardly an inspiring start to my career as a litigator, but I felt proud just to have spoken coherently under the judge's impatient stare while a stenographer etched my words into the permanent record.

We worked the calendar in pairs, and my first time out, in early October, I teamed up with my friend Jim Bronson, soon to distinguish himself as the star lawyer of our class. Jim and I arrived at the bureau early Monday morning and, over large cups of coffee, methodically stapled notes to each of 250 files: the day's caseload. Cases were heard in random order, and ADAs and Legal Aid lawyers had too many matters scheduled every day to be present on every one, so we all wrote brief explanatory messages to our representatives in court. The note system generated a good deal of delay and confusion, but it seemed the only way to move the heavy volume of cases through the system toward trial.

At nine-thirty Jim and I carried our files across the street to court. The scene outside AP-2 was a mass confusion of humanity reminiscent of Dickens. Snappily dressed attorneys from well-to-do law firms jostled in the dark, noisy hallways alongside threadbare solo practitioners awaiting court-appointed cases. Beleaguered Legal Aid lawyers stood amid circles of people who all seemed to be asking questions at once. Mothers carried crying babies, nervous young couples held hands. Jim and I pressed through the crowd and headed for the prosecution table.

The courtroom was full. A few families were scattered among the rows of wooden benches, but mostly the seats were occupied by defendants. They included a catalogue of lowlife: gamblers, pushers, exhibitionists, prostitutes, con artists, drunks who had refused to move along, pimps with long, pomaded curls and rakish black hats, token-suckers, pickpockets, and always a few lunatics. Among them sat felons awaiting indictment, people who drank too much before driving home, shoplifters, bodybuilders who got into fights, and even a few student protesters. These were the accused who either had been released on their own recognizance or could come up with enough money to make bail. The really heavy offenders and the down-and-out waited inside holding pens and spent their nights in the Riker's Island prison or the Tombs.

Across the room from the prosecution table, I noticed a group of Legal Aid lawyers preparing their own stacks of files. Defenders looked different from ADAs. They wore tweed jackets, blue jeans, and sneakers; one of the men had a pony tail that hung halfway down his back. Every male prosecutor I had seen came to work in a dark suit, starched shirt, and silk tie. Female ADAs, too, wore "power clothes." Though we were all lawyers just beginning our careers, we had apparently chosen sides: ADAs were the State, Legal Aid was Everyman, and each looked the part.

At a quarter to ten, from behind a door hidden in the rear of the courtroom, a black-robed judge emerged and walked briskly to the bench, flanked by court officers wearing gun belts. One of the officers stepped before the judge's bench and delivered the oyez-oyez in a thick Brooklyn accent: "All people having anything to do before this Honorable Court shall draw near, give their attention, and they shall be heard. Be seated and take all your conversations and other matter outside. Criminal Court is now open for business." The audience quieted down.

Despite their designation as All-Purpose, the AP Parts handled neither hearings nor trials: they dealt strictly in paper, the interim phase between arraignment and trial. All day motions, responses, affidavits, lab reports, certificates of grand jury action, and other arcane documents shuttle back and forth, from defense to prosecution, prosecution to defense, while defendants stand silently before the court.

At first, Jim filed papers and fielded questions from the judge while I hung on the telephone trying to reach the ADAs whose notes were missing, or spoke to witnesses who wandered into court. One woman in a flowered dress came up to the railing at the center of the courtroom and called over to me, "Mr. DA, sir." A court officer was about to intervene, but I waved him away and took the woman into a back hallway. She said she wanted to drop petit larceny charges against her son. "He's a good boy," she said. "I just want him to stop stealing my money." I asked her if she had been threatened. "Not really," she said, "only by my husband." I told her to call the ADA assigned to the case.

When I returned to the courtroom, Jim handed me the file on a case involving possession of some stolen blouses. The complaint had been filed almost seven months before, and the judge now threatened to dismiss it sum-

marily under the Speedy Trial Act. Jim had requested a
second call—shorthand for having a case re-called later in
the day—and I got on the "DA phone" to reach the prosecutor in charge.

"There's no note down here," I said, "and the judge says
he's going to dismiss it."

"Oh, Christ," said a harried-sounding young woman, "I
know the case is getting old, but I still haven't heard from
the store security guard. Try to get a plea to *Attempted*
Possession of Stolen Property, and let the defendant do
community service instead of jail time. Just try to get
something out of it."

When the case was re-called, the defendant refused the
offer, and the judge dismissed the charges.

Throughout the day, Jim and I alternated jobs. We read
notes and blindly followed their instructions although we
had no idea whether we were being unreasonable or just:
these weren't our cases. In the crush of the calendar some
of the morning's notes inevitably got lost and we were
often left empty-handed before an increasingly impatient
judge.

"Where is the People's motion response in calendar
number 124?"

"I don't know, Your Honor," I would choke out.
"There's no note on the file and the ADA is on trial."

"You mean you don't know if the ADA has spoken to the
witness about dropping the charges? The case is three
months old!"

"Your Honor, there's no note."

Legal Aid fared no better. They missed deadlines, forgot about clients, lost notes, and fended off tirades from
judges. They also routinely obtained postponements
whenever the People (short for the People of the State of
New York) were ready for trial. Under the Speedy Trial
Act, the DA has six months in which to answer, "Ready,"
but there is no such law urging defense lawyers forward.
Judges became livid when they sensed defenders stalling
for time, but they had no power, beyond holding a lawyer

in contempt of court, to force a defendant to trial. Sometimes a judge would appoint new counsel, but that remedy only added to the delay, which, short of acquittal, was just what defendants wanted most. Called in by our office to testify, police officers and witnesses often waited in the wings for half a day only to be informed that trial had, once again, been postponed. Angry accusations of bad faith volleyed back and forth between Legal Aid and the People. Occasionally, the routine was broken by a defendant who changed his or her mind and pled guilty.

The speed of the proceedings in calendar also kept me perpetually off balance. Each of the two to three hundred cases we handled every day received about a minute and a half of court time. The moment one case concluded, the clerk read the next defendant's name. I scribbled down the judge's ruling and then frantically dug through the files or ran to the DA phone if my partner was dealing with a walk-in witness. To make matters worse, the prosecution table was so low that I had to bend halfway over to take notes. By the end of the first day, my throat was hoarse from shouting, my feet were tired from standing, and my back ached. Back at Bureau 20, Jim and I collapsed into chairs. Only four more days to go. Time to hit Forlini's.

Our bureau chief, Mitchel Nelin, had said that our time would be our own so long as we got the work done, but that promise turned out to be a little misleading. After my first week of calendar, I immediately returned to ECAB, starting on a Saturday. Though I lost the weekend, I still looked forward to working the complaint room. The city generated countless weird varieties of crime, and interviewing cops in ECAB was like going on an anthropological field trip—though far from an academic pursuit. Learning the strange facets of street crime was a part of the job.

Cops from Public Morals, like transit police, figured among the regular members of complaint-room society. At some point during every shift these jaded officers brought in their catches, known in the trade as "pros" cases. They were probably the most cynical members of the New York City police force, and, from what I could tell, they had reason to be. Making pros collars, they said, is like shooting fish in a barrel. They brought cases downtown in bulk, three or four to an officer, and we wrote them up three or four cops at a time. Our write-ups read simply, *LFP:* Loitering for Prostitution.

From the officers I learned that a blow job from the low-class Eleventh Avenue hookers who service their clients as they ride through the Lincoln Tunnel costs as little as ten dollars, while the ritzier Park Avenue South set charges seventy-five for the same service in hotel rooms. "Around the World" means a kinky combination of oral and anal sex, and the less honest hookers pick their john's pockets while the john's attention is elsewhere. Some girls work for abusive pimps who threaten them if they try to walk out, others are self-employed. Some johns are cocaine addicts who pay prostitutes a hundred dollars an hour just to watch them get high. Every perversion has its market—cross-dressing, bestiality, S&M, B&D; it is merely a question of taste and price.

The prostitutes themselves, from what I could tell, seemed resigned to being continually arrested and rearrested by Public Morals. Every night they were rounded up, herded into police wagons, and brought down to court. They rarely resisted arrest and sometimes even became friendly with the arresting officers. But their willingness to put up with the weary cycle of arrest and release had an edge of desperation about it. One woman who called herself Cherise pleaded with her arresting officer, "Hank, I just got out of the Women's House last week. If you let me go I'll give you the righteousest blow job you ever had." Another girl, who worked the Holland Tunnel giving oral sex to New Jersey commuters, bragged, "I could suck the head off a nail."

Public Morals cops were glad to kill time teaching a rookie prosecutor about street life, and they loved to tell crime stories, but they never completely lowered their guard. I may have been a member of the "law enforcement team" and therefore privy to certain inside information, but because I was also empowered to prosecute them for police misconduct I was not quite a full NYPD insider. When I asked, for example, why they never arrested the johns, they put me off: "That's the policy, Counselor."

Relations between police officers and prosecutors were often strained, even though we were "on the same side" of the law. In one training lecture we had been instructed that a recent judicial decision deemed our Loitering for Prostitution complaints too vague and therefore invalid under the so-called Void for Vagueness doctrine. The office had since met the court's mandate with a form complaint that spoon-fed the information to the officers:

Deponent observed defendant at the above public place stopping male *passersby (or) motorists* and engaging them in conversation for the purpose of prostitution. Deponent further states that he observed defendant for a period of about *(must be more than 20)* minutes during which time defendant was seen stopping about *(must be more than 5) passersby (or) motorists.* Deponent further states that defendant's general deportment indicated that defendant was engaging in prostitution in that *(describe circumstantial evidence that defendant was engaging in prostitution, e.g., location known to be frequented by prostitutes, defendant dressed in manner typical of prostitutes etc.)* .

Officers soon memorized the new form, and they all wrote in their memo books that they had observed the girls, or the boys, for "twenty minutes," and that each one had beckoned to "at least five male motorists." To vice cops with years on the job, however, the twenty-minute requirement seemed absurd. One seasoned officer joked that the best-looking hookers got picked up so quickly by johns that they would probably never get arrested.

Officers also grumbled that their innumerable arrests only forced prostitutes to move from one neighborhood to another, usually in response to whichever community complained the loudest, and that ADAs—who never pressed for heavy sentences on pros cases—were only too willing to let officers waste their time. I couldn't offer them much consolation. No one, not even the most hardened prosecutors, pretended that Public Morals could rid Manhattan of prostitution. Still, cops slept on the complaint-room floor, dozens of hookers took up space in the pens, and we cranked out endless amounts of paperwork. None of it seemed to have been affected by the doctrine of Void for Vagueness.

Of all the petty crimes we sifted through, misdemeanor drug possession dominated ECAB. At random days and times, the police department ran drug sweeps—mass arrests carried out by a phalanx of officers ambushing notorious city blocks—and the "in" misdemeanor basket overflowed with drug arrests. Most possession cases hinged on only two issues: whether the drugs were real and whether the officer had "probable cause" to search the defendant. If the drugs were "beat," then the defendant hadn't committed any crime. If the search was illegal, then the drugs would be suppressed at a hearing and the charges dismissed. Laboratory analysis took a few days to complete, so in ECAB we concentrated on the search.

Under the Fourth Amendment to the United States Constitution, an officer may search a suspect only if there is "probable cause" to believe the person has committed or is about to commit a crime. If the officer actually sees the crime occur, by definition he has cause to immediately arrest and search the criminal. Such, at least, is the textbook law.

But in ECAB we ran up against "dropsy." In dropsy cases, officers justify a search by the oldest of means: they lie about the facts. *As I was coming around the corner I saw the defendant drop the drugs on the sidewalk, so I arrested him.* It was an old line known to everyone in the justice system. One renowned federal judge many years ago complained that he had read the same testimony in too many cases for it to be believed any longer as a matter of law. I thought that after His Honor's scathing public condemnation dropsy had died out.

During my first experience with the aftermath of a drug sweep, one officer told me he had observed a man holding a vial of cocaine up to a streetlight, another patrolman reported seeing a teenager drop six packets of heroin to the ground, and a third cop said he had arrested a woman when he noticed two syringes with needles sticking out of her shirt pocket. Later that night I heard other variations: one cop had removed vials of cocaine from a seller's mouth, where he was holding them "like a chipmunk"; another had arrested "the Claw," a lifetime junkie whose habit of shooting up in the same arm caused his hand to swell to the size of a baseball mitt, when he saw the man clumsily open a packet of heroin on the subway. (The officer added that Bellevue Hospital offered a substantial sum to ensure that the hand would be donated to their lab upon its owner's demise.) Three cops said they had seen dealers swallow glass vials of crack and, for lack of a more serious offense, charged them with Obstructing Governmental Administration. There must have been plenty of good arrests mixed in with cases that fit the dropsy profile, but at times I entertained the bleak notion that some officers just made up better lies than others.

In each dubious case I cross-examined the officers, warning them that judges are skeptical of dropsy searches: "If you just tell me the truth, Officer, we stand a much better chance of winning a suppression hearing." But patrolmen were not about to give themselves up. "Counselor," one replied angrily, "that's really the way it happened. You should come out on the streets and see for yourself. When we come walking down the block, the mopes all try to get rid of whatever they're holding. It's incredible. Maybe they think that if the stuff isn't found on them they can't be charged. Besides, you guys are going to bargain the case down to a Dis Con [Disorderly Conduct] with a fine, so who cares?"

As part of the interview routine, we always asked whether the defendants had made any incriminating statements and if *Miranda* warnings—the classic list of rights recited even by TV cops—had been properly given. John Patton repeatedly advised us that "defendants always say something." Getting a defendant's side of the story early on, he said, would prepare us for what might come out in court and help weed out bad searches.

In ECAB, officers readily admitted that they forgot to read defendants their rights. They knew that most offenders pled guilty at the first opportunity and that the question of *Miranda* warnings would never be raised. The statements they attributed to defendants, however, seemed to have been edited down just to avoid an ADA's criticism: "You got me"; "Don't call my probation officer"; "It's only one bag." I felt that I was getting close to the truth when one cop told me that a defendant had said, "Take your fucking hands off me. I didn't do anything. I want a lawyer."

It soon became painfully obvious that taking statements would not help cure the dropsy syndrome. Even if the defendants themselves had come to the complaint room to give me their versions of the arrests, I would still have to choose between believing the officer or a person whose main interest is in getting out of jail as soon as possible. I was in a position to remedy police misconduct by dismissing unconstitutional arrests outright, but doing so on the basis of a hunch or a defendant's uncorroborated word was not a realistic alternative. Instead, I accepted the officers' versions of events at face value and sent complaint after complaint off to the typists. I had the strange sensation of being co-opted by the police.

* * *

Many crimes, fortunately, had little to do with an officer's honesty. One cop said he had recently come across a new Mercedes that had been ravaged by vandals. Its windows were kicked in, upholstery slashed, and dashboard set on fire. Inside the car he found the owner's sign reading NO RADIO. On the other side of the sign, the vandals had written, "You should of had a radio."

Another cop had been summoned to a Greenwich Village apartment on the report of a burglary in progress. When the patrolman arrived he asked the young male occupant where the burglar had tried to enter. The tenant said, "All right, I admit it, there was no burglar, but how about having sex with me?"

"Forget it," said the cop.

"Oh, come on," the tenant persisted. "I'll go downstairs, buy some crack, we can get high and screw."

The patrolman noticed a vial containing some white powder on a coffee table. "What's in the vial?" he demanded.

"Oh, just some coke," said the young man, "but it's not enough for the two of us."

"Okay," said the cop, "you're under arrest for falsely reporting an incident and possession of cocaine. Where's your telephone? I have to report this to my sergeant."

"Don't call your sergeant," said the kid. "I don't do threesomes."

I began to understand why officers treated defendants with such contempt. Every day they risked their lives on the streets, walking targets for harassment or violence, only to be questioned and criticized by a fresh-faced ADA or by a judge who makes three times their salary, neither of whom has ever entered a crack house or stopped a man not knowing whether he might pull a gun or sue for illegal arrest.

As part of the orientation program, each rookie spent a night in the backseat of a patrol car. My assignment was Alphabet City, a notoriously drug-infested neighborhood filled with ramshackle walk-ups used as shooting galleries and crack manufacturing plants. The officers who took me out explained that I was being given cream-puff treatment: no heavy radio runs to shootouts or raids, just a nice, safe patrol. That night we walked through abandoned alleys looking for lost children, served subpoenas on reluctant witnesses, and went into a blacked-out basement on the report of "a disturbance." Every corner presented a possible hiding place for a crazed, violent junkie or cop-hater. I tried to recall the officers' bravery whenever I found myself becoming too contemptuous of how they treated criminals.

It wasn't long before our class realized that trials were, for us, months off. The vast majority of defendants pled guilty at arraignment. A few of the surviving cases made it to brief hearings before retired judges known as judicial hearing officers, but the rule of thumb among older prosecutors was that out of a hundred misdemeanors squeaking past arraignment, two might reach trial. In the meantime, our job was to keep the wheels of the busiest and probably most chaotic court system in the world turning or, more appropriately, grinding.

Every other week we were back in the All-Purpose Court Part, offering excuses to judges, arguing with defense lawyers, and scrambling to keep our petty-crime prosecutions from falling into complete disarray. We came to know court officers, judges, and stenographers by name, and we learned some basic courtroom skills, maintaining stamina not the least among them. But being in court, a phrase that had suggested arguing before a jury or cross-examining a witness, in fact meant stapling notes to files, serving laboratory reports on defense lawyers, reciting other rookies' notes, getting rid of old cases. One afternoon, a friend from outside the office came to AP-2 to watch me in action. He seemed impressed by Criminal Court but surprised at the uneventful routine. "It looks to me like all you're doing is filing papers," he said. "I guess it's just over my head."

After a month and a half in ECAB and AP-2, I began to see Bureau 20 only as a place to stash my law books—which I still hadn't used—and a safe haven at the end of the day; more a prosecutor's locker room than a law office. Still, I glimpsed a ray of hope when, after weeks of institutional assignments, cases began to appear in my mailbox. At first I had five. Within a week, twenty. After three weeks, forty, and then I stopped counting. To help us cope with the growing caseload, the office hired trial preparation assistants, usually one for every two or three rookies. I was assigned Ida Valdez. TPAs were like courtroom clerks. They knew all the really useful details of legal practice, from where to file motion papers and which cabinet held subpoena forms to the names of judges who were lenient about deadlines. Ida, I gathered, was supposed to help me get started.

When the TPA assignments were announced I went right to Ida's work station in the bureau hallway to introduce myself. She was away from her desk, but a look at her cubicle served as a good introduction. Its movable walls were papered over with Bob Marley reggae posters, flower-power stickers, and an array of male sex-machine pin-ups prominently featuring *Miami Vice* cops. A few ostrich feathers had been glued to the edge of her desk, making a bizarre sort of canopy, a beat-up old radio sat in the corner, and a couple of paperweights declared BE YOURSELF and LESS MUGGING, MORE HUGGING. I left a note on her chair and went back to my office.

As I was muddling through my first five cases, wondering what I should do about an assault with a bicycle—was a bicycle a weapon under the Penal Code?—a short, slender Hispanic woman wearing an oversized pair of green-framed eyeglasses appeared at the side of my desk. She had a large mouth that shimmered with red lipstick and she wore her hair plastered in a large swirl that ran around her head and disappeared over her shoulder.

At first Ida proved a tremendous help. "Did you call the witnesses?" she asked. "In most cases, they won't come downtown unless you drag 'em or serve 'em with subpoenas." It had never occurred to me that crime *victims* would resist following through on their cases, so at her suggestion I put technicalities aside and tried to track them down. Out of five victims, only three had telephones, and of those with phones, one was home. When I explained that I was from the DA's office, he hung up on me.

The man who hung up on me, however, agreed to come downtown after talking to Ida. Ida soothed a woman crying hysterically in the hallway and scolded a kid into promising to stop smoking crack. By example, she taught me how to communicate with people from backgrounds entirely different from my own, people afraid of lawyers and unused to articulating their problems. Dealing with the poor and uneducated, who most often were our witnesses, was a subject never mentioned in lecture.

But during the year it became increasingly apparent that Ida also had her weaknesses. There was no shortage of paperwork, and by December it piled up on Ida's desk and deadlines started to slip by. My officemate, Annette, who shared Ida's services, complained bitterly to John Patton and tried to have Ida transferred to some more menial position. But Ida stayed on, which was just as well as far as I was concerned. Ida might not have been as organized as some of the more buttoned-down TPAs who were applying to law school, but her warmth and humor helped to humanize the sometimes grim atmosphere of 100 Centre Street. Whenever I felt fed up with the pace of Criminal Court or the armies of cops with drug cases, I retired to Ida's feathered cubicle, listened to the radio, and relaxed.

Accepting Ida, however, meant doing all my own paperwork. During one lecture entitled "Trial Preparation," we had been told about a case called *People v. Rosario.* Our lecturer, a respected member of the Appeals bureau, talked about *Rosario* the way a preacher refers to the Ten Commandments. "At the start of a criminal trial," he said, "you absolutely must give the defense a copy of every document concerning the case signed or written by every witness, police officer, or detective. Failure to turn over *Rosario* material results in an automatic mistrial. Remember, *an automatic mistrial.*"

Assembling *Rosario* material proved to be a more formidable task than I had expected. Like all bureaucracies, the New York City Police Department generated sheaves of forms, as various as insect species, and they were continually growing in number. Memo books, property vouchers, stop-and-frisk forms, on-line booking sheets, rap sheets, UF-61s, follow-up UF-61s, radio transmissions, accident reports, breathalyzer calibration sheets, IDTU worksheets, ballistics reports, drug analyses, and "aided cards" all had to be assembled, organized, and xeroxed. Just before trial, every rookie went ferreting through police files in a last-minute attempt to retrace the paper trail running from the scene of the crime to our offices.

The two most common forms were the Complaint Report, also called the UF-61, and the Arrest Report. The 61 contained a police officer's concise statement of the case and the names and addresses of witnesses. It was clear, easily read, and well organized: the corporate charter for any criminal case. The maniacally intricate Arrest Report, by contrast, was an oddity.

I had glanced at these reports in ECAB but never taken the time to read one closely. In forty-one lines, subdivided into more than eighty categories, the report describes the crime, the defendant, the time and place of occurrence, and the officer's name, rank, shield number, tax registration number, and command code. Under a multiple-choice section called "Nature of Crime," it lists "Robbery, Larceny, Drugs, Other," although it provides no spaces for Assault or Weapons Possession. If the crime is a robbery, the form becomes more specific, though it remains just as selective: "Purse Snatch, Payroll, Neck Chain, Hijack, Bicycle, Other."

Three separate sections—one at the top of the page,

one in the middle, and one at the bottom—describe a defendant's physical appearance. Two of the sections, entitled "Defendant Information," include age, sex, race, skin tone, height, weight, eye color, and hair color. The third section, "Physical Description," offers twelve choices alone to describe "Hair": under "Hair Length" it offers "Short, Long, or Normal," and further on, it lists "Unusual Teeth," "Wig/Hair Dyed," "Limp or Foot/Leg —Missing/Deformed," "Part Bald," "Unusual Ears/Hearing Aid." Twenty choices describe "Body Marks." In the last line above the officer's signature, the report concludes with "Other Identifying Data: Homosexual, Team Member, Gang Member." Officers spent hours filling out these reports, which few lawyers ever bothered to read carefully. Still, without them, we were not ready for trial.

Of course, preparing a case also involved interviewing cops. And having the officers' precinct telephone number already in the file, I assumed that I might actually use the number to set up appointments. A few days before my first misdemeanor hearing, I telephoned the precinct and asked to leave a message for an Officer Rollins. My call was transferred to a division called Roll Call, where a woman informed me perfunctorily that I hadn't filed a subpoena with the Appearance Control Unit.

The subpoena turned out to be yet another preprinted form, automatically replicated in triplicate, with blanks for the officer's name, command code, and shield number, the name and docket number of the case, my name, my telephone extension, the top pending charge, and other increasingly irrelevant information. By mid-January, my file drawers held more than a hundred misdemeanors, yet I couldn't interview a single officer without filling out a subpoena. I often learned, a day or two before trial, that I had requested the officer's RDO (regular day off) and would have to reschedule. The Speedy Trial clock ticked away, and my telephone, unused, sat on my desk mocking me.

* * *

At one time, the idea of preparing a case for trial held a certain allure. I imagined myself alone in an office late at night, sifting and resifting testimony. The phone rings: a new development, a fingerprint matches, a ballistics report ties spent shells to the defendant's pistol. Strategy planned like a chess game. The reality—xeroxing, filling out forms, writing notes to be read anonymously in the All-Purpose Court Part—was more like file-clerking.

As caseloads grew, forms of every stripe came to pervade our lives in the trial bureau. In my first Driving While Intoxicated case, I received a thirty-five-page motion from Legal Aid. It challenged the use of Breathalyzer machines, questioned the validity of the New York drunk-driving laws, and demanded, among other things, the victim's psychiatric records—the latter request seemed particularly odd since in this case there was no victim. I expected to spend days researching the issues. Then a second-year ADA told me that the hefty-looking motion was a standard printout to which our office had responded thousands of times before. He xeroxed a twenty-page form brief that I filed with the court. A few days later the judge denied Legal Aid's motion.

Soon I couldn't imagine wasting time over anything that added to the workload. In case after case, ancient memoranda filled with outdated case law passed back and forth in the guise of legal argument, and I resigned myself to fighting Legal Aid's boilerplate with ours. It was assembly-line litigation, the battle of the forms.

FOUR

Doing Justice

According to a well-known anecdote, Oliver Wendell Holmes, Jr., was climbing the steps of the United States Supreme Court one morning when he was greeted by one of his law clerks. "Do justice, Judge Holmes," said the clerk. "I don't do justice," Holmes replied. "I merely apply the law." Whether or not that remark was intended seriously, it has forever since made clear that law and justice do not always go hand in hand.

In the complaint room our job was merely to apply the law. It made no difference whether the person who beat the subway fare or stole stockings from Macy's was a college student or a junkie with a fifteen-page criminal record. And in the AP Parts, reciting notes and filing canned briefs, we simply helped cases limp forward to trial.

By early November, John Patton and Mitchel Nelin had decided we were ready to begin working AR-1, the primary arraignment court in Manhattan. There we received our first lessons in doing justice.

The arraignment court operates like a twenty-four-hour clearinghouse for the newly arrested. In the course of an eight-hour shift, as many as a hundred and fifty defendants pass before the presiding judge. Even at four A.M. the courtroom is alive with lawyers haggling over bail and plea bargains, white-shirted corrections officers escorting prisoners in and out of the pens, a judge drinking coffee at the bench, and a prosecutor standing behind a stack of cases fresh from the complaint room. There are brown linoleum floors, brown walls, brown chairs for the lawyers, and brown benches for the onlookers. The judge's bench and chair are brown. Banks of fluorescent lights suspended from the ceiling project a flat illumination that washes away color and reduces everything, even faces and clothing, to a muddy gray-brown, like a faded newspaper photograph. At the rear of the room, half of the bulbs are burned out, and the farthest corners recede into shadow. Because it may take as long as forty-eight hours from the time a defendant is arrested until he is "produced" in court (federal orders notwithstanding), friends and family members wait, bleary-eyed, in the pews amid police officers, detectives, defense lawyers, and a few scattered observers.

Upon entering Bureau 20, I was told to spend some time getting a feel for AR-1. For one afternoon, I watched from the sidelines as an ADA, alone at the prosecution table, argued case after case, picking up facts from our files as he went along. Judge, prosecutor, and defense lawyer all shouted in legal shorthand, trying to be heard over the hum of conversations in the audience.

"Your Honor," yelled an attorney on behalf of a youth accused of robbing a woman on the subway, "the People have asked for $5,000 bail in a case where, by their own statements, the only crime committed is a GL 3. My client doesn't even have any priors. It's obvious this won't be presented to the grand jury by one-eighty-eighty day. I'm asking for the Court to set no bail at all."

"Mr. DA," said Her Honor, glowering at the prosecutor from the height of her bench, "your office seems to be all over the place with its bail requests. It's just outrageous that in a case like this, which should be a misdemeanor, in my opinion, you ask for such unreasonably high bail. The defendant is seventeen years old and has never been ar-

rested. I'm granting the defendant's application for ROR
and setting the matter down for eleven one in AP-7."

"For the record: over the People's request for $5,000
bail, Your Honor," shouted the prosecutor in response. He
jotted down the judge's ruling and turned to read through
a file on the next defendant.

"Nice try, Mr. DA," smirked one of the court officers,
"and great training for the rookie, too."

I was too embarrassed to ask what "GL 3," "ROR," and
"one-eighty-eighty day" meant.

Arraignment, like most Criminal Court procedures, had
been refined to a swift routine. The defendant and his
lawyer come before a judge, the clerk reads the charges,
and the defendant pleads either guilty or not guilty. In
misdemeanor cases, if the defendant pleads guilty, he is
sentenced immediately. If he pleads not guilty, the court
decides whether to release him outright or to set bail.
Those, at least, were the minimal legal outlines. Under old
English law, however, "to arraign" meant "to set in order," and in a broad sense that was still arraignment's true
function. Our complaints, drafted on the basis of a police
officer's testimony in the sealed ECAB complex, were
placed in the context of the defendant's criminal history
and his or her side of the story.

Arraigning defendants, even misdemeanants, took real
skill. We had to know "black letter law," criminal procedure, and be able to think on our feet. Our files on each of
the defendants were kept in numerical order on a table—
yellow covers for felonies, blue for misdemeanors—and
as in AP-2, there was no warning about which case would
come next. The clerk read a defendant's name and we
snatched up the file, made a hasty argument to the court
and then listened to the defendant's side of the story. We
had about three minutes in which to decide who deserved
a break and who didn't.

Jim Bronson quickly impressed everyone with his flu-
ency in legal terminology and ability to react under pres-

sure. Handsome, poised, and intelligent, he stood coolly before angry judges, spouted case law and legal citations, and seemed to win every issue. From the start, he was slated to distinguish himself. For the rest of us, the experience was a roller-coaster ride.

My first week working AR-1, I was supervised by a senior ADA—a fortunate state of affairs, since I had enough trouble just making sense out of the stapled mass of papers in each file. At times I became so involved trying to locate all the pertinent facts that I arraigned defendants without even looking up at their faces.

One man had been arrested for low-level gambling charges. "Tell me about the facts of the case, Mr. DA," the judge asked.

In a one-line scrawl, the write-up read, *Policy—more than 500 MHRP slips*. It looked as if it had been dashed off at the end of a night shift. I had no idea what MHRP slips were, so I cleared my throat and answered, "Your Honor, this is a policy case."

"I know that, Mr. DA," he retorted icily, "but what are the facts?"

I had done my best to make the spare write-up sound like a serious criminal matter, but with this next unanswerable question my hands went cold. Should I tell His Honor on the record that the DA's office had no idea why the defendant had been arrested and had spent a night in the pens?

As I shifted from foot to foot searching for an answer, my adviser slipped the file from my hand, pushed me gently to one side, and said, "Your Honor, the defendant was arrested at the time and place stated in the complaint with more than five hundred MHRP slips on him."

"That's more like it," said the judge, and turned to the defense lawyer. "Counsel, the offer is a two-hundred-dollar fine if your client pleads today, five days in jail if he fails to pay."

I looked over for the first time at the defendant, a short Hispanic man about forty, who must have been watching

as I quailed before His Honor. I was so obviously a rookie
—I spoke too quickly, lacked confidence, didn't know the
facts of the case—that the situation probably seemed
grimly humorous to him. After a brief consultation with
his attorney, he pled guilty. I suppose that meant "we"
had won.

On the cover of the file I wrote my initials, the date, and
a note: *PG: 225.15, SI: $200/5 days.* (Pled guilty to Posses-
sion of Gambling Records; sentence imposed: two-hundred-dollar fine or five days.)

Later, I asked my adviser what MHRP slips are. "Who
knows?" he said. "They're illegal—something to do with
horse racing. I see them in gambling cases all the time.
But listen, next time a judge asks a question you don't
know how to answer, just read him the write-up or say,
'Your Honor, I don't know.' He'll get mad, but you're
supposed to take some heat down here."

In addition to the write-up, every file included an array
of paperwork—police reports, property vouchers, and the
CJA sheet (which listed the defendant's address, the
names of family members, and current employment). But
the only other really crucial document was the rap sheet.
When I first heard the term, it reminded me of television
detective lingo, but even the most intellectual judges,
slated for the appellate courts, talked about "sheets" and
"raps." Nobody said "criminal history."

Rap sheets come from a vast computer bank in Albany
known as NYSID (New York State Identification System),
and they range from one page to the proverbial phone
book. In the Corrections Department's system of shorthand, they list a defendant's every in-state arrest, sentences imposed, dates of release from prison, arrest warrants, open cases—even the *false* names, social security
numbers, and addresses given to the police. Reading a
defendant's sheet in arraignments lets you know whether
the man charged with exposing himself on the subway is a
first-timer or has just been released from Stormville
Prison after doing ten years for rape.

The great majority of misdemeanors were "disposed of" through plea-bargaining. Judges, unlike prosecutors, have virtually no power to dismiss cases or reduce charges, other than on technicalities, so the onus to fit the punishment to the crime and the criminal rested initially on us. If the crime was minor and the defendant's record minimal, we reduced the charge—most often to Disorderly Conduct, known as "Dis Con"—in exchange for a guilty plea. The public saves time and money, the defendant gets off lightly: more or less an even exchange. With repeat offenders we made deals by recommending low sentences in exchange for top-count pleas, and judges, who had complete discretion in sentencing, were only too happy to see one fewer case clogging the system. It was known as keeping dispositions up.

The stakes for misdemeanants were never high: should a defendant do sixty or ninety days for his sixth shoplift? By law the sentence could never exceed one year, regardless of how many offenses a defendant had racked up. For punching a stranger in the face (a class A misdemeanor), a man with twenty convictions for violent assaults faced the same one-year maximum as a first offender. But even given the one-year cap on petty crimes, arraignment court remained a legal battleground, one in which ADAs had to fight if we hoped to be effective. It was a lesson I learned during one of my first solo negotiations.

David Middleton, a sixteen-year-old felon with three aliases, had been arrested for beating the subway fare. *Manipulating a turnstyle. $24.00.* The case, like all farebeats, was probably a winner. When Middleton's name was run through the computers, a bench warrant "dropped." It had been issued in a shoplifting case when Middleton skipped out. Judges usually gave teenagers the benefit of every doubt, since the more time kids spend inside, the less likely they are to reform. But Middleton had worn out his welcome. In only three years, he had amassed a felony conviction for robbery and two drug-related misdemeanors, not to mention the open shoplift case. He wasn't old enough to drink legally, yet he probably knew the arraignment process better than I did.

Middleton had served first fifteen and then forty-five days on his two drug convictions and he was still on probation for the robbery. He faced up to one year or a one-thousand-dollar fine on the farebeat alone. Our class had recently been instructed that, as a matter of policy, sentences should increase with every new arrest. Sixty days, therefore, seemed about right.

One of the court officers announced, "The People versus David Middleton, Docket Number 5N078546," and Middleton, a handsome, well-built youth, got up off the defendant's bench and strutted over to the defense table. Expensive basketball sneakers. Padded leather jacket. The usual.

"Your Honor," said Middleton's Legal Aid lawyer, "may we approach to discuss a disposition?"

"Gentlemen, step up," said the Honorable Louis Friedland. Friedland, a heavy-set man with a shock of black hair, was a seasoned jurist who prided himself on running a tight ship. Cases proceeded quickly in his court, so quickly, in fact, that he often requested that overflow cases from secondary arraignment parts be added to the day's work. He was known as the Tsar of Arraignments.

"Mr. DA," he asked the moment I arrived at the bench, "what are you looking for to cover the farebeat?"

"Well, Judge," I answered nervously, "the defendant got fifteen days for his first misdemeanor and forty-five days for his last offense. It seems to me the penalties should go up with each subsequent—"

"Cut the crap, Mr. DA, and just tell me what you're looking for to cover the farebeat." I should have known I didn't have to explain sentencing policy to a judge with twenty years on the bench.

"Sixty days," I answered.

Friedland froze for a moment. Then he pounced: "Sixty days for a farebeat? Listen, Mister, you better get it together or you'll be practicing law in Poughkeepsie. You don't give two months to a sixteen-year-old kid for beating the fare unless you're out of your fucking mind. Who the hell told you a kid should go to jail for two months over a one-dollar token? You're lucky I don't call your bureau chief."

"Sir." Friedland turned to the tired-looking Legal Aid lawyer, who, decently enough, had stepped back, "tell Mr. Middleton that the offer is thirty days—to cover the shoplifting case as well."

As I returned to the prosecution table, I felt as if I had just committed an unpardonable error of judgment. For the rest of the morning the word echoed in my ears: "Poughkeepsie."

Back at Bureau 20 at the end of a long day punctuated by Judge Friedland's continual verbal barbs, I went to see John Patton about the David Middleton incident. Better that he hear about my incompetence from me than from the Tsar. Patton, who was involved in a game of poker, didn't seem to take Friedland's criticisms at all seriously. "It's just business as usual," he said. "You'd better get used to it, you're going to hear much worse. By the way," he added with a sly smile as I left his office, "sixty days was way too high."

Hanging around the office one evening, I complained about Friedland to my officemates. They both responded with stories that matched my own. "One judge made me feel like such a dope," Arnold said. "He really rubbed it in. He said, 'Sonny, why don't you call upstairs and we'll get a real ADA down here?' What did he expect? He knows I've only been on the job for a month." "That's not half as bad as a woman from Bureau 40," Annette joined in. "Judge Kleiman kept yelling at her until she cried." Judicial hazing, apparently, was a longstanding tradition, and rookies were supposed to be thick-skinned enough to take it. Still, I didn't look forward to hearing worse.

Abuse from judges was only one of many disconcerting realities we encountered in arraignment court. For the first time we faced serious opposition from defense lawyers. Defenders knew that ADAs missed deadlines and let cases languish in their file drawers, and that their clients—guilty or not—were often the victims of police misconduct. No respectable defense lawyer, therefore, would allow a client to toss away even five days of his or her life or add one more conviction to a rap sheet simply on the say-so of the DA's office. A successful argument often made the difference between a defendant's walking out the courtroom door and his returning to the pens.

But the new crew of Legal Aid lawyers weren't thrown into court quite as rapidly as ADAs. They learned from the examples of their supervisors, and the supervisor I encountered most frequently was a twenty-year veteran and notorious eccentric named Jeffries. At first, his behavior came as something of a shock. Throughout the day, Jeffries, whose thick mane of gray hair set off a sallow courtroom pallor, strode about the room, ranting to the judge that his clients "were not being produced from the pens fast enough." Whenever the Court refused to rule in his favor, he shot back, "Your Honor, your idea of fairness is a one-way street." By example, Jeffries instructed his pupils in the fine arts of complaining, cajoling, and wheedling. And he did well by his clients.

I first opposed Jeffries in a heroin-possession case. The defendant, Leticia Gómez, had allegedly been caught by a patrolman as she held a glassine envelope of heroin up to a streetlight. After placing her against a wall, the officer found fifteen more packets of heroin in Gómez's socks. According to Gómez's rap sheet, she had been arrested thirty times in the last three years for trespassing (which meant shooting up in an abandoned building), prostitution, and drug possession.

When the clerk called her name, she got up from the prisoner's bench and walked haltingly over to the defense table, where a pink paper arrow ordered, in black marker, STAND HERE. I noticed her swollen hands, a telltale sign of a long-term junkie, and I could smell her from across the courtroom. She looked miserably down and out, a "skel," as the cops would say. I think the term was short for human skeleton.

Judge Berthe Winfrey, one of the many Criminal Court judges who rotated through arraignment court, liked to keep a vase of flowers next to her on the bench. That day, in spite of a fresh cutting of carnations, she was in a sour mood from having had to deal with one recidivist after another and chose to direct her invective more at defense lawyers than at ADAs.

Winfrey looked at the pathetic woman with her filthy clothes and matted hair and asked, "Back again, Ms. Gómez? What is it this time?"

The defendant started to answer, but Jeffries put a hand over his client's mouth and said, "Don't speak. Remember? I told you that already. Don't say a word. Your Honor," he continued, "I demand that the Court not speak with my client. You've been interrogating defendants all day long, and I think it's an outrageous practice!"

"Mr. Jeffries," said the Judge, "confine your remarks to this case. My practice today has been the same as it always is. I have in no fashion threatened your client's rights. Now, tell your client I'm making a one-day-only offer to her—plea to the charge and five months."

"But, Your Honor," the defendant broke in, crying, "I was told I could get three months."

Jeffries's hand swung up again. "I told you not to say a word." Gómez wiped the tears from her face with her misshapen hand.

"Your Honor"—Jeffries turned toward the bench— "that's too long. Plenty of other judges would give her thirty days. My client will accept three months, but not a day more. Otherwise, she wants to fight the case. She says that the police came up to her and searched her without any reason. They just put her up against the wall and rifled through her belongings." Gómez nodded.

"Mr. Jeffries," said Her Honor, sardonically, "let's hear from the assistant DA."

"Your Honor," I began, knowing that my services had

been enlisted by the court to help squeeze a plea out of Ms. Gómez, "we are informed by Police Officer McDonough that he observed the defendant holding a glassine envelope of heroin up to the streetlight. That gave him probable cause to search her, and the search revealed fifteen packets of heroin in her sneakers—a quantity of drugs consistent with more than just personal use. Your Honor, the defendant faces up to one year on this case. The People recommend at least eight months. In the past the defendant has received sentences of—"

"Thank you, Mr. Prosecutor," said Winfrey across the carnations. "Now, Ms. Gómez, you understand that I'm giving you a break. Fifteen packets. Mr. Jeffries, advise your client to accept the Court's generous offer of five months. The time will only go up if the case gets adjourned. Of course, she can take the case to a hearing and try to suppress the evidence. The choice is hers. But the offer of five months is for today only."

"But Your Honor," Jeffries whined, "the case is just her word against the police officer's. The search was obviously unconstitutional. And I resent the DA's suggestion that my client was selling drugs. There's absolutely no evidence to support that charge. In any event, my client can't control herself; she's a drug addict. Locking her up won't do anyone any good at all. Wouldn't you consider putting her into an outpatient drug rehab program? That's the only way she'll ever be able to help herself."

"Mr. Jeffries," said Judge Winfrey, "if you took the time to read your client's rap sheet, you might notice that she was in fact placed on probation for her last offense, *which she violated.*" Winfrey drew out the phrase for maximum effect. "My papers indicate that she was given a break specifically to enroll in a drug program, but that she failed to do so. That's why she violated her probation. Now, does she want the five months or not? I'm warning you, if she doesn't make up her mind, I'll recommend to the next judge who sees her case that she get at least six months."

Gómez started crying again. Her swollen hands on the defense table looked grotesque.

"But Judge," Jeffries continued, "she's got three kids on public assistance. What do you expect her to do about them? Who's going to take care of them?"

"Mr. Jeffries, what kind of mother supports her drug habit through prostitution? The offer remains five months."

The lawyer whispered to his increasingly distraught client.

"Four months, Judge?" asked Jeffries. "Please?"

"Five months was the offer, Mr. Jeffries. Take it or leave it. The district attorney wants eight months. Isn't that right?" Her Honor turned to me.

At this point I felt like dismissing the complaint and letting Gómez back out on the street to pursue her drug habit. Jeffries's pestering began to grate, and I felt only pity for his client. As Patton had said, "They're only misdemeanors." Gómez's tired, sickly face looked pathetic. What difference did it make whether she spent an extra month in Riker's Island? Still, she had broken the law countless times and it was my job to ensure she received an appropriate punishment. On behalf of the People of New York County, I answered, "That's correct, Your Honor. And the case is solid. We have the testimony of a police officer who personally recovered the drugs from Ms. Gómez."

"But Your Honor," Jeffries continued tirelessly as his voice rose, "you're not being fair. You've questioned my client on the record and threatened her with a higher sentence if she doesn't plead out. You've robbed her of her right to go to trial!"

"Mr. Jeffries!" shouted Judge Winfrey. "How dare you state on the record that I have deprived your client of the right to a trial? I have merely informed her that I will recommend to whatever judge next gets this case that she not be re-offered five months. She can go to trial if she wishes."

"But Your Honor, couldn't you do any better than five months? It's just a possession case."

"All right, all right. Four months," said the Judge as she looked deep into the carnations. "Does your client want it or not? This is the last chance."

"Thank you, Your Honor, thank you," said the defendant through her tears. "I want the four months."

"Are you sure?" asked Jeffries audibly.

"I want it, I want it. I'm guilty."

After a few stints in AR-1, I decided that it was better to concentrate on serious offenders, give marginal offenders a break, and help free up the overburdened court system. Taking someone like Leticia Gómez to trial would be a waste of time and resources. Sometimes, however, defendants wanted to litigate their cases and refused any sentence no matter how low. This posed a real problem. After seeing a defendant reject an offer of Disorderly Conduct with five days, I couldn't back down and dismiss the case.

"Mr. DA, I'll hear the State on bail," one judge said every time a fair offer was refused. Eventually, I understood. This innocent-sounding remark struck fear into the hearts of defendants, as it was intended to. "The People are requesting a thousand dollars, Your Honor." For the down and out, even a hundred dollars' bail guaranteed their waiting in Riker's Island Prison for a trial that might easily be six months away. The message was loud and clear: take my reasonable offer of five days or you're going to rot in Riker's fighting the issues. The defendant's eyes bug out; half-heartedly he pleads guilty. Strong-arming defendants into a plea was rough justice, but it kept the number of dispositions up, the number of "bodies in the system" down, and sped cases along to a conviction. I followed this dubious practice more often than I care to remember, but I was learning the game.

Despite some tough tactics, judges generally indulged defense lawyers, even veterans like the whiny Mr. Jeffries, and kept prosecutors tightly reined in. The DA's office had a built-in advantage over defense lawyers, and judges knew it. We spoke to witnesses, police officers, and detectives in the privacy of the complaint room, where we could sort through the charges. By the time our papers arrived in court we at least had a coherent theory of the case, even if it had been compressed into two scribbled lines on a Data Sheet.

Legal Aid lawyers interviewed their clients in a holding cell minutes before arraignment. The clients often lied, and the lawyers just as often came to resent it. In many cases the only question worth asking was, "What is the least amount of time my client can get?" Guilt was a foregone conclusion. Defenders, therefore, had to use any means at their disposal to help their clients, and judges, accordingly, gave them latitude. It was a standing joke among ADAs that Legal Aid had three basic approaches to weak cases: whining, shouting, and crying.

But just as in the complaint room, the marching line of petty criminals was occasionally interrupted by comic scenes. After hours of heated argument, everyone—even prisoners on the bench—welcomed a chance to laugh, albeit with gallows humor.

Hookers came through the system by the dozen, and judges, concerned about precious jail space, never took their cases seriously. These men and women, who had lists of arrests so long that the NYSID computer operators devised a shortened format to fit more convictions on each rap-sheet page, were rushed through a guilty plea and thrown back onto the street, no questions asked.

One afternoon, the clerk announced, "Vanity Valdez, Docket Number 5N093520. Charged with Penal Law two-forty-thirty-seven. Loitering for Prostitution."

A woman stood up from the defendant's bench. Six feet tall, leggy and lanky, she was an Amazonian wonder wearing all the cheap attractions of the street—false eyelashes, a swooping black wig, and thick make-up. Her rounded hips were wrapped in a blue miniskirt with the words GO-GO printed in large black letters over the cheeks of her buttocks. She sauntered over to the paper arrow on the defense table. Without looking at Ms. Valdez, John Baltimore, a private attorney who made his living representing prostitutes, turned to the court and said, "May I approach, Your Honor?"

Judge Friedland, the Tsar, back on the bench, waved us both up.

Baltimore nonchalantly leaned one arm on the judge's bench and asked, "Judge, what are you giving out to pros cases? Time served or a fine?"

"John," responded Friedland with a smile, "these days I go by the pound. If her rap sheet weighs more than this" —he held up a slim legal periodical—"then it's three days. Your client's only been arrested hooking ten times, so, since she's a newcomer, time served. But warn her, the more she does this, the more the sentences will go up. Now step back."

He withdrew and we were back on the record.

"Your Honor," said Baltimore, earning his fifty-dollar arraignment fee, "my client authorizes me to enter her plea of guilty to the charge of Loitering for Prostitution, a class A misdemeanor. She stands ready for sentencing."

"Ten years," said Friedland, looking down at Valdez's horror-stricken face as Baltimore shuffled through his files with a look of satisfaction. "No, no, no," the judge corrected himself with a laugh. "Time served." He turned to the elderly man hunched over his stenographic machine and added, "You don't have to put that in."

"Don't worry, Judge," he replied knowingly.

Vanity Valdez spun around and, tripping on her high heels, ran past a court officer, who pulled aside the metal chain at the center of the courtroom. Everyone watched as she hurried down the aisle and out the rear door, GO-GO swinging back and forth like a metronome.

Late one Friday, a man who called himself Chester Crumberbatch came before the court. He had been bothering people on a Times Square subway platform, and when an officer asked him to leave he tried to punch the cop in the face. By New York standards these were minor crimes—Harassment, Attempted Assault, and Resisting Arrest.

Judge Leonard Balkin, one of the kindliest jurists I encountered in my rookie year, said to Crumberbatch's lawyer, "He's a sad-looking case. If he pleads guilty, I'll give him five days. Go talk it over with him."

As the defendant contemplated his options, the court officers started getting restless, rolling their eyes, and murmuring, "Come on, take the five days. Corrections'll let you out in three."

"Now, sir," continued Balkin, "do you wish to plead guilty and take the five days?"

"Yes," said Crumberbatch, looking distractedly at the lights suspended from the ceiling.

One of the court officers leaned over to me, flashed a thumbs-up, and whispered, "All right, one more for the gipper."

"And by pleading guilty, it's the same as if you went to trial and were found guilty. You understand that?" continued Balkin.

"Oh, come on!" said Crumberbatch, smiling.

"I assure you it is, sir. Now, do you understand?"

Crumberbatch looked nervously at his lawyer, who, in turn, prodded him, "Don't look at me. Just tell the judge what you think."

"Yes, Your Honor, sir. But what about my animals? They're at home without me."

"Mr. Crumberbatch," said Balkin, "just answer my questions."

"I'm trying, sir, but what about my animals?"

"I don't know about your animals. Just tell me: Do you need more time to talk with your attorney?"

"No, sir," he said promptly, "but my animals—I'm happy to go to jail, but I got to make a call. You see, my house is full of animals, some snakes, four cats, mice, birds, and they need to be taken care of over the weekend."

"Don't worry, you can make a call," said Balkin.

"Okay, I plead guilty so long as I can make a call."

Standing up in arraignments, deciding whether to give defendants a break, was a heady feeling, even in a courtroom as crowded and busy as AR-1. Defendants eyed ADAs with a mixture of fear and contempt and I often felt I held the keys to jail cells in my hand. But the effects of power were tempered on one side by the judges, who usually encouraged us to be lenient, and on the other side by Dave Ames, the chief of the rookies. They were the good and bad angels sitting on our shoulders, each offering different counsel.

ADA Ames set prosecutorial policy for Criminal Court, although he once instructed us that our office had "no official policies." He regularly called emergency meetings of the rookies at which he pressed us to request higher bail and make fewer plea-bargains, since the statistics were down: too many cases reduced to Dis Cons this year. His hair looked as if it had been grayed by years of worrying over the picayune crimes that flooded Criminal Court. Someone once remarked that Ames had the most unenviable job in the world.

Ames routinely sent memos around the office announcing the newest changes in DA policy. One memo read, in substance: "The office has received numerous complaints about drug use in public parks. Last week an innocent bystander was killed in crossfire between dealers. Henceforth, our position regarding drug-possession cases in or near a public park is to require a plea to the top charge and to request the maximum sentence of one year."

To the annoyance of judges and defenders, some rookies picked up an excessive amount of Amesian zeal and followed his memos to the letter. During that fall it was Ames's parks policy that brought matters to a head. I happened to be in arraignment court one afternoon when Alex Barnette, one of my officemates, demanded one-year sentences for a group of NYU students with no criminal records who had been caught passing a joint in Washington Square Park. The judge wanted to adjourn the cases and dismiss them in six months if the kids stayed out of trouble, but Alex doggedly adhered to Ames's new memo and threatened to go on record.

The marijuana law was unusual. It was the only statute that allowed judges to dismiss charges against first offenders over the DA's objection. But this judge took Alex's threat seriously, and after some harsh words they reached an impasse. Determined to get his way without public criticism, His Honor demanded that the author of the inhumane parks policy come to court and account for himself. Expecting a fireworks display, I stuck around to watch. Instead, when Ames arrived the judge began cordially, "Dave, what is this thing your office has against the NYU students? One of your assistants has been asking for a year, and frankly, I think it's totally inappropriate."

"Your Honor," Ames replied, "it's a legally authorized sentence. How else do you expect the police to clean up the parks?"

"Dave, come on. You know perfectly well I can't give these kids a year."

"Judge, that's our position. The parks situation is a serious matter. You know about the crossfire last week. I'm willing to authorize a reduced charge in this case, but I expect higher sentences for defendants with records."

The one-year policy was reasonable—at least arguably —as long as it was applied to coke and heroin possessors with substantial criminal histories. But Alex Barnette, my enthusiastic officemate from California, would gladly have sent that group of students to jail for a year—given them a bullet, in court parlance.

Ames's policies notwithstanding, I tended to be soft on misdemeanants. It was a trait that, if nothing else, made for smooth relations with judges and defense lawyers. Watching a person leave the courtroom headed for a prison as grim as Riker's was a depressing sight. And knowing that my intransigence might have added a few

FIVE

Hospital Hearing

When we were not writing complaints, arraigning defendants for eight hours a day, or filing documents, we spent a week—or, if we were lucky, two—preparing cases for trial. But since it took months to accumulate a caseload of any significant size, there were days when we had nothing pressing to do.

One afternoon I was lounging in my office with Jim Bronson, thinking about running in Central Park before the sun set and wondering if I could leave early without being too conspicuously absent, when John Patton leaned his head through my doorway. My feet left the desktop and I sat up straight, trying to look as though I had been thinking of search and seizure law.

Patton said he needed a lawyer to do something called a hospital hearing at Columbia Presbyterian that afternoon. I volunteered for the field trip. Inside Patton's office, a worried-looking senior prosecutor handed me a slim file containing an even slimmer summary of the case: *Deft. attacks C/W [complaining witness] in Central Park with machete. Housing police arrive while assault is in progress. C/W receives injuries to hand and neck.*

The senior assistant hurriedly explained that bail had been set at $10,000, but in order to keep the defendant in jail any longer we were required to hold a hearing to

"show reasonable cause to believe the defendant committed a felony." I reminded John that I had yet to do any
type of hearing whatsoever, much less one involving a
felony, and asked if he was sure he wanted to send such a
neophyte. In his casual, confident manner, he assured me
that the whole thing usually takes only ten minutes once
everybody arrives: "All you have to do is put the victim on
the witness stand, ask him about the event, and rest the
People's case. It's pretty hard to screw these things up,"
he added, making me feel, if anything, less secure, since if
I did lose the hearing, the fault would clearly be my own.

I started to ask a long list of questions about what to say,
where to stand, and the like, but Patton rushed me out of
his office. A car was leaving for the hearing in five minutes, and I shouldn't be late.

Outside 100 Centre Street I found the driver, judge,
stenographer, clerk of the court, and guard standing next
to a large blue station wagon (I had hoped for a police car).
His Honor and I shared the comfortable middle seat,
while the guard, stenographer, and clerk crowded into a
small folding seat in the rear, each clumsily maneuvering
his or her respective gun, transcribing machine, or note-
book.

As we drove up the FDR Drive and snaked through
crosstown traffic to the hospital, I talked with the judge.
He was a man of about forty-five with a bushy red beard
that partially covered a pockmarked face. I tried not to let
on that this would be my first appearance in court, apart
from institutional assignments, and that I barely understood the rules of evidence, much less those governing a
hospital hearing. Fortunately, His Honor and I shared a
number of extralegal interests, and we spent the time
discussing a music review from a recent *New York Times*.

At the 168th Street entrance to Columbia Presbyterian,
we were greeted by a young orderly who escorted us past
security desks and up in a stainless steel elevator. The
elevator doors opened onto a hallway where frowning
doctors, their attention buried in charts and folders,

walked briskly beside nurses pushing IV rigs and trays of gleaming surgical instruments. A sign on one of the swinging doors explained the rush of activity. We were in the critical ward.

The orderly led us into a small white room that he announced would function as the courtroom. The stenographer unpacked her transcribing machine, the clerk arranged his papers on top of a desk that now became the bench, and the judge examined the court file. Having no idea what to do next, I took a seat and reread the three-sentence write-up in my file. Though I tried to appear confident, I was amazed to find myself the sole representative of the People of the State of New York in the critical ward of a major metropolitan hospital. Plea-bargaining shoplifts was one thing, but litigating a felony seemed well beyond my grasp. I had the queasy, dreamlike sensation of sitting down to take an examination utterly unprepared.

The young orderly appeared again and asked, "DA?" I nodded.

"Would you like to speak to the witness before the hearing starts?"

"Absolutely," I said, embarrassed not to have thought of this most rudimentary detail of preparation on my own.

He took me through more swinging doors and into a room containing a number of patients, each of whom looked like an anatomy textbook illustration. One man had recently received a skin graft to his forearms. Both arms were covered with a criss-cross pattern of incisions and looked as if they had been cooked over a grill. Another patient, the gray color of a cadaver, lay motionless under an involved series of tubes leading into his arms and mouth. More bodies were partially hidden by rolling dividers.

"Mr. Straight," said the orderly to a comparatively healthy-looking young man lying on a rolling cot, "this gentleman is from the District Attorney's office. He's here to represent you at the hearing. You know how to ring for

me if you need anything," he added, and withdrew from
the room.

I introduced myself and explained to the witness that
my job was to make sure that the man who had attacked
him with a machete would stay in jail. Since I sincerely
believed myself to be Straight's protector, or at the very
least not his enemy, I expected some sort of positive response. Instead, he eyed me suspiciously and remained
silent.

"Mr. Straight," I asked, "do you understand that you are
about to be a witness in a hearing?" He lowered his head
and gazed at his right hand, suspended above the railing
of his bed by an elaborate set of pulleys. The hand itself
was encased in a plaster cast and pierced by a matrix of
thick metal bolts. Straight's fingers stuck out of the end of
the cast and were held in place by a network of clear wires
attached to the fingernails.

"Mr. Straight," I continued, "I'm not here to hurt you.
All I want to do is find out what happened to you."

Suddenly Straight looked up at me, and his face contracted into a horrible grimace. "My hand," he said, "he
cut off my hand." A stream of tears rolled down his cheeks
and fell onto the bedclothes.

I sat quietly and Straight eventually began to talk. On
the night of the crime, just thirty-six hours ago, he had left
a party uptown in Manhattan at about two in the morning
and hailed a livery cab to take him to his car, which he had
parked in the Bronx. Once in the cab, Straight discovered
that he had only a few dollars in his wallet and couldn't
afford to pay for the ride. He explained the problem, and
the cabbie agreed to let him phone a friend who could
lend him some cash. As it turned out, the friend wasn't
home and Straight got back in the cab to apologize that he
couldn't pay the fare.

By that time the meter read nine dollars. The cabbie
became furious, accusing Straight of trying to beat the
fare, and an argument ensued. Then, without warning, he
electronically locked the rear doors and sped off, swerving

wildly from side to side. He drove the cab, with its terrified rider trapped and tossed in the backseat, off the main
streets and into Central Park. Once parked on a turnoff by
the shoulder of the road, the cabbie reached under his
seat and pulled out a two-foot-long machete. As Straight
tried desperately to unlock the passenger doors and make
his escape, the crazed cabbie leaned over his seat and
began swinging the knife.

*How many times did he hit you? Show me exactly where
the blade made contact. How many times did he cut at
your wrist before it severed your hand? Did you use your
free hand to open the cab door?* Questions came out of my
mouth as I delved into the gruesome details.

Straight said that the driver had first tried to cut off his
head. He pointed to two large, clear dressings covering
broad areas of his neck where the skin had been cut away,
exposing the yellowy tissue beneath. To protect himself,
Straight blocked the machete with his right forearm while
using his left hand to unlock the cab door. The cabbie
brought the blade down over and over onto the wrist.
Finally, the door opened and Straight escaped, reeling
onto the empty lanes of the street. As he ran from his
attacker, he cradled the severed hand in the crook of his
left arm. The last thing he remembered was the blinding
approach of headlights. A police car stopped and took him
to the hospital. Since arriving a day and a half ago, Straight
said he had been awakened by the recurring vision of his
hand dangling by a small shred of skin.

The arrest report showed that the defendant, Hector
Ramos, had been on the scene, standing by his cab when
the Housing Authority Police just happened by. A bloody
machete was found underneath the livery cab. According
to his rap sheet, Ramos had recently come to New York
from the Dominican Republic. This was his first arrest.

To my surprise, I wasn't overpowered by Straight's
breakdown, although the brutality of the crime itself was
appalling. Instead, I was sobered by a self-conscious
awareness that I was seeing things that few people get to

see, and that I was present in a position of importance. My
job *required* that I draw out every gory detail of the assault, that I pry into the victim's life, under the sanction of
the State's imprimatur.

As I started to explain to Straight what little I knew
about the format of the impending hearing, the orderly
returned to the room and announced that the judge was
ready, the defense lawyer and Ramos present. The orderly transferred Straight, pulleys and all, to a wheelchair,
and we left for the courtroom.

I strolled alongside as he wheeled the patient down the
bustling corridors and, hoping for some objective data
about Straight's condition, asked, "How badly was his
hand cut?"

"When he came into the emergency room, the hand
was hanging by a piece of skin. Every bone and tendon
was completely cut through."

"It's a miracle you could re-attach it."

"Well, you must see this sort of thing all the time down
at the DA's office."

"Oh, yeah," I answered uneasily. There was no point in
letting Straight in on the secret that his case was being
handled by someone whose prosecutorial experience consisted of filling in form prostitution complaints and arraigning trespassers.

When we reached the makeshift courtroom, the orderly leaned over to me and whispered, "Don't tell him,
but there's still a chance that the microsurgery performed
on his hand won't be successful and we'll be forced to
amputate."

Inside, the stenographer sat ready at her transcribing
machine, and the clerk had the file open. My attention,
however, was drawn to a short, stocky Hispanic man with
a wispy mustache. Seated next to his defense lawyer, the
man calmly rubbed his wrists to restore circulation to the
areas where handcuffs had pinched too tightly. I had
never been so close to a violent felon, yet even at this
range he appeared neither sinister nor evil. Not a trace of

depravity showed in his round face; his arms weren't especially muscular. In his polyester shirt and dirty blue jeans, he looked strikingly ordinary.

His Honor glanced at the file and then looked around the less-than-magisterial setting. He and the clerk shared the only desk. The rest of us shuffled papers on our knees.

"Mr. Prosecutor," said the judge through his red beard, "are the People ready to proceed?"

Things were moving faster than I had expected. There was no discussion among counsel, no coaching from my supervisors. Not even a bench conference. It suddenly flashed through my mind that the DA's office must be terribly negligent to send out a rookie, barely more than a law student, to handle a serious felony. Maybe I should have gone to a safe, secure corporate firm.

"Yes, Your Honor."

"Very well. Proceed."

"The People call Andrew Straight."

Straight, who had been sequestered outside the courtroom, was wheeled next to the witness stand by the orderly, who remained standing behind him. The clerk swore the witness in, and I began direct examination. Though I was nervous, starting was easy. First I elicited the so-called pedigree information—name, occupation, place of residence—that forms part of every direct case, and Straight responded predictably. Moving on to the facts of the case, I began with a question suggested in one of our training manuals.

"Mr. Straight, directing your attention to shortly after three A.M. on November 12, on the 96th Street crosscut in Central Park, would you tell the court if anything unusual happened to you?"

"Unusual?" Straight looked at me as if I had compared his traumatic experience to missing the bus on the way to work. Then, completely disregarding me, he turned to the judge and cried, "Oh, God, this is the first time I've seen a judge since this happened." He leaned toward the defendant and, pointing with his uninjured hand, moaned, "He cut off my hand. My hand was just hanging off my arm."

Silence filled the little courtroom as Straight wept quietly on the witness stand, too overcome to continue. The defendant, sitting only a few feet from his accuser, remained apparently unmoved.

I was about to resume direct examination when the judge took matters into his own hands.

"Tell me," said His Honor in a solicitous tone. "Tell me exactly what happened to you."

The judge's concern for the victim was a good sign, but it also made me wary. As a lawyer, I knew that witnesses should never recount every detail of their testimony in the preliminary stages of a case—their recorded words provide savvy defense lawyers with added material for cross-examination if the case ever comes to trial. From a purely strategic point of view, Straight's testimony should be kept to a minimum. But I was not about to cut off His Honor. Well aware of my inexperience and fearing a tirade of the sort delivered by Judge Friedland, I looked on helplessly as Straight rambled on for forty-five minutes in response to questions from the bench.

Finally Straight finished his gruesome account and I sat down, having nothing more to ask after the Court's excessively thorough interrogatory. I had slipped in a few questions and hadn't been disgraced, but on the whole I felt rather useless.

The judge then turned to the defense lawyer and asked, "Ms. Chasson, any cross-examination?"

Dana Chasson, Ramos's private defense lawyer, stood up and looked imperiously around the courtroom. A woman of about forty, Chasson had a squarish, pale face that sagged as if pulled down by the weight of her large gold earrings. "No cross-examination, Your Honor," she said, and then paused for a dramatic emphasis as if putting on a grand defense for a full-dress jury trial. "However, my client, Mr. Ramos, wishes to take the witness stand to testify on his own behalf." Her numerous gold bracelets rattled as she crossed her arms.

My throat tightened. The hearing was supposed to take ten minutes and involve only one witness. I had already been in the hospital for two hours. No one had told me I would have to cross-examine a defendant accused of a vicious felony. Proper cross-examination is one of the most difficult tasks a prosecutor can perform, and defendants rarely take the witness stand, so no one back in Bureau 20 would have foreseen this situation. What if the judge believed the defendant's story and let him free? I imagined my name in a *New York Post* headline: DA BLOWS HEARING: MACHETE SLASHER FREED.

"Your Honor," I said, rising to my feet, "I didn't anticipate that Mr. Ramos would be taking the stand. Because his testimony might run on for some time, I would like a brief adjournment to call my office and let them know I won't be back as early as I had expected." It sounded better, I thought, than explaining that I needed my deputy bureau chief's guidance on cross-examination.

The judge allowed my request, and we took a ten-minute recess. The orderly wheeled Straight from the courtroom. I reached Patton at his office and in desperate tones explained my predicament. True to his jaunty style, John made it all seem easy. "Just let the defendant talk as much as possible. If he's lying, he's bound to trip himself up." Probably to calm me down, he added, "Listen, if he's telling the truth, all the cross-examination in the world isn't going to get you anywhere, so just do the best you can. Have fun; it's a good experience." Armed with these rules of thumb as my sword and a yellow note pad as my shield, I returned to do battle in court. I would try to have fun.

Chasson called her client to the stand, the clerk administered the oath, and we were again under way. Seated next to the burly, red-bearded judge, the defendant looked small, smaller certainly than his alleged victim. To his further advantage, Ramos also appeared composed, although perhaps excessively so for someone facing serious charges.

From the witness stand, he told a story that, like Straight's, began with an unpaid taxi fare and ended with a slashing. In fact, his supposed explanation sounded much like a confession, corroborating all the details leading up to the critical event in Central Park. They had quarreled over the fare. They had driven around trying to find Straight's friend who would lend him some cash.

But Ramos claimed they had driven onto the shoulder of the highway in the park so they could come to an agreement about the fare. Once by the roadside, Straight came at him with a knife and tried to steal his payroll and his taxicab. In order to defend himself, he drew a machete from underneath his seat and used it to fight off his attacker. If Straight got the worst of it, Ramos said, that was his own doing.

"No further questions, Your Honor," said Chasson with a flourish, and sat down, evidently content with her client's performance.

"Your witness, Mr. Prosecutor," said the judge.

"Thank you, Your Honor," I answered, and began firing my first shots into the darkness. There seemed no point in going over aspects of the case that had, by virtue of the defendant's testimony become common ground for defense and prosecution, so I went right into Ramos's defense: that Straight had tried to rob him at knifepoint.

"How big a knife did Mr. Straight threaten you with?"

Ramos indicated a blade about three inches long. Was he joking? Using a machete to fend off an attack with a penknife?"

"Did he merely threaten you with it, or did he cut you?"

"He cut me first." The defendant appeared quite unharmed, so I followed Patton's advice and let Ramos spin his tale out further.

"How badly?"

"Very badly."

"Really? Would you show the Court where your scar is?"

He held out his left-hand ring finger, which bore a well-healed scar no longer than a half an inch. Ramos's defense was rapidly turning into a dark parody. Even if Straight *had* given Ramos this small cut, it provided no legal justification for hacking off his hand. Yet Ramos sat there under oath, repeating a patent lie and asking to be released. To my surprise, I *was* having fun.

"So, after he cut your ring finger, you took out your machete?" "And then you began to cut off his hand, isn't that right?" "How many times did you have to cut him before he dropped the knife?" "You didn't try to get out of the car, did you?" "Did you cut Mr. Straight's neck before or after you cut off his hand?" "You never told the police that Mr. Straight had attacked you first, did you?"

After twenty minutes, I felt confident enough to sit down. My nervousness had been transformed into righteous indignation, and I only hoped it was as obvious to the judge as it was to me that Ramos was lying.

Both sides rested, and His Honor asked whether defense counsel wished to make a closing statement. I assumed that, in light of her client's outrageous assertions, Chasson would simply rest her case. But a timeless lawyers' adage counsels that if the facts are on your side, hammer on the facts; if the facts aren't on your side, hammer on the law; and if neither the facts nor the law are on your side, hammer on the table. Dana Chasson chose the table.

"Your Honor," she began, still arguing before an invisible jury, "I submit the evidence shows that my client has been wronged in numerous respects. He was the victim of a serious robbery. A *knifepoint* robbery, a robbery during which he received physical injury, and an injury that the court itself has seen today. Yet what does the district attorney's office do about it? They accuse my client, the victim! At this point, Your Honor, I am asking the representative of the district attorney's office to bring charges on behalf of my client and have Mr. Straight, the *supposed* victim, the real criminal, arrested. Further, I am asking the Court to release my client so that he can more effectively fight these unfounded charges of felonious assault. I have nothing more to add." Bracelets clanked as Chasson threw herself back into her chair.

"Thank you," said the judge, impatiently stroking his beard.

"Mr. Prosecutor, do the People wish to respond?"

I briefly pointed out some of the more obvious contradictions and absurdities of the defendant's story, and emphasized that even if Straight had attacked the defendant, the small wound inflicted provided no justification for brutally hacking at someone's hand and neck until they are literally in pieces. As to Chasson's request that the DA's office prosecute Straight instead of her client, I suggested that she arrange for Ramos to come to the complaint room and speak to an ADA about the robbery.

The judge thanked both sides and immediately stated that the People had more than met their burden of showing that it was likely the defendant had committed a felony. Bail would remain at $10,000. He then added, to my delight, that the defendant's "justification" appeared to him to be no more than a perjurious veil of lies to cover up his inexcusable brutality.

After court adjourned, the orderly let me visit Straight in his room. The same patients I had seen earlier lay in the same positions on the same rolling metal cots. When I entered, Straight looked up with anticipation.

"Sir," he asked, "what happened?"

"Well, Mr. Straight," I said, basking in the afterglow of my success, "the judge agreed to hold the defendant in jail on ten thousand dollars' bail. We couldn't have done better!"

Straight grasped my hand. "This renews my belief in justice. I was sure they would've let the man go. But you know, I was praying, and it shows that when you're right the Lord stands behind you. Sir, you did a great job. I don't know how to thank you enough."

Soaking up Straight's praise, I was only too pleased to

accept full credit for this victory on behalf of the State of New York. I left the hospital swollen with pride and, on the subway ride home, mentally replayed scenes from Ramos's cross-examination. This first contact with heavy crime made up for weeks in ECAB and the deadly grind of Criminal Court. I thought that for the first time I understood the real function of the DA's office: prosecuting serious cases. Misdemeanors had to be handled, but that was just a phase of the career to be endured, not necessarily enjoyed. For one afternoon I had had a chance to do something that made a difference.

But my complacency about Straight's case was shortlived. As I mulled over the facts, certain details jarred. Why did Straight leave his car parked in the Bronx and take a cab into Manhattan? How did the defendant, a recent immigrant, manage to afford an expensive private attorney? Why would a cab driver bother to hack off a farebeater's hand over a nine-dollar fare?

Later that year, the felony ADA who had originally handed me the case dropped by my office.

"Remember Mr. Straight," he asked, "the man who thanked the Lord that justice was done?" I proudly recalled my success.

"Turns out our victim did a stretch of two years in New Hampshire for forgery. So much for his being some sort of choirboy. But what's really interesting is that our Mr. Straight used to work as a disc jockey in Florida, the major point of entry in this country for cocaine.

"Anyway, I imagine Ramos and Straight were involved in some sort of coke deal that didn't go down as planned, and Ramos was out for revenge. That's why he basically parroted the same dumb story Straight told on the stand. Neither of them wanted to get into worse trouble, since the sentences for drug dealing are a hell of a lot heavier than for assault."

"Isn't there anything we can do about it?" I asked.

"Forget it. It's still a crime to hack off someone's hand,

SIX

Christmas

In early December I was assigned to night tour in ECAB, better known as "the lobster shift." Named after lobstermen, who go to work in the early-morning hours, lobster is the midnight-to-eight-A.M. shift, and it runs for seven consecutive nights.

At home after my first night's work I lay in bed, kept awake by the winter sunlight streaming through the shades and the image of dozens of police officers coming into my cubicle with crack-possession arrests. When I finally fell asleep, I dreamed about arraigning the defendants I had written up the night before. The next night I woke at ten, dragged myself to the subway, and arrived at 100 Centre Street ready to turn around and go home. By the end of the shift my throat was sore and my vision blurry. Feeling lightheaded on the subway ride back uptown, I tried to pick out the faces of drunks, junkies, and farebeaters from the press of commuters and to imagine what their rap sheets looked like. Wednesday night I again headed down to Criminal Court. I had slept for six hours that afternoon and altogether felt steeled to face the hordes of police officers and the institutional environment with its bolted-down furniture.

The snowy, wind-blown street outside Criminal Court was deserted, but inside the lobby there was plenty of activity. A crowd milled in front of the twenty-four-hour arraignment court: lawyers in suits; a circle of burned-out prostitutes wearing leopard-print stretch pants and miniskirts; men and women in their best attire, hoping to make a good impression on the judge. They checked and rechecked lists of cases taped to the wall by the courtroom door, and nervously smoked cigarettes like expectant fathers outside a hospital delivery room.

Armed with my usual cup of coffee, doughnut, and Penal Code, I climbed the curving stairway to the second floor. Halfway up I passed two more prostitutes sitting on the stairs and smoking cigarettes. Some judge must have just finished giving them time served. Along the walkway that looks down over the South Entrance Hall, a crowd of officers hung around joking. "Evening, Counselor." "How ya doin'?" "You writin' up misdemeanors? I got a great farebeat for you." A row of sleeping cops stretched down the corridor past the ECAB doorway and disappeared around the corner. The police waiting room was standing room only. I squeezed through and headed for my cubicle.

On the wall someone had posted a sign announcing, ONLY 21 MORE SHOPLIFTING DAYS UNTIL CHRISTMAS. Through my window, I watched the wind blow a fresh dusting of snow across a playground bordered by Baxter Street and the southern end of Chinatown. Two officers walked in tandem across the street, presumably for a quick bite at Wo-Hop, the cheapest and closest Chinese restaurant, or a beer at the Recess.

The misdemeanor basket in the supervisor's office overflowed with new arrests. The topmost envelope contained a group of shoplifts from Alexander's department store: twenty-three arrest reports all charging Petit Larceny and Criminal Possession of Stolen Property. I went to the officers' waiting room and called out, "Officer Pinto." A twenty-two-year-old man in a white shirt and blue jeans stepped energetically through the thicket of blue-uniformed legs. "Let's go, chief," he answered. "I've been waiting here almost seven hours." I recognized Pinto from previous shifts. He worked for the Stores' Mutual Protection Agency, a quasi-police force organized by the major Manhattan department stores. On the job, SMPA officers wore official-looking uniforms, and at the end of their shifts they brought the daily catch of shoplifters downtown en masse. Somewhere along the line, police officers probably signed off the arrest reports and handcuffed the prisoners, but I never stopped to ask.

Back inside my cubicle, Pinto leaned forward in the plastic folding chair opposite my desk. "I got a date tonight," he said, "so if you can get me out of here right away, I'd appreciate it." He handed me a stack of papers. "Look, I even filled out the complaint forms for you." He was a welcome contrast to the tough, jaded cops sleeping in the halls.

"Officer," I said, hefting the packet, "what did you do, arrest everyone in the store?"

"Counselor, it's Christmas. We always get jammed up this time of year." The sign in my cubicle was clearly no joking matter to Pinto. Blouses, stockings, jewelry, and fur coats found their way into handbags and briefcases, even inside underwear. One woman tried to leave the store wearing four shirts and carrying three dresses inside a shoulder bag. She had stolen everything, even the bag. A youth had been caught in the first-floor perfume department carrying three bottles of Oil of Olay under his leather jacket. I thought, "One bottle for Mom, one for an aunt, and one for his girlfriend." Merry Christmas, everybody. Pinto said he had barely needed to wait for these two perps to trigger the alarm, since he had arrested both for shoplifting at least three times before.

The next case came in as a two-forty-thirty-six: Loitering with Intent to Use Narcotics. I asked the patrolman to give me the facts. "Well, Counselor," he began, "originally there were three kids on the corner of one-o-seven and Amsterdam, which, as you know, is a drug-prone location—"

"Officer," I interrupted, "as far as I'm concerned, all of Manhattan is a drug-prone location. Every cop tells me about drug-prone locations whenever he has a weak case. Just tell me about what you saw, all right?"

"Okay, okay, Counselor. I was in the RMP [radio motor patrol—police car] with my partner at the corner of one-o-seven and Amsterdam and I saw these three kids smoking crack in a glass pipe. It was easy to spot." I glared at him knowingly. "I mean," the officer corrected himself, "I had a clear view of them from the vehicle. My partner and I approached the suspects and told them to stay put. Anyways, two of the perps ran down the street, but we did manage to arrest the third mope."

"Did you search him?"

"Affirmative, but he had nothing on him."

"Did you see him hand off the pipe to one of his friends? Why didn't he have anything on him?"

"Well, he was just hanging out with his friends. I never actually saw him with the pipe. That's why we charged him with Loitering to Use Narcotics."

"Listen, Officer, if you never saw him smoking crack, how am I supposed to prove he intended to use narcotics? After all, that's the crime you arrested him for. For all I know, the kid never smoked crack in his life."

"Counselor, if you want to DP the case, it's all right with me. We've each got our job to do."

I explained that unless he could give some more incriminating details, I would indeed DP (decline to prosecute) the case. Usually cops put up a healthy fight to keep a good collar from getting DP'd on a technicality, but this officer didn't even try to justify the arrest.

"Have it your way," I said. "I'll fill out the dismissal form and get you out of here."

"Listen, Counselor," he said sheepishly, "could you kinda sit on the papers for a couple of hours? You know, I made this collar right at the end of my tour, and I was counting on the overtime. I promised my kid a new bike for Christmas, and I figured I'd have to wait at least two more hours. You kinda caught me by surprise when you called the case so soon."

The officer's request was outrageous, but it was nothing new. Over the last few weeks I had learned that cops often tried to soak a few extra hours of overtime out of the complaint room. In fact, every prosecutor had to deal with the problem at one time or another. Learning about overtime was just another phase of our initiation. Like my colleagues, then, I mildly bawled the officer out, reminded him he was asking me to commit a crime, and sent him on his way.

The first time an officer had asked me to lose his papers, I immediately went to see the ECAB supervisor. I felt bad about turning in the tired-looking patrolman and quite probably damaging his career, but my duty seemed clear. He was, after all, stealing taxpayers' money.

The supervisor that day was an ADA who looked about thirty. Although only a few years older than me, he smiled cynically when he sensed my shock. "Listen," he asked, "do you really want to put together some kind of corruption case against this guy? Just tell him to watch out. It happens all the time."

Certain officers were especially shameless about arresting people to make Christmas money, what they referred to as "collars-for-dollars." On days when a Forty-second Street patrolman feels like getting home in time for dinner, he tells the pot-smoking kid on the corner to put it out and move along, but come Christmastime he hunts down arrests, and, if nothing better presents itself, brings in some homeless person for urinating in public, or, worse, an innocent "victim" like the teenager charged with loitering. Whether or not the case is eventually dismissed, his six-to-eight-hour Christmas wait in the ECAB hallway will be compensated at time and a half.

After dismissing the Loitering for Drugs case, I wrote up a couple of farebeats, a dozen pros cases, and a husband-and-wife assault before taking a meal break. Some

ADAs called it a lunch break, but that name never sat well with me in the middle of the night.

By the time I left the complaint room it was about two-thirty. Sarah Sturges, a pretty, red-headed rookie from Ohio, stopped me in the lobby. I had first met Sarah early in the fall, when we had worked the four-to-midnight shift together. That evening we went out for dinner on a thirty-five-dollar stipend provided by the office to cover the expenses of night work. Sarah and I had decided to spend it all on a good meal in Little Italy. Drinking Chianti at an intimate restaurant, both of us in formal dress, had a pleasantly intoxicating effect. It was like some sort of blind date. Though the return to the grubby ECAB cubicles broke the romantic mood, our friendship remained.

Tonight, Sarah was working lobster arraignments—what I called "a thousand and one arraignments at night" —and she seemed on the verge of tears. "It's murder," she said hoarsely. "There's a million drug cases coming through and the Tsar's on the bench. He's furious about all the bad searches and wants me to dismiss everything."

"It's not your fault," I said. "Besides, he's probably right: most of them are beat cases."

"I know," she sighed. "But I'm supposed to start three trials tomorrow morning and the last thing I need is to be humiliated all night by a judge and then read a bunch of notes from Dave Ames in the morning."

"Good luck," I said, and left for "lunch."

Outside Criminal Court the sidewalks were empty. To the south, in Foley Square, the neoclassical government buildings looked ghostly blue in the streetlamp light. Across Centre Street, bands of homeless people huddled together under the wing of a modern courthouse, and wrapped themselves in enormous sheets of white plastic. They looked like Roman statues topped with grotesque, misshapen faces. Every night for the past few days I noticed the group sleeping under the courthouse eaves, and every morning they disappeared, leaving behind a few cardboard mattresses and empty wine bottles.

I walked past the bums in togas, down the streets of Tribeca and into Chinatown. I avoided junkies who had stumbled off into the night after being released from the pens, and watched cars with nervous-looking drivers pick up prostitutes coming out of night court. I strolled through public parks frosted with snow where the wind spun pieces of newspaper in icy whirlpools, and eventually went down a side street to a twenty-four-hour basement restaurant where Chinese cooks stirred pots of noodles. As I entered my glasses frosted over with the change in temperature, and when I took them off the restaurant became a blurry, greasy-smelling haven, alive with the chatter of after-midnight diners who looked over at the young man in a suit and tie sitting by himself in a corner. I wiped off my glasses and read a book over a bowl of soup.

At three-thirty, meal break was over and I returned to the fluorescent lights, the forms, and the cops. A tall stack of misdemeanors was waiting in the "in" basket. The first officer I interviewed announced that there was a "precinct condition in the o-six," so a drug sweep had been mobilized. "My partner and I were coming up to the corner of Avenue A and Third," he said, "when the perp drops a package to the ground and runs. I pick up the bag and find thirty-seven tinfoils of coke. My partner runs after the defendant and grabs him. He struggled as we were cuffing him, so I added Resisting Arrest."

It was a typical dropsy case, but there was no point in challenging the officer. Either he saw the defendant drop the bag or he was lying—an hour of cross-examination in my cubicle would achieve only a greater backlog of bodies in the system and reward overtime-hungry officers. If the case someday went to a hearing on the validity of the search, I suspected that the evidence might well be suppressed, the complaint dismissed, and the defendant, probably a dealer, given the number of packets he carried, set free.

In law school I had been a staunch supporter of the Fourth Amendment suppression rule. According to the

United States Supreme Court, suppressing evidence illegally seized by the police would deter officers from shaking down suspects. The rule had sounded like a good idea
at the time, but from my vantage point in Criminal Court,
suppression seemed largely ineffective. Officers knew
that a vast majority of defendants would rather plead
guilty to a plea bargain or accept a light sentence than
fight a case in court. If one or two perps won a misdemeanor hearing every few years, so be it.

Suppressing evidence also had the unpleasant side effect of shaking the public's faith in a court system that
releases the guilty on technicalities. Perhaps because of
the collars-for-dollars mentality, it occurred to me that a
better way to prevent official misconduct would be to
impose heavy fines against offending officers, coupled possibly with police department sanctions, but allow the evidence to be used. If both an officer and a defendant have
violated the law, both should be punished. The risk of a
heavy penalty will deter officers from making illegal
searches, and the defendant can still be held responsible
for his own misdeeds—which have nothing to do with the
officer's misconduct. But this was ECAB, not a classroom. I
dashed off a complaint without even reading the defendant's name.

After the officer left, I looked out at the courtyard below
100 Centre Street. A faint blue glow behind the neighboring buildings indicated that sunrise was not far off. Under
the streetlamps, wisps of snow appeared and then disappeared into the fading darkness. They were like the cases
that came through my cubicle, evanescent and ghostlike.
I wondered whether I was still enjoying the job. The run-
down surroundings had started to bother me, the cop's
slang sounded less amusing, and there seemed to be fewer
interesting crimes. Just more farebeats, pros, drugs, and
the occasional assault. The tiny, human differences between one case and another, details that had seemed so
colorful only a few months ago, had become distractions.
Just give me the facts; things are busy.

By eight, the sun had been streaming through my window for over an hour. My eyes ached and I was beginning to get writer's cramp. I had interviewed twenty officers since the drug sweep came in, all of them bringing PCP, coke, or heroin cases. The day shift arrived on time but there was more work waiting at the bureau. My caseload, now up to a hundred and fifty misdemeanors, required daily attention whether or not I was on lobster.

Across the street, Bureau 20 was still deserted. I found a mass of stapled rap sheets and DA write-ups stuffed in my mail box. Twenty-six new cases. It was as if everything I had written in ECAB had rematerialized in the mail. In addition to performing triage on these new matters (some cases appeared too tenuous to merit more than a phone call or two), I had fifteen cases calendared in AP-2 and each one required a note. There were phone calls to return, motions to answer, and witnesses to interview.

That winter my wife, Kate, spent a few months working in Boston. Although she was spared having to observe some of my more bizarre behavior and mood swings, I missed having someone to complain to at the end of long nights. Kate sounded a bit worried when she called one morning and found that I had been drinking beer for the last hour. For me it was the end of another day of lobster ECAB.

And as the night shifts came and went, I contracted cold after cold—the result of losing sleep and working among groups of chronically ill street people. But I was not entirely alone. My officemate Annette said that she could never sleep during the day. Whenever she worked lobster, she looked as drawn as an insomniac. One January afternoon I found Jim Bronson dragging around the office. Usually alert and energetic, he looked haggard. He told me that after a night of lobster he had come back to the bureau and stayed the whole day just to try his first hearing. "I won," he said with a weak smile.

* * *

By this time, 80 Centre Street—the Louis J. Lefkowitz State Office Building—had become familiar territory. Every day I walked under its white sculptured ceiling highlighted in gold leaf, skirted lines at the Department of Motor Vehicles, and waited for the slow, rickety, manually run elevator cars. At night I was let in through a side entrance by one of the elevator operators, who, like the rookies, rotated through graveyard shifts.

The elevator operators themselves ranked among the building's natural wonders. Some were balloon-fat, others crabbed and sticklike, as odd-looking as gargoyles, but all were full of cheer. Mary, with her big, round, motherly face; Freddy, who played the electric guitar in the basement; Charles, the gentleman, whose clothes were always immaculate; and Harold.

Harold and I met during my first night shift. At three A.M. I climbed the back stairs up to my office to take care of some paperwork. Work stations, secretaries' desks, and offices were deserted, and a faint white light filtered in from the streetlamps outside. The time-clock hummed. Walking down the bureau hallway, I listened for footsteps, for the mad defendant who crept about the DA's office at night. Santa Claus faces, taped to the walls in anticipation of a Christmas party, leered at me.

I hurried through my paperwork and ran back to the darkened sixth-floor lobby. The elevator arrived with a loud ping and a blood-red "down" light flooded the lobby. A hand with long, dirty fingernails pushed the door aside, and the red overhead light bathed Harold's face in a ghoulish chiaroscuro. Huge, watery eyes looked out of sagging sockets, his broad mouth had a dozen teeth left, unwashed silver hair curled around his large, waxy ears, and he had a hunchback. "Going down, buddy?" he asked.

It wasn't long before I looked forward to seeing Harold's unforgettable face and bantering with him on the ride upstairs. He told the same stale jokes over and over, but they provided some comic relief from the courtroom grind and the extreme seriousness of police officers and lawyers. "How's the job going, Harold?" I asked as part of our daily ritual. "All right," he answered through toothy gaps. "It's got its ups and downs." "Might go a little better if you washed your hair," I kidded. "Okay buddy, just step to the rear."

Christmas week I worked the five P.M. to one A.M. shift in arraignments. John Patton had offered us a choice of Thanksgiving or Christmas and I chose night court on Christmas.

After dark the arraignment court felt more like a police station than a hall of justice. The judge's bench was lit by a glaring desk lamp, the floor was dirty, and my ears rang with the drone of the court proceedings. The sweaty odor of men and women falling asleep on the pews in the audience and acrid disinfectant in the holding cells mixed with the smell of burnt coffee rising from the wastepaper basket under my table. The stenographer, an elderly man who wore the same plaid shirt each night, took down our every word like an automaton.

Defendants continued to look pale, poorly nourished, and angry as they emerged from the pens, and I still felt inclined to believe them when they alleged beatings, illegal searches, or shakedowns at the hands of the police. But while I hadn't forgotten that many of these "criminals" were driven to crime by poverty, racism, and other social ills, I could hardly expect an offer of Disorderly Conduct to miraculously change their lives. Too many were repeat offenders who abused the leniency shown to them on their first few brushes with the law. They had turned right around and gotten rearrested a day, a week, or a month later.

With the approach of the twenty-fifth, new arrests declined sharply, not because the crime rate slowed or because fewer officers were on the street, but because most cops just weren't interested in putting in overtime right before the holidays. Still, arraignment court was never empty. As usual, prostitutes were rushed through by the dozen. They all had phone-book rap sheets, and, one at a time, they unquestioningly pleaded guilty.

At sidebar one night, a visiting judge from Queens explained that it was her policy to give prostitutes three days instead of time served. "Under the Corrections Department's system," she said, "every defendant serves only one-third of her sentence before release. Three days means that the girls are due to be released immediately after arraignment—the same as Time Served. Corrections doesn't like it because it creates more paperwork, but I think three days looks better on their rap sheets." I nodded politely.

Having worked arraignments for the past three months, my colleagues and I finally were trusted to arraign the full spectrum of criminals, felons and misdemeanants alike. Handling felonies, even if only at arraignment, helped put the grind of petty crime into perspective. Every night one or two serious cases came through the system that, like Andrew Straight's hand-hack, made prosecuting seem worthwhile. As rookies, however, we remained under the strictest orders not to make offers and get dispositions on felonies. Our task was solely to convince a judge to impose whatever bail had been decided upon by senior prosecutors in the complaint room—who, unfortunately, lacked the benefit of a rap sheet. Whatever the merit of a defense lawyer's argument on behalf of a client, we had to blindly follow our orders. In certain cases, like a vicious murder or a large-quantity drug sale, a rap sheet made little difference: bail started at $50,000 or more, even for first offenders. But in the dozens of robberies that came through, a clean sheet could keep a defendant from spending days or even months in the pens wondering how to raise bail.

There was a muscular young man with tattooed arms and black hair slicked back like a fifties greaser. He had robbed a string of ice cream stores and each time shot one or two innocent bystanders. One of the victims had nearly bled to death. Though he had only one misdemeanor conviction, I asked for $100,000 bail. After a long-drawn-out argument from the defense attorney, the judge set $75,000.

A young man was accused of robbing a liquor store. He was a twenty-year-old black college student who had never been arrested before. He claimed that his was a case of mistaken identity: the officer had caught him blocks away from the scene of the crime, and the store owner, who was brought around, had confused him with the real robber. His mother and father sat in the front row of the audience. Over my request for $2,500 bail, the judge released him.

A skinny man named Angel was caught with 800 packets of heroin in his bicycle knapsack. I requested $50,000 and got it: this was his third felony.

One middle-aged woman was arrested when the police recovered three kilos of cocaine and two Uzi machine guns from her kitchen cabinets. Inside her bedroom, the officers found $200,000 in cash. Another ounce of cocaine turned up in her baby daughter's crib. Though the felony prosecutor in ECAB knew that this was the woman's first arrest, he told me to ask for $250,000 bail. It sounded high, but he turned out to be right. The defendant's lawyer said that her brother would post the money in the morning.

When I wasn't reading through our files constructing a bail argument, I often watched the prisoners seated on the bench and tried to pick the felons out of the crowd of misdemeanants. In one file, I read about a defendant who had taken his eleven-month-old daughter, climbed to the top of a stepladder, held the child at arm's length and dropped her on her head while the girl's mother stood by screaming. Then, in the words of our felony complaint, "the defendant scratched at her face with his fingernails, causing lacerations requiring plastic surgery." For some reason, I first imagined this child abuser as a meek family man who snapped under the pressure of work and debts. Then I suspected he might be a frenzied dope addict wanting to dispose of an unnecessary responsibility.

The clerk called the defendant's name and a man wearing a bushy goatee and a long, uneven Afro stepped to the paper arrow. His body was slender and sinewy. Glazed but aware eyes stared out from beneath hooded eyelids and looked boldly at the judge. When His Honor glanced up after reading the complaint, the defendant's expression and demeanor shifted. His hip swung to one side, his limbs relaxed, and a smug defiance showed in the trace of a smile. It was as if he were saying, "I'd do it again. Nobody knows my reasons, but they're all that protect me from you and whatever crazy punishment you choose for me. I'm laughing at you. Maybe to protect my self-respect, maybe because I'm crazy." Bail was set at $10,000. Two court officers attached themselves to the man and hustled him back into the holding cells.

There were moments that winter when I leaned toward becoming a hardened prosecutor who fought for ever higher sentences and bail, but inevitably I slipped back. Misdemeanors just seemed too picayune to fight over, and the social gains from ensuring higher sentences for minor offenders appeared, at best, uncertain.

In December, the mayor instituted a policy forbidding homeless people to sleep on the streets when the temperature falls below freezing. To enforce the rule, he ordered the police to round up street people and take them to shelters on icy nights. Many of the homeless resisted being herded into the shelters, where they claimed robberies and assaults were commonplace, and so the police occasionally were obliged to arrest the most recalcitrant of the street sleepers.

On New Year's Eve an elderly woman named Virginia Lee was brought before the court on a charge of Resisting Arrest. The write-up said that the police had found her sleeping at the Staten Island Ferry terminal and she had refused to leave. Dave Ames had recently informed us that we should assist in enforcing the mayor's new policy: no plea bargains.

Ms. Lee, a short, thickset woman wearing a moth-eaten fur coat and a filthy hair net, walked to the defendant's table. Despite her frowzy appearance, she carried herself with considerable self-possession, and looked Judge Fallan, a kindly, soft-spoken man, in the eye. She appeared angry, but also deeply wounded, as if someone had evicted her from her own home. I pictured her at the ferry slip, huddled amid her possessions, watching the lights flicker on the shore across the river.

Fallan and I had worked together for three evenings in a row and had developed a good rapport. He looked at the old woman and then at me. What difference did it make whether Ms. Lee pled guilty to a misdemeanor?

"The People offer Disorderly Conduct with a sentence of Time Served to cover the instant complaint," I said.

"Ma'am," Judge Fallan addressed the shrunken figure before the court, "how do you plead, guilty or not guilty? Before you answer, I am telling you now that if you admit to being disorderly, you can go home tonight. Do you understand?"

She entered her plea.

Clearly disturbed by the great void that loomed before this woman, Judge Fallan said, "Okay, ma'am, we're going to let you go now. But where are you planning to stay?"

"Your Honor, I'm going back to the ferry."

"But you can't sleep there. The officers will just bring you back to court again. Isn't that right, Mr. Prosecutor?" he asked.

"That's right, Judge," I said, having no idea whether in fact the police might not just let her alone from now on.

"Why not, Judge?" she asked. "There's lots of people sleeping there. Why can't I stay there too? I've been sleeping there for years."

"Don't you have any relations? The Mayor says it's against the law for you to go back there tonight and stay."

"No, Judge, I don't. I came here three years ago from Alabama and I've been sleeping at the terminal every night. Now all of a sudden I can't do that no more. If I can't, I guess I'll go back down south to my family.

"Some city," she rambled on. "You know who wrote the Constitution? Not the mayor, I'll tell you that much. If I was a drug dealer or a prostitute, they'd leave me alone. They'd just come, pick me up, let me out, and I'd be right back in the same old place. But no, they got nothin' better to do than pick on and harass some old lady."

Fallan cut the matter short. "Thank you, ma'am. Please step out. Mr. Clerk, call the next case." The following morning I found a note from Ames in my mailbox: "Why Dis Con?"

As we settled into the job of prosecuting petty criminals, we also settled into various camps. At Forlini's, where we used to gossip and trade anecdotes, I now overheard my friends calling Legal Aid lawyers "sleazy," and ridiculing lenient judges as "morons." Like every rookie, I resented being verbally abused by judges and positively hated listening to defenders' harangues on behalf of junkies and token-suckers, but judges and defenders seemed no more or less laudable a part of the system than prosecutors. Throughout my class, however, there was a growing sense of self-righteousness, as if being an ADA were the most noble of all legal existences, and being a team player meant not questioning that we were the good guys. Even Jim Bronson fell in with the mainstream, and our differing attitudes took a toll on our friendship.

The camaraderie that I enjoyed in Bureau 20 also began to demand a degree of conformity as a quid pro quo. One Legal Aid lawyer asked me, in all seriousness, whether ADAs were required to wear dark suits, white shirts, and red ties. Whenever I deviated from the starched Brooks Brothers norm, someone in the bureau would inevitably remark, "That's a nice shirt, but you look like a goddamn defense lawyer." My worn wingtips marked me, in Jim Bronson's words, as "suspiciously academic." The jokes were telling.

More unsettling still, few of my colleagues admitted to being disturbed by prosecuting homeless people or teenagers from the ghetto. The most gung-ho members of our office demonstrated a disturbing zeal for "locking up the scum," and I overheard one rookie remark with disappointment, "I thought we were going to be allowed to carry guns." We all tacitly recognized that the overwhelming majority of the people coming through Criminal Court were poor and from minority groups, but black and Hispanic prosecutors—who rarely went to Forlini's and complained about its clubhouse atmosphere—were the only ones I ever heard discuss the subject. Others just didn't want to talk about it. Questions about social injustice or the fact that jails only made defendants more deeply embittered brought unencouraging answers: "The slimeball shouldn't have been there in the first place." "You know what they say: 'Don't do the crime if you can't do the time.' "

It wasn't hard to understand why we fell in as we did. We all felt the siege mentality in court and knew that the system was functioning above capacity. Some ADAs sincerely believed that by regularly demanding heavy sentences they were doing the city good, keeping crime down, and justly punishing the guilty. Others, like myself, just as earnestly thought that it was better to reduce the number of marginal cases burdening the system, and to give petty offenders a break. The subject generated a lot of unspoken resentment.

I remembered that Scott Pryor, a rookie in Bureau 20, had once worried about becoming hardened by the job. At the time, it seemed an unlikely prospect. But the mounting pressure and frustration, I now understood, were bound to force us into one camp or another.

SEVEN

The People Are Ready

My first trial, *The People of the State of New York v. Eddie Martínez,* began on April Fool's Day. It had been assigned to me by a felony prosecutor after he reduced the charges —Assault and Criminal Possession of a Weapon—to misdemeanors. Eddie was a Puerto Rican in his fifties who, though arrested time and again, had always avoided being convicted. As his court-appointed attorney, Lawrence Millman, never tired of repeating to me during breaks in the proceedings, "Eddie has nine lives."

The case arose one night in Spanish Harlem out of a drunken argument between Eddie and his neighbor Hector García. The write-up read like a scene out of *West Side Story.* Eddie was in his third-floor tenement apartment when he heard Hector closing up his storefront. "Goddamn Dominicans, you work too fuckin' much and you make too fuckin' much noise," Eddie shouted out his window. "Go fuck yourself, Eddie," Hector retorted, and continued closing his store.

That, apparently, was enough to set Eddie's blood afire. Furious, he came downstairs with Victor, his thirteen year-old son. Victor climbed up on the roof of a car, hit Hector over the head with a crowbar, and ran back into the apartment building. Alone on the street with his dazed and staggering nemesis, Eddie pulled a knife and stabbed Hector in the abdomen. The police arrived minutes later and found Eddie upstairs.

On the morning of trial, the day after the case was assigned to me, I met my two witnesses for the first time. Misdemeanor trials on a day's notice were not out of the ordinary, even in a large, ostensibly well-organized prosecutor's office. The arresting officer, Police Officer Mark Shelley, wore a tie and a jacket with his shield pinned to the breast pocket. His blond hair was cropped close, and his eyes were blue and clear. He was eminently presentable. In a dirty shirt and blue jeans, Hector García, my star witness, was a mess. "We don't pick 'em," I thought, and sent Ida off to borrow a jacket for Hector to wear in court.

After a fifteen-minute interview, I xeroxed some police reports and took García and Shelley over to 100 Centre Street. It wasn't how I had pictured starting my first trial —thrown into a maze of facts, having to write my witnesses' names and the time and place of the crime in large block letters on a legal pad in case I blanked them out under the pressure of the moment. As we crossed the street on the way to court, the severity of the crime hit home: Hector had been stabbed with a knife and had spent ten days in the hospital. Even the one-year maximum seemed low.

Leland Sklar was presiding in Jury Part 15 and would be my trial judge. I knew Judge Sklar from night court and, like many ADAs, thought of him as one of the most even-tempered, intelligent members of the Criminal Court judiciary. Word at 100 Centre Street was that Sklar gave both sides a fair trial, a commodity apparently in short supply.

His Honor called us up to the bench.

"Counselor," he said to Lawrence Millman, Eddie's attorney, "I presume you're ready to go?"

"Yes, Your Honor. Mr. Martínez is ready, as you can see." He motioned over his shoulder toward a pale, almost gray-complexioned man with long, greasy hair who slumped casually behind the defense table. A tuft of gray hair grew out of a pronounced mole on his chin. Eddie looked even more disheveled than Hector.

"No way to dispose of this?" asked Sklar.

I had been on the verge of trial with at least ten other cases—witnesses ready, paperwork complete, defense lawyer and client present—only to have the court promise the defendant probation or a fine in exchange for a guilty plea. Eddie's case, however, was no ordinary misdemeanor. Sklar said he couldn't offer anything less than ten months—just two months under the maximum. I drew a breath of relief: Eddie risked almost nothing by fighting the case. I would be the third rookie in Bureau 20 to enter the almost sacred realm of being On Trial. John Patton would have to find someone to cover for me in night arraignments this week. I was "OT."

Sklar announced that we would begin at two-thirty that afternoon. I took him literally, and at the appointed hour I was standing outside the locked courtroom door with a file full of *Rosario* material, and questions for prospective jurors on my lips. At a quarter to three the court officers returned from lunch, and by three Eddie and his lawyer were at the defense table.

Judge Sklar assumed the bench.

"Gentlemen," he began, "thank you for being on time." Sklar then turned to his clerk and said, "Floyd, bring up a jury panel."

Everything I knew about picking juries—a procedure known as voir dire—I had learned in a training lecture delivered by Tom McGillicuddy, a bureau chief and top homicide prosecutor. He was an intense man with straight black hair and glasses, and he spoke with a smug exuberance untempered by his twenty years on the job.

"Some people say my notions about fit jurors are offensive," he had told us, months ago, "but they're wrong." A woman sitting next to me leaned over and whispered, "I hate him already."

"I wouldn't want him on my jury," I agreed.

"Above all," McGillicuddy said, "use voir dire to keep

nuts off the panel. For most cases, you want a middle-class, middle-aged jury, the types who have held the same job for a number of years and, preferably, who have children. They should be no-nonsense people who don't mind following orders and have a stake in the community." Warming to his subject, he continued, "Let's get down to brass tacks. No artists or musicians—they're too spacey and can't remember complex fact patterns." What about a Rachmaninoff piano concerto? I thought. "Writers are okay, but they tend to be too liberal and look for the defendant's motivation. You want 'Did he do it or didn't he?' types. No doormen. They always acquit. Janitors can be okay, but security guards will give you trouble."

The unabashed generalizations poured forth like a series of intentional faux pas, but McGillicuddy was serious. The Irish make bad jurors, but blacks are okay. Hispanics are only so-so, especially in domestic dispute cases. "Remember," he concluded, "you can win or lose a case during jury selection." The reasons for these assertions, I gathered, were self-evident.

"Judge," said Floyd, putting down the receiver, "if you're willing to wait about half an hour, I can get you a fresh panel." Jurors are shuttled around the courthouse in groups of fifty referred to as panels. An "old" panel can be filled with all the people who for one reason or another have not passed muster in other cases: kooks, illiterates, drunks, religious zealots, public-spirited elderly men and women with defective hearing aids, maybe even doormen. We all agreed to wait.

By a quarter to four a fresh panel was herded into the courtroom, and when all fifty had taken their seats Judge Sklar began: "Members of the jury, before we get into the case, do any of you have personal reasons why you would not be able to serve?" Ten hands shot up in response.

One by one the ten jurors came up to the bench and explained their problems. One young woman had recently injured her leg and couldn't sit for prolonged periods. She was excused. A vague young man wearing a beaded necklace said that he felt awkward. "Your Honor, you know, I'm not my brother's keeper. How can I say whether someone's guilty or not? It just doesn't seem right to me. Our task in life is not to judge one another, you know?"

"Sure," said Judge Sklar, casting me a sidelong glance. "You're excused."

A tense, angry man said that his best friend had been wrongly convicted by "Morgenthau's office" and that "anything coming out of there is full of shit, Your Honor." Another woman said she had been raped three times and robbed at gunpoint more times than she could remember. She felt she could be a fair juror but was nervous about being in the courthouse with so many criminals around. Eventually we weeded out the reluctant jurors, and I returned to the prosecution table ready to proceed.

"Members of the prospective jury," said Sklar, "it's now nearly four-thirty. I think it would be best for all if we reconvened tomorrow morning at nine-thirty sharp. Is that a problem for any of you?" The forty remaining jurors kept their hands in their laps. "Very well. Floyd, swear the panel in and send them home."

I had been on trial for nearly a full day and hadn't even started selecting a jury. I hadn't even opened my mouth.

That evening I interviewed both Officer Shelley and Hector García at greater length and then met with John Patton. Between drags on cigarettes, Patton gave me pointers on basic technical details like introducing hospital records into evidence and phrasing objections. But the best piece of advice he offered was, "Don't read from a piece of paper to the jury. Not that it's bad form, but they'll see it shaking in your hand."

After the coaching session, I left the office. On the subway ride home, over dinner with Kate, in front of the bathroom mirror, and fitfully through the night, I rehearsed my questions to the jury, opening statement, and direct examination of both witnesses. I was determined to nail the man who had stabbed Hector García. By the time

I left for work, I had tried the case five times over and was in typical trial lawyer's form: keyed-up, obsessed, and red-eyed.

As Sklar had ordered, I appeared in court at nine-thirty. Eddie and his lawyer were there, but only half of the panel had shown up, so again we waited. Delay, I sensed, is inseparable from the jury system. No wonder my friends kept asking me if I could get them off jury duty.

Hector and Officer Shelley had spent the previous day in a sealed witness room, and it looked as if their wait today was just beginning. At ten-fifteen, I stopped in to tell them that we were about to select jurors.

"Can't I go take care of some business while you're picking a jury?" Hector asked.

"Sorry," I answered. "We might finish early and you're the first and most important witness." If I don't win this case, I thought, he'll kill me. First he nearly gets stabbed to death, now he's going to be bored to death.

By one o'clock our jury—six main jurors and two alternates, one of the half-size juries that decide misdemeanor cases—had been selected and sworn in. At last we would begin.

"Members of the jury," said Sklar, "you are all excused for lunch. Return here at two-thirty." Delay, delay, delay. Waiting for the starting pistol.

Some lawyers say they never eat during trials, but I found food to be the only thing that stopped me from pacing maniacally around, tapping pencils on my desk, and rereading every note in my file ad nauseam. I ate two large sandwiches and an ice cream cone. On the way back to court, I grabbed a hot dog. Feeling somewhat weighted down but considerably less nervous, I arrived in Sklar's courtroom. For once, everyone was on time.

We began.

During my opening statement my voice quavered, I looked at the floor, and without the podium that I expected would be between me and the jury I searched in vain for a comfortable place to keep my hands. Most of what I said was boilerplate from the DA's trial preparation manual, but I tried to give a convincing performance. I told the jury that an opening statement is like the table of contents of a book or a movie preview. I listed the names of my witnesses and gave a brief summary of the case. Halfway through, I remembered to make eye contact with each juror. There were three men and five women. In voir dire I had followed McGillicuddy's rules—at least those about no-nonsense people—with one exception, a young woman from SoHo who dressed in black: an artist. She seemed intelligent and interested in the case, and I had many friends who are artists, so I offered no objection. I also wanted to prove that McGillicuddy's offensive generalizations were wrong. Now, seeing her in the jury box wearing what seemed a skeptical expression, I had second thoughts.

At the close of my speech, I quoted the DA's recommended ending word for word: "After you have heard all the evidence, I'm going to ask you to go to the jury room and reach the only just verdict possible, given the testimony you will hear. I'm going to ask you to find the defendant, Eddie Martínez, guilty of Assault in the Third Degree and Criminal Possession of a Weapon in the Fourth Degree. Thank you."

Millman's turn. He was a smooth old pro, tall and graceful, and I envied his ease before the jury.

"My client," he said pointing at Eddie, "is presumed under the law to be innocent. He and I could sit at the counsel table and play cards during the entire trial, and if the DA failed to put forward enough evidence you would have to find him not guilty. That's the law. It's the assistant DA's party." Millman turned to me, open palms facing up. "He invited you here; he has to provide the entertainment. And you have to be entertained *beyond a reasonable doubt.*" He let the words hang in the air.

I felt eight pairs of eyes boring holes into me. I was asking the jury to find a fellow citizen guilty of a crime, to strip him of his presumption of innocence. Millman was the poor soul's protector. The jurors laughed at Millman's jokes; they were charmed by his style. He wore his tie slightly askew. I wanted to tell the jurors that they could trust me, too. After Millman tossed off a few more folksy examples that made my burden of proof feel like the Earth itself on my shoulders, he sat down.

I called my first witness.

Hector García was led to the stand by a court officer. At my urging, Hector had worn a cleaner shirt and a jacket. He looked better groomed than the day before, and he testified with disarming sincerity. Hector had no trouble pointing out Eddie as the man who had stabbed him, and when he lifted up his shirt to show the jury his stab wound, I heard their quiet, involuntary expressions of shock. Leaving Hector on the stand, I introduced the hospital records into evidence under a provision of the Criminal Procedure Law that dispenses with the need for a witness from the hospital. Good luck, Mr. Millman, I thought.

"Mr. García," Millman began without losing a beat, "did you sign a complaint report in this case?"

"Yes, sir," Hector answered.

"And you read it and swore to it before you signed it. Isn't that right?"

"Yes."

"Now, you just testified that my client stabbed you with a knife. Am I correct?"

"That's correct."

"But, sir, the complaint report you signed says Mr. Martínez stabbed you with a *crowbar*. Isn't that true?"

"No, sir, that's not true." Hector looked over at me, nervous and confused.

I dug through my trial folder and found the report. It was signed by both Hector and Officer Shelley. Oh, God, I thought, it says "crowbar"! How the hell did I miss that? I looked over at the jury, feeling them staring me down again. Millman handed a copy of the report to the clerk, had it marked Defense Exhibit A, and then read it aloud.

When he reached "crowbar," I blushed and wanted to skulk out of the room.

"Mr. García," Millman went on, now indignant, "you swore in the complaint report you were stabbed with a crowbar, did you not?"

"I must have," Hector said.

"Now, today, you are swearing you were stabbed with a knife. Right?"

"Uh-huh," mumbled Hector.

"Were you lying then, or are you lying now?" asked Millman, looking at the jury.

I objected to the question and Sklar ordered it stricken from the record, but the damage had been done. By the time Millman finished with Hector, the jury, especially the SoHo artist, looked angry. Even I was beginning to have a reasonable doubt about the case. On redirect examination I asked Hector whether he was sure he had been stabbed with a knife. He said he was sure. "First the kid hit me with a crowbar, then Eddie stabbed me." But the jurors continued to look at me quizzically. As they filed out for the day, Millman leaned over from his table and said, "I told you. Nine lives."

I went directly to John Patton's office.

"Did Millman use the 'It's the DA's party' or the 'We could sit here and play cards' line in his opening?" he asked as I walked in.

"Both," I said. "But John, I'm afraid he made Hector look pretty bad. Millman introduced the complaint report into evidence and it says Martínez stabbed Hector with a crowbar, not a knife. He basically made Hector out to be either a liar or an idiot."

"That means you've won," said Patton. This was news to me.

"First of all," he said, "impeaching a witness with the complaint report is the oldest trick in the book, and it almost never works. If that's all Millman used against Hector, it means he's got nothing to go on. Those reports are always full of mistakes, and nobody reads them carefully.

Besides, in your case Hector had been stabbed just before he signed it. He couldn't have read the report carefully. You mentioned that in redirect exam, didn't you?"

"Well, not exactly."

"Okay, so you screwed that one thing up. You'll still win. What's Millman going to argue? That Hector wasn't stabbed with a knife? It's impossible to stab someone with a crowbar. You don't have to be a rocket scientist to understand that. Tomorrow morning, have Officer Shelley testify about Hector's condition at the time he signed the report. It might even be more dramatic that way."

I felt better about Hector's testimony, but far from relieved. The jury didn't have John Patton to guide them.

Walking to court the next morning I envisioned Officer Shelley on the stand, calmly dismantling Millman's innuendos.

"The People call Police Officer Mark Shelley."

Shelley walked to the stand, looking his usual well-dressed and clean-cut self. The SoHo artist sat with her arms crossed defensively across her chest as he swore to tell the truth. The rest of the panel leaned forward in their seats, as if to say, "This had better be good."

After some preliminary testimony, Shelley read the complaint report on the stand, identified the crowbar mistake as his own, and explained that Hector had signed the report while in his hospital bed.

"Officer," I asked, "please describe Mr. García's physical condition at the time he signed Defense Exhibit A."

"Hector's condition? He was a wreck. I mean, he had just been hit over the head with a crowbar and stabbed in the stomach. Let's just say he wasn't at his best."

The effect on the jurors was palpable. They relaxed in their seats, the SoHo artist uncrossed her arms, and the foreperson looked up at me approvingly. Okay, Mr. Millman, we're even. "No further questions, Your Honor."

Millman lit in aggressively, voice raised from the first. "Officer Shelley, isn't it true that when you arrived at the scene, there was a crowd of people gathered around Mr. García?"

"I don't exactly recall, sir." It was the first I had heard about a crowd.

"Officer, isn't it true that there was in fact a crowd, a large crowd, at the scene when you arrived? Surely you wouldn't forget an important fact like that?"

"Sir, as I think about it, there was a crowd."

"And isn't it also a fact that people in the crowd told you a young boy had assaulted Mr. García?"

"Sir, people were saying a lot of things." Shelley was starting to sound like the cops in ECAB with dropsy cases.

"Officer Shelley, I asked you a question."

"Well, sir. Yes, I believe one or two people said a kid had hit the complainant."

"Officer, did you take down their names?"

"Negative, sir. I did not." I tried to keep my distress from showing as Millman did a mock double take.

"Wait a minute, Officer. Are you saying that there were witnesses who identified *another person* as the real criminal, but you arrested my client instead?"

Shelley got angry. "Listen, Counselor, I arrested the perp because Hector García told me, 'Eddie Martínez stabbed me.'" *The perp.* I cringed at Shelley's defensive tone.

"But, Officer, didn't you just testify that Mr. García wasn't 'at his best' that night?"

"Yes, sir. But—"

"And you also testified that other witnesses identified a young boy as the real criminal? Isn't that also true?"

"Yes."

"But you chose to believe a man bleeding on the street, over two voluntary witnesses. They weren't bleeding too, were they?"

"Objection."

"Never mind," said Millman, laughing. "I withdraw the question." The SoHo artist crossed her arms again. "Now,

Officer, you never recovered the knife from the scene of the crime, did you?"

"No, sir. I looked around but didn't find one."

"But you didn't go back to the scene of the crime later that night to look further, did you?"

"No."

"You just took Mr. García's word for everything, isn't that right?"

"Objection."

"I withdraw the question, Your Honor. Officer, did you ever stop to ask Mr. Martínez his version of what happened?"

"Yes, sir. He denied the crime."

"And you didn't believe him?"

"Correct, sir."

"And," Millman continued belligerently, "you never read him his rights, did you?"

Shelley looked over at me. I knew he hadn't given Martínez his *Miranda* warnings, but legally it made no difference; the arrest was still proper. Failure to read the warnings affected only the use of any incriminating statements Eddie might have made. The effect on the jury, however, was something unforeseen. They waited, rapt, for Shelley's answer.

"No, sir. I didn't." Their backs stiffened, faces hardened.

"Now, Officer Shelley, one more item. You found a thirteen-year-old boy with Mr. Martínez when you went up to his apartment, isn't that right?"

"Yes, sir. The defendant's son."

"You didn't arrest him, even though witnesses said a young boy had assaulted Mr. García, did you?"

"No, sir, I did not."

"Officer, you knew Eddie Martínez from the neighborhood before this incident occurred. Correct?"

Shelley shifted uncomfortably. "I don't know what you're driving at, Counselor."

"Officer, isn't it true that you saw Mr. Martínez almost

every day on your patrol and that you didn't like Mr. Martínez?"

"Negative. Eddie and I had had words on one prior occasion. He had been drinking in public, and I told him to move along."

"Did Mr. Martínez move along as you requested?"

"Only after I threatened to arrest him for blocking pedestrian traffic."

"But Mr. Martínez wasn't lying across the entire sidewalk, was he?"

"Objection," I said. Once more Millman had turned the case inside out.

"That's okay, Your Honor," he laughed. "I withdraw the question. I'm through with the police officer." Millman spat out the last words as if they had a sour taste.

That was my case: a victim who signed whatever the police put in front of him and a cop who had a grudge against the defendant, didn't read him his rights, ignored witnesses, never searched for the assault weapon, and failed to arrest the more likely perpetrator, Eddie's son. I had promised proof beyond a reasonable doubt and instead I had been publicly humiliated.

"Your Honor," I said, rising to my feet, "the People rest."

Over lunch I paced up and down in Patton's office and complained that things had gone from bad to worse. "You worry too much," he said. "I've been doing this stuff for years, and I still never know what a witness will say in court. No matter how many times you go over it in your office they say something you don't expect in court. The only thing you can be sure of is that it'll be different. That's the fun of it. Next time you'll know to ask your cop whether he knew the defendant. Anyway, you're still going to win."

Back in court, Millman rose and said, "The defense calls Victor Martínez." A skinny young boy wearing a T-shirt and jeans was led to the stand by a court officer. Apart from his deep brown eyes, he looked a little too tough for a thirteen-year-old. His hands were dirty and his hair, like his father's, was stringy and greasy. I wondered whether Victor would try to take the heat for his father by claiming that he had stabbed Hector.

Millman went slowly through the pedigree: State your name, your age. Where do you live? What school do you attend? What courses do you take? The jury soaked up every word.

"Tell the members of the jury what happened the night your daddy got arrested," Millman asked.

"I heard my father shouting, and I went downstairs with him. The man who owns the store underneath us yelled at him some more. I got scared for my father so I stood up on the roof of a car and hit the man over the head with a crowbar."

"Did you see what your father did?"

"No, I ran away after I hit the man." Victor looked over at his "daddy," that poor, oily-haired man facing criminal charges. He lent the case an air of tragedy. Only thirteen years old, Victor had to come to court to defend his father.

Cross-examination required a soft touch. Gently, I asked Victor two questions.

"You didn't stab the man after you hit him with the crowbar, did you?"

"No, sir."

"After you ran away, your father stayed with the man, didn't he?"

Victor paused. He looked at me, at Eddie, at the judge. "He stayed with the man," Victor said to Judge Sklar in an almost confessional tone.

"No further questions." I had finally won a round.

Millman called Eddie as the last witness. Predictably, he denied everything. "Yeah, I argued with Hector, but I didn't stab nobody. I'm a peaceful man. Hector and the cop don't like me. That's why they framed me."

I had nothing concrete, so I began cross-examination with a long shot.

"You had been drinking the night Hector García was

stabbed, hadn't you?" The question was objectionable—
no blood alcohol test had been taken that night—but Millman didn't try to stop me.

"Yeah," said Eddie. He could have said no, and that
would have been the end of the subject. Now the door was
open.

"In fact, you had been drinking a lot. Isn't that right?"

"Yeah."

"How much is a lot, Mr. Martínez?"

"I think I had seven or eight vodkas." I heard a murmur
pass through the jury.

"And that was just before you went downstairs to argue
with Hector García, right?"

"Yeah." I sat down.

That afternoon we delivered closing arguments. As defense counsel, Millman went first, and, as usual, he was
good.

"My client is protected by a stone mantle," he began,
one hand resting on the jury box, "a mantle called the
presumption of innocence. The DA has tried to chip away
at that mantle, but I think it's safe to say the mantle is still
intact.

"Who are the DA's witnesses? A store owner who said
my client stabbed him. But what kind of mental state was
he in when the crime occurred? He had just been hit over
the head with a crowbar. A *crowbar*. Think how clear your
perceptions would be if that happened to you. What did
the police officer say? 'Hector was a wreck.' Who knows if
Hector ever clearly saw the face of the person who
stabbed him? He was in such a dazed state, he couldn't
even read the complaint report—an important police
document. But would you sign one without reading it
carefully?

"And Officer Shelley, a cop who calls the defendant the
'perp'—how many of you even know what that word
means?—and neglects to read his own prisoner his constitutional rights. What kind of a public servant is that? He
can't even tell a knife from a crowbar. And more impor-

tant, Shelley had it in for Mr. Martínez, as he told you himself. This case provided a golden opportunity to get even. The witnesses at the scene all said a boy assaulted Hector. Shelley found a boy—Victor—who admits at least to using a crowbar on Hector, but what did he do? He arrested Eddie.

"And, finally, Eddie Martínez himself took the stand. He didn't have to, you know that. He has a right to remain silent. But Eddie Martínez broke the silence because he wanted to tell you the truth. He didn't want to leave any worries lingering in your minds. He even admitted to you he was drunk that night. He could have denied it, but he wanted to tell you the truth, the whole ugly truth, and that's just what he did. When he told you, 'seven or eight vodkas,' you probably wondered for a moment. But now you can see that those vodkas are the badge of truth-telling, a sign of honesty.

"Before I sit down, let me remind you of what I said earlier. The DA alone must prove his case to you beyond a reasonable doubt. This one doesn't even come close. Eddie Martínez is not guilty."

When I stood up, I noticed John Patton and a group of rookies from Bureau 20, including Jim Bronson, sitting at the front of the audience, here to watch me lose my first case. The panel looked up at me, expectant.

"Members of the jury," I began, my hands trembling, "remember your reaction when Hector García took the stand. Remember his scar, remember his honesty. That's what this case is about, not a police report or a son's loyalty to his father. The only witness to contradict Hector about the stabbing was Eddie, and no one in the world has a greater interest in the outcome of the case than he does."

I reminded the jury that even Victor, Eddie's own son, agreed that Eddie was the last person to be seen with Hector. I quoted the hospital records that confirmed Hector had been stabbed. "It's a big city, ladies and gentlemen. Do you really expect a police officer to comb through alleyways and garbage cans looking for a knife?

He already knew who committed the crime and had a bleeding victim to care for."

I ended on my strongest point. "Why do you think all the witnesses on the street said a young boy assaulted Hector? I'll tell you. Victor stood on the roof of a car and swung a crowbar over his head. Anyone standing around could see that. But Eddie, the last person to be seen with Hector, stabbed him in the stomach—at a level that no one could possibly observe. All the evidence points in one direction and one direction only. Eddie Martínez is guilty of both Assault and Criminal Possession of a Weapon."

Sklar read the jury their instructions, dismissed the two alternates, and sent the remaining six off to deliberate. The next few hours were an agony of waiting, a painful suspended animation. John Patton and Jim Bronson both shook my hand after summations and said I had done a fine job, but I hardly heard their praise. For the first time I realized how badly I wanted to win.

At five-thirty my phone rang. Floyd, the clerk, said, "There's a verdict." My heart beat in my eardrums. Walking across the street, I took deep breaths to keep calm, and bought a hot dog.

As the jury filed in, they all deliberately avoided my gaze. A woman in the front row handed the verdict sheet to Sklar, who asked, "Madame Foreperson, have you reached a verdict?"

"Yes, we have, Your Honor."

"As to Count One of the complaint charging Eddie Martínez with Criminal Possession of a Weapon in the Fourth Degree, how do you find?"

"Not Guilty."

My stomach contracted. I felt numb. What would I tell my colleagues, Patton, Hector?

"As to Count Two of the complaint charging Assault in the Third Degree, how do you find?"

"Guilty."

I wanted the foreperson to repeat it, just so I could be sure I hadn't misheard. What did it mean? Eddie had assaulted Hector, but without a weapon? The two counts were both class A misdemeanors, so it didn't matter that Eddie had beat one. He still faced the maximum of a year.

"Mr. Millman, does the defendant wish me to poll the jury as to their verdict on Count Two?"

"Yes, Your Honor."

Each juror rose and, watching Eddie, clearly and loudly said, "Guilty." Except the SoHo artist. She was the last to speak. When Sklar asked, "Do you agree with the verdict as to Count Two?" she hesitated and in a halfhearted manner said, "Yeah."

Eddie had used up his nine lives.

The verdict in, Patton again congratulated me. This time his praise penetrated. Law school was still a recent enough memory to make evaluations feed my ego like manna, and I repeated his words to myself for days.

After Eddie's case, I went back to ECAB, arraignments, AP-2, night work, day work, answering motions, filling out forms. The criminal justice machine kept churning in the background, always ready to swallow us up.

Soon enough, however, other trials came my way. The second took place before a single judge, with no jury, and involved two members of a Colombian pickpocket team who stole a woman's wallet during the San Gennaro festival in Little Italy. My main witness, Detective Monica Troia, twenty years on the force, stole the show. Again I won.

Another case involved a defendant who collected money at the door of a Forty-second Street massage parlor. An undercover officer had gone to one of the booths and asked the masseuse for her menu of prices. After she rattled off a list of illegal acts, the officer went to the man at the door and complained about the excessive price of a blow job. When he convinced the masseuse to lower her price by ten bucks, the officer arrested them both. The masseuse pled guilty and got time served, but her co-defendant—essentially the manager of the parlor—would not get off as lightly, so he held out for a trial. The case was also tried without a jury, but still all the testimony had to be transcribed, in this instance by a diminutive, white-haired woman who had only recently come to Criminal Court.

"What did you say to the woman in the massage booth?" I asked the undercover officer.

"I asked what her prices were," he answered.

"What was her response?"

"She said, 'It's forty dollars for a hand job, sixty for a blow job, eighty for fuck and suck, and a hundred for around the world.' "

"Excuse me, Officer," the judge interjected, "but those terms will not suffice under the Penal Code. You'll have to give us more literal definitions."

As requested, the officer graphically defined all the terms. When he arrived at "around the world" I glanced at the stenographer. She transcribed every word, but looked a little uncomfortable.

The trial took a surreal turn when the defendant took the stand to explain that he had a hearing defect. He said that when the officer complained about the price of a blow job, he didn't understand what the "customer" was saying. The defendant had even hired a hearing expert to testify about his impairment. The judge convicted the man immediately.

Winning seemed so simple: just put the witnesses on the stand, ask them to tell their stories, and sit down. By the time I reached my fourth trial, I felt invincible. This one involved an assault on a Sanitation Enforcement Officer, a member of a unit I nicknamed the "garbage police." One Saturday morning, a garbage cop spotted a truck driver illegally unloading styrofoam boxes into a city-owned garbage can. When the officer tried to write the truck driver a ticket, the driver pushed the cop to the ground and began kicking him. A fellow sanitation officer saw the fight, pulled the two apart, and arrested the driver. At the time, the driver was on probation for a violent felony.

The injured sanitation officer arrived in my office accompanied by two serious-looking men who described themselves as "inspectors." They had come along, they said, to make sure the case got taken seriously.

The officer himself was a cheerful, round-faced black man. "I don't know why the guy hit me," he said. "I just wanted to give him a ticket. It was only a ten-dollar ticket, too. But then he just starts slamming me. I never even got a chance to defend myself."

After the interview, I felt certain that he had done nothing to provoke the fight. That he was attacked in the line of duty made the crime seem all the more outrageous. "There will be no plea-bargaining in this case," I told the stony-faced inspectors.

A month later we went to trial, my second experience before a jury. After a day of jury selection and false starts, I delivered my opening statement: "Members of the jury, this case involves an unprovoked assault on a sanitation officer, a city official who, at the time, was carrying out his duty." It sounded convincing. The jurors looked impressed. The defense chose not to make an opening statement.

I called the round-faced garbage cop to the stand and he testified in the sincere, wide-eyed manner that had initially won my confidence. My opponent, Earl Pines, a rookie Legal Aid lawyer, had a sly look about him that gave me some unease. My humiliation at the hands of Lawrence Millman, though by now a few months old, was not forgotten.

"Isn't it true," Pines asked the roly-poly garbage cop on cross-examination, "that you first hit my client, not the other way around?"

"Objection." I sprang to my feet.

"It's cross-examination," said the judge, "Mr. Pines should be allowed some leeway. Answer the question, sir."

"No, of course not," the victim calmly responded. "I just wanted to give him a ticket. Then he jumped on me."

"Isn't it true that you yelled at him first, that you provoked him?"

"No."

Every suggestion and leading question met with the officer's calm denial. Earl seemed to be getting nowhere. The defendant, a tall, sinewy man with deep-set eyes, sat stiffly at the defense table. My direct case completed, I awaited his side of the story.

The first defense witness was a man wearing a windbreaker and jeans. He had a three-day beard, and tattoos on the backs of both hands. When he took a seat before the jury, his jacket pulled open to reveal a T-shirt that said FULL MOON SALOON over a crude rendering of a naked woman with her buttocks in the air. Between his T-shirt and his having nothing to say about how the fight got started, he ended up making the defendant look worse.

"No cross-examination, Your Honor."

Next, the defendant walked to the stand. He folded his large hands in his lap. The clerk swore him in and asked, "State your name and county of residence."

"My name is . . ." He paused and then started again. "My name is Richard . . ." Then he stopped.

All eyes were on this skinny, dark-eyed man who seemed unable even to remember his own name. Losing the struggle to keep his composure, he wept. In arraignments defendants often cried, but something about this man's quiet tears was especially disturbing.

The court called a recess, and when we returned the defendant told his side of the story. "The officer started it all," he said. "He ran over to me, yelling right from the start. Then he began pushing and threatening. After a few pushes, I admit I did fight back, but I had no choice."

Cross-examination was easy. As I went over the defendant's past crimes and the fact that he was currently on felony probation, he twisted in his seat and fingered the arms of the chair. He became angry as I forced him to go over in detail exactly what the cop had said and done. "In your direct testimony you said that the officer had first swung a fist at you. But just a moment ago you said he first tried to kick you. Which was it?" "The officer never used his nightstick, did he?" "He didn't use his gun?" "But he attacked you with his bare hands?" I sat down, victory assured.

"Your Honor," said Earl Pines, "there is a witness on his way over to court as we speak. Could we adjourn for fifteen minutes?" Feeling that Pines's first character witness had only hurt his client's case, I offered no objection: more equivocal testimony from the Full Moon Saloon could only speed the jury toward conviction.

When we reconvened, an unassuming man wearing a shirt and tie took the stand. He swore to tell the truth. "I own a bar across the street from where that guy over there"—he pointed at the defendant—"got arrested. I was working that morning, opening up shop, when I heard somebody shouting. I looked out my window and saw a big fat cop screaming at the guy. He was just putting these styrofoam containers into a garbage can. Next thing I know, the cop starts swinging at him out of nowhere. After a few swipes from the fat cop, the guy swung back and then they both hit the ground."

On cross-examination, I looked unsuccessfully for loopholes. The witness didn't know the defendant, hadn't been coached by the lawyers, and had never seen the officers before. He had had a clear view through the barroom window and had watched the entire episode from start to finish.

The jury came back in less than half an hour, and I breathed a sigh of relief when they acquitted.

Though I always enjoyed the drama, jury trials seemed oddly out of place in the 100 Centre Street assembly line. After months of two-minute court appearances and negotiations in which guilt was more often than not presumed, a case suddenly ballooned into a week-long examination of fact. Trials happened almost at random—some defendants pled out earlier on, some didn't. It had little to do with the severity of the offense or the likelihood of conviction. And with hundreds of cases in my file drawers, I could never be fully prepared on each one.

Many prosecutors resented the jury system, and at times I shared their feelings. By definition jurors were not insiders. They had never heard the "DA's party" or "stone mantle" lines. The stock arguments of counsel, which would have bored an experienced judge, impressed them. The standard excuses offered by defendants came as revelations. They rendered bizarre verdicts, as in Eddie Martínez's case, and generated endless delays. "Twelve peers, good and true" seemed a far cry from six jurors, no artists or doormen, herded into the Criminal Justice Building and then picked over for hours by lawyers. In a trial-advocacy lecture we were warned never to ask jurors after a trial how they had reached their verdict. Their answers would be too disturbingly unrelated to the facts.

EIGHT

Con Games
and Guilty Victims

As the weather turned warmer and tourists thronged Rockefeller Center and Times Square, I noticed a new species of crime arriving at 100 Centre Street: con games. During training, a pair of seasoned detectives had lectured to our class on the subject. They distributed a manual entitled "Pickpockets and Con Games: Research and Personal Experience" and showed us filmed re-enactments of schemes ranging from three-card monte to a high-stakes swindle perpetrated by a team of sophisticated professionals. Some of the scams seemed so transparent I couldn't believe that they fooled even the dullest-witted hayseed, but as the cases came through the system I realized that their success depended upon a principle entirely different from trickery, and more insidious.

One night, two young Swedes on vacation in New York showed up in the complaint room. They were both burned-out hippies with long blond hair and love beads, and they looked as if they had taken too much LSD. In the interview they were alarmingly slow on the uptake.

The previous day, on Forty-second Street, the pair had met a fellow tourist who handed them a piece of paper bearing an address that he said he was having trouble locating. As the three vainly searched for the building, the tourist talked about how untrustworthy and suspicious people seemed here in Manhattan, so unlike the honest folk in his home country. Before long, the group determined that the address on the note was incorrect.

"Now I don't know where to go," the tourist complained. "Would you mind waiting for me while I make a phone call to a relative of mine who lives here?"

The Swedes were only too glad to help.

"Thank you," he said, "but I really feel uncomfortable carrying around all my money." He flashed a thick wad of twenty-dollar bills with which he hoped to get started in the city. "I tell you what, you hold my money while I make the phone call. Okay? I know it will be safe if I leave it with you two." They agreed.

"I appreciate it," the tourist went on, "but I want you to treat my money just as carefully as if it were your own. In my country we carry our money in a handkerchief tied with a special knot—like this." He demonstrated a complicated system of knotting a red bandana around his fist-sized bundle of cash. Then he added, "Just to make me feel better, you put your valuables together with mine in the handkerchief so I know everything will be safe. Okay?"

The slow-witted Swedes handed over their cash and return tickets to Stockholm, and the tourist knotted up the loot in the handkerchief.

"Now," he said, "you must carry the handkerchief in your coat—just like this—so nobody comes along and picks your pocket." He slipped the bundle inside his coat and drew out an identically knotted handkerchief. The Swedes took the packet and agreed to rendezvous in ten minutes. When the tourist failed to return, they untied the substituted handkerchief and found a wad of shredded newspaper.

Against all odds, the Swedes recognized the con man the next day standing on a subway platform. One of the two travelers approached him and said, "Hello, remember me?" The swindler pushed his former victim away and bolted—straight into the arms of a policeman summoned by the other Swede to watch the confrontation.

When the case arrived in ECAB, we learned that the Swedes were leaving the United States permanently in two weeks. Trial, obviously, could be months away. Knowing that the case would never pass muster as a felony, the ECAB supervisor reduced the charges to misdemeanors, and handed the file to me. The crime was known on the street as "the Spanish-handkerchief switch," and prosecuting it required a bit of bluffing, a con game in its own right. I wrote across the Data Sheet: *Offer 90 days. CONFIDENTIAL: witnesses leaving town.* From the con man's point of view, the lenient offer presented an interesting dilemma: demand a trial and find out that the Swedes are students who plan to return to Hunter College in the fall, or take ninety days in Riker's. The con man, I discovered two days later, took the safer route: three months in Riker's.

There were many other con games played on the street besides the handkerchief switch, the most elaborate being "the pocketbook drop." This scheme, I was told, once ended with two elderly sisters committing suicide after it had stripped them of their life savings. Although I never handled one of these cases directly, I learned about the game from a pair of detectives who had spent ten years on pickpocket patrol in midtown Manhattan.

The con usually begins when the first con artist "finds" a pocketbook on the street and asks a potential victim if it belongs to her. Together they open the bag and discover a bankroll, in some cases thousands of dollars, with no identification. While the two finders discuss what to do next, a curious passerby stops and inquires. The passerby says that he has a friend who works in a bank across the street and who might be able to tell them what to do. After a brief discussion, the pocketbook is given over and the victim and the first con artist watch as the stranger disappears into the bank.

Minutes later, the stranger returns. His banker friend, he says, warns that they are all legally bound to give the money to the police so that the rightful owner can claim it, and that in his experience finders of property rarely get to keep their windfall, even if it goes unclaimed. The banker will agree to keep quiet about the whole operation in exchange for a share of the profits. For their mutual protection, however, he wants to verify that each finder is well enough off to hide his or her sudden wealth: he wants to see a thousand dollars cash apiece. Hearing this, the first con artist says that the whole thing has gotten out of hand and he no longer wants any part of it.

But before he can walk off, the second con man tries to convince him that there's nothing to lose if everyone cooperates. The first con eventually agrees, withdraws a thousand dollars from his bank, and quickly returns. The second man takes the money and runs over to the bank. While waiting for his friend to return, the first con bemoans his own stupidity to the victim: he has lost not only their newfound money but a thousand dollars of his own as well. To the great surprise of both, the second con returns and hands over the security money and a quarter of the treasure.

The moment of truth having arrived, both con artists exhort the victim to play along. Having seen with her own eyes how trustworthy both of these happily met strangers are, she goes to her own bank, withdraws a thousand dollars, and gives it to con man number two, who runs across the street and disappears as before. The first con suddenly recalls an appointment and leaves the victim, a thousand dollars poorer, alone on the street waiting for the second con man—who, of course, never returns.

More sophisticated con artists take the crime one step further, preying upon the victim's desire for retribution. A new member of the con team telephones the victim after the crime, identifies himself as a New York City detective, and asks if she has recently been swindled: some of his operatives spotted her with two well-known con artists wanted by the authorities. An appointment is set up, and a day later a detective and uniformed patrolman arrive at the victim's home.

They listen sympathetically to the victim's tale of abused trust. Could she identify the men if she saw them again? Yes, she's sure she could; she is willing to do anything to help catch these ruthless criminals. The detective explains that the police also suspect one of the tellers in her bank. The problem, however, is that they need more evidence linking him to the crime. Would she withdraw a large sum of cash from her savings account? She needn't fear for her money—all the bills will be marked, and she will receive a police department check in place of the evidence.

She says she is willing to do anything.

The next day the three meet at the bank, where the victim again hands over a large slice of her savings. The new con men take the money, issue a bogus check, and then disappear as mysteriously as they entered her life.

Gambling cases, which constituted a surprisingly large class of crimes, also proved to be a species of con game. Every New Yorker recognizes the fast-talking three-card monte dealers on the midtown boardwalks, shuffling three ragged cards on top of a cardboard box while trying to hustle a couple of out-of-town suckers. The dealer places the cards—one red and two black—face up on the table, flips them over, and with a few deft motions rearranges them before the bettor's eyes. The game pays two-to-one if the bettor picks out the red card. Under the Penal Code, monte constitutes illegal gambling, but as played in New York City, it is a con game.

To pique a bettor's interest, dealers begin by losing large sums of money to plants in the crowd. Playing against these "strangers," the dealer clumsily moves the three cards, or "inadvertently" marks the corner of the red card so the victim eventually believes that the sucker is on the opposite side of the table. As the plants win hand after hand and the dealer complains how much the game is costing him, the conned victim decides to get in on the action. Once the victim puts down his cash, however, the game shifts course.

In one scenario, by far the least odious, the dealer fixes the inadvertently marked card and deals with remarkably improved ability. Taken off guard, victims lose a few hands and walk off, forty dollars poorer. In another variation, a plant walks past the table and says, "Police," just after the bettor lays down his wager. The dealer and his cronies pick up the cards, take the victim's money, and run, leaving the ragged cardboard table as the only hint of their presence.

In the nastiest of all monte scams, the victim is allowed to win a few hands. No matter the size of the bet, the dealer uncomplainingly pays out two-to-one winnings and eventually allows him to walk off. At either end of the block, however, members of the team wait to retrieve the winner's windfall and his wager, either by intimidation or by force.

When possible we prosecuted monte dealers, but they had an easy time of it at the hands of judges concerned about limited jail space. Many forty-time offenders walked cockily out of arraignment court with nothing more than a hundred-dollar fine due in a month. Gamblers, after all, posed little threat of violence—better to save the cell at Riker's for a gun-possessor. The officers, however, made no secret of their frustration at seeing the people they had arrested days before back on the street, making enough money each week to pay their fines twenty times over.

At first I tended to side with judges about giving monte dealers a break. The game itself seemed on a par with the unwinnable tests of "skill" at traveling circuses, in which tourists lose dollar after dollar and consider the money well spent on a good time. It was the gambler's risk. And if he or she was robbed afterward, we should prosecute for robbery, not waste time over a gambling complaint.

Some cases, however, made the question seem a bit more complex. Barry Gold worked as a teller in a midtown bank. One July afternoon while on his lunch break, Gold walked by a game of one hundred operated by an ex-felon named Clarence Smith. In one hundred the bettor rolls three marbles down an inclined board punctuated by a series of marble-sized holes numbered from one to one hundred. If the numbers of the holes where the marbles land total exactly one hundred, the bettor wins one hundred times his wager. The odds, of course, favor the house astronomically.

Gold bet ten dollars on the game and lost. For some reason, perhaps a latent gambling addiction, Gold, who had never so much as been arrested, returned to the bank where he worked, withdrew three thousand dollars out of a stranger's account, and raced back to Smith and his game. Over the next half hour, Gold's wagers increased from ten to fifty to one hundred dollars, and eventually the whole three thousand flowed into Smith's pocket. Hopelessly ensnared by his wrongdoing, Gold went back to the bank and dipped into another stranger's account, this time for five thousand dollars.

All afternoon Smith's take swelled as Gold gambled and lost twenty-nine thousand dollars stolen from five different accounts. Returning to the bank for what he vowed would be the last time, Gold withdrew a final three thousand. He walked mechanically through the midtown crowds back to the scene. In the meantime, Smith had been joined by a man in a white suit who leaned casually against a red cadillac. Gold handed the whole three thousand to Smith as one bet and, with the feverish intensity of a person trying to rescue himself from inevitable tragedy, rolled his marbles down the board. Gold added the numbers—a perfect one hundred.

Beaming ingenuously, he turned to Smith and said, "I won, don't you see it? You owe me three hundred thousand dollars!" Smith walked over to the white-suited man sitting on the hood of the car and exchanged a few words.

"What's wrong?" Gold demanded, sensing his victory ebb away. "Give me my money."

"Sorry, man," said Smith, "but we weren't finished counting your bet yet, so it's no good. Why don't you try another roll, now that we're set?"

Gold was about to insist on his due when three bruisers loomed out of nowhere and stared him down. After wavering between revenge and fear of the repercussions of his own theft, Gold eventually turned himself in at the local precinct and led an officer back to where Smith was still hawking his game of chance. Both Gold and Smith were arrested and prosecuted. For his promise to repay the stolen cash (which had disappeared, presumably in the Cadillac) and testify against Smith, Gold pled to a misdemeanor. Smith was indicted for Grand Larceny.

The real art in gambling cases and con games lay not in duping the unsuspecting but in baiting the avaricious. Many "robbery" victims later admitted in our offices to having been conned. They lied about the crime, they said, because they felt embarrassed by their own illicit motivation. The tourist holds his "friend's" handkerchief in part because he himself may make off with a quick buck; the pocketbook drop victim hopes to walk away with someone else's lost treasure; the gambler risks a week's pay for an easy windfall. In each case, the con man dangles a bauble in front of the greedy.

And gambling and con cases were not the only matters in which victims came to court with some share of guilt on their hands. Among the misdemeanor cases in Criminal Court truly innocent victims proved to be something of a rarity.

In my first battered-wife case I felt outrage on behalf of the victim. The complaint room summary read: *C/L [common-law] wife, Rita Alvarez, argues with husband, who comes home drunk. Argument escalates and husband repeatedly punches wife in head and body.* Nobody much cared about a junkie trespassing in a shooting gallery, but a battered wife deserved justice. Even defense lawyers confessed they had little enthusiasm for representing abusive husbands. Of the seventeen cases I had found in my mailbox that morning, this one got my full attention.

Rita Alvarez had no telephone, so I subpoenaed the arresting officer, Mark Assad, and sent him out to her apartment on Malcolm X Boulevard. The following afternoon she called me from a pay phone.

"Excuse me, sir," she said, "but, like, I don't want to go to court over this. Can I just forget about it and get my husband out of jail?"

I had been forewarned about battered wives refusing to follow through once their husbands had been taken away and sobered up. Ordinarily, I would have dismissed the complaint and moved on to the next matter in my files, but Rita's case seemed to have real merit. Hoping to convince her not to forgive too quickly, I insisted she come downtown for an interview.

The following morning, Rita Alvarez was waiting outside my office with a young girl, presumably her daughter. I introduced myself and invited them inside. As she followed me in, Rita carelessly pulled her daughter by the wrist like a Raggedy Ann doll. I flipped through a pile of manila folders on my desk, searching for Rita's husband's case, and glanced up at the victim. In the stark light of my office, Rita looked wan and weary, though still youthful. I didn't detect any bruises or swelling on her face, which probably meant she hadn't been beaten too severely.

I found the file, opened it, and asked her to tell me the whole story.

"Listen, sir," she began, speaking quickly, "I really don't want to talk about it. I just want to drop the case. I mean, can't I do that?"

I explained that once someone files charges, only the DA's office can dismiss the case. "Basically," I said, "you have to convince me that there is a good reason to let your husband go free."

"Well, I love him. What else do I have to do?"

"Why don't you start by telling me why you are so eager to drop charges? If you're being threatened or if you're afraid your husband will hit you again, I can get you an Order of Protection. You know, you may feel sorry for him today, but you may just find yourself back here again, only next time you could be hurt much worse."

She paused as if considering my advice but continued to insist that she wanted to drop the charges and get her husband out of jail.

"Ms. Alvarez," I said impatiently, "you've got to have some kind of reason why you want to let your husband off. If it's a good reason, I'll consider dropping the case, but you've got to tell me the truth or I'm going to prosecute your husband, whether or not you cooperate." This, of course, was practically impossible, but most witnesses were sufficiently intimidated by a few threatening words never to call my bluff. And in Rita's case, I hoped my adamancy would save her from another beating.

"All right," she said. "Let me tell you what happened. On the day my husband, you know, did what he did, he came home and he was pretty mad at me, you know?"

"Why was he mad at you? Were you cheating on him?"

"No, no, nothing like that," she said. "But, I like to do some coke sometimes, you know. Smoke base and stuff. And that day I had taken a lot of his money, and I was kind of high when he got back, and he could tell 'cause I'm kind of, you know, hyper when I'm high. So he starts yelling at me and getting real mad."

"Was he drunk?" I asked, remembering the write-up.

"Yeah, he was drunk, but not like real messed-up or anything. So, anyway, he's screaming at me that I'm a junkie and spending all his money and shit. So, I took a pair of scissors and stabbed him in the arm. That's when he started punching me. After that, I'm not too sure what happened, but eventually the policemen came and I told them that my husband was beating on me, so they arrested him."

It was entirely possible that Rita had fabricated the

story to get her husband out of trouble. The arresting officer, after all, hadn't mentioned any wound on the defendant's arm. Rita had lied either to the police or to me; at this point, it didn't much matter which version was true. Both stories would come out before a judge or a jury and destroy her credibility. And, on top of it all, Rita didn't want to cooperate. Hers was a case for social workers or the police, not the court system. I said that her husband would be released from jail sometime that afternoon. She thanked me, jerked her daughter's arm to get her attention, said goodbye, and left.

John Patton had, in fact, warned us all early on, "The legal work is easy. In six months you'll see that the hardest job is to find out whether your witnesses are telling the truth." As usual, he was right. Witnesses—a category that included victims, police officers, and bystanders—could lie to us for any of a number of reasons. The job, however, *required* that we try to get at the truth. It wasn't long, therefore, before I habitually eyed witnesses' stories through the same skeptical lens I once reserved for dropsy cases. Unfortunately, training at the DA's office did not include any instant lie-detection methods. We all had to learn through experience.

The police arrested a woman for picking a priest's pocket. In my office, I told the priest that the defendant, who had a record for prostitution, claimed he had paid her ten dollars to feel her breasts. He decided not to press charges and left in a hurry.

A man on probation for murder was arrested for violating a court order of protection after he slapped his wife across the face. When I asked the wife, a black woman, if she had done anything to provoke her husband, she became furious and accused me of being a racist. I told her to come back the next day when she felt a little calmer. She never came in again or returned my calls, so I dismissed the complaint.

On Fourteenth Street and Second Avenue, at three

A.M., a man was arrested for throwing a woman to the sidewalk and cursing at her. In my office I dared to ask the victim the inevitable question. "Please don't be offended," I said, "but are you a prostitute?" Without missing a beat she said she was. I told her that as long as she was willing to admit her profession on the witness stand, we could go forward with the case. On the day of trial, the defendant pled guilty.

An affluent New Jersey family man said he had been assaulted at one-thirty in the morning on West Forty-fifth Street, an area notorious for prostitutes, drug dealers, and other unsavories. The victim, who had bandages and bruises on his head, said that he was walking down the street when a stranger asked him for a match. As the victim fumbled in his pockets, the stranger took a long piece of wood, hit him on the side of his head with it, and took his money. Fortunately, said the victim, he saw the perpetrator disappear into a nearby building, and when he returned with a police officer the culprit was still inside.

The bloodied bandages on the victim's head testified unequivocally that he had been injured, but the episode rang false. Truly unprovoked assaults, I had learned, were a rarity, and nice family men don't go sightseeing on West Forty-fifth Street after midnight.

"Look," I said, "you've given me absolutely no reason why you were in that neighborhood at one-thirty in the morning. If we go to trial on this case, the truth is going to come out, and my opinion is that you were down there to pick up a prostitute. Isn't that right?"

Denials, protestations, and angry threats followed. A few months earlier I might have backed down, but this time I warned him that perjury is a class E felony and carries a three-year prison term. Then he quietly confessed: "All right, it's true. I was there to find a girl; but I swear José hit me. He's her pimp. Listen, please, if my wife finds out I don't know what she'll do. I can't get up in court and say why I was there."

"Just tell me the whole story now, and we can decide what's the best course to take."

Though I believed I was slowly becoming more discerning about credibility, a sense of my own naiveté was driven home when I began picking up "SAP cases," disputes from the Summons Arraignment Part. These troublesome matters begin as private disputes in which one of the parties eventually files a civilian complaint and serves a summons on his or her opponent. In the SAP, a judge decides whether a prosecutor should be assigned to look into the matter. My only long-drawn-out experience with a "SAP case" involved Ellys M. Ellys. From our first telephone conversation I should have known this "victim" couldn't be trusted, but I was determined not to let my growing skepticism get in the way of giving a witness a fair hearing.

"Hello," said a male voice.

"Yes," I replied. "May I please speak to Ellys M. Ellys."

"I'm sorry. Ellys is not in right now."

"Do you know when he'll be back?" I asked.

"No."

"May I leave a message, then?"

"Okay."

"Please tell Mr. Ellys that the district attorney's office called about the case he brought against a man named Tillden."

"Oh, hello," said the voice. "This is Ellys."

We scheduled an interview, an appointment I hoped he would miss, giving me an excuse to drop the case. But Ellys showed up right on time. In fact, Ellys M. Ellys, in his wrinkled suit and tie, and with his wiry black hair combed more or less in place, looked surprisingly respectable. His only unusual feature were the preternaturally dark circles under his eyes. They gave him a slightly reptilian look.

Ellys had written a five-page, single-spaced account of the dispute that had led to the current charges. It began: "Continuing his long-standing vendetta against me, my employer, Mr. Christopher Tillden, has resented my diligent work and taken out his resentment through a series of harassing and assaultive encounters beginning before the coming of Christmas and continuing up until his unilateral termination of my employment at . . ."

After I read this odd and confusing summary, Ellys gave an equally strange, though internally consistent, verbal account. Ellys had worked as an insurance agent for a firm during the past year. He had given Christmas gifts to his fellow employees and claimed to have gotten along well with everyone except his immediate superior, Tillden. Shortly after the holidays, Tillden told Ellys that he had taken too many days off work and that his pay would be docked. Ellys argued the point, but Tillden wouldn't give in. As Ellys pressed the issue, Tillden started to yell obscenities and then tried unsuccessfully to kick him in the legs and groin. Ellys filed charges.

To Ellys's disappointment, I explained that under New York law a person must suffer physical injury to bring an assault charge, and Ellys hadn't alleged any injury. The harassment charge seemed justified, however, and I agreed—against my better judgment—to go to trial on that count. I sensed that Ellys was an oddball, but he claimed to have been wronged, and besides, no victim of mine had ever taken the trouble to write a factual summary of the crime. He deserved the benefit of the doubt.

The harassment had taken place months ago, and when I called the personnel department at Ellys's former office, I learned that the witnesses had all taken jobs elsewhere. Ida tried to track them down, but, not surprisingly, she also came up empty-handed. "That's no big deal," said John Patton, the week before Ellys's trial. "I used to try felonies with just one witness. You just put 'em on the stand, ask your questions, and rest the case. Just be sure Ellys is telling you the truth. The case sounds fishy to me."

On the day of the trial, I still had only Ellys's word to go by. Tillden had since refused the most lenient offer possible: Adjournment in Contemplation of Dismissal, a procedure that voids all charges after six months; it was even lower than Disorderly Conduct. He didn't even want a lawyer. When Ellys and I walked into the courtroom, Tillden, a sandy-haired man about sixty years old, stood up and shouted, "Ellys, you idiot! You forced me to come all the way downtown on your complaint. I don't know what you're trying to do. You're crazy!"

Ellys, with his lizard eyes, looked coolly at his former boss and said, "I'm not speaking to you. Talk to my lawyer."

"I'm not your lawyer, Mr. Ellys," I said. "I'm here because you brought criminal charges against Tillden, that's all."

In the clarifying light of a courtroom, Ellys looked stranger than usual, even a bit shady. Yet I was lending him a government stamp of approval.

The charge against Tillden, harassment, was a violation one step below a misdemeanor. In Criminal Court, violation trials last an afternoon, and most formalities are forsaken. There isn't even the option of a jury. Getting right down to business, Judge Carol Marbell called the case into the record and I made a brief opening statement.

"Call your first witness, Mr. Prosecutor," said Her Honor.

Ellys slithered to the stand with slow, self-conscious movements. He gave his name and address and swore to tell the truth.

"Now, Mr. Ellys," I said, "please tell the court exactly what happened to you on December twenty-ninth at your place of employment."

Ellys turned to the judge and began: "Well, Your Honor, everything I say will be one hundred percent the truth. I swear on the Bible."

"Thank you, Mr. Ellys," said Marbell. "Now please tell me what happened."

"Yes, Your Honor, yes," Ellys went on. "Continuing his longstanding vendetta against me, my employer, Mr. Christopher Tillden, has resented my diligent work and taken out his resentment through a series of harassing and assaultive encounters beginning . . ." Despite my coaching, Ellys launched into a verbatim recitation of his five-page account. With various interruptions, I urged him to relate a chronology of events as he had in my office, but he continually returned to the script like a trained bird. Things had gone too far. Ellys's demeanor on the stand was even more bizarre than in my office—at once strident and unctuous, as if he were trying to convince not only the court but himself that he was telling "one hundred percent the truth." Unable to look either the judge or the defendant squarely in the eye, he stared at me the entire time, bent upon borrowing my credibility.

Somewhere in the middle of page two of the summary, I screwed up my resolve. "Your Honor," I interrupted. Judge Marbell looked startled. "May I approach the bench, please? Something pressing has just come to my attention."

"When I was a prosecutor," she said, "cutting off one's own witness was considered rather bad form, to put it mildly, and I can hardly imagine what came to your attention in the last sixty seconds. But this is a bench trial," she sighed, "so I'll permit it."

"One more thing, Your Honor," I asked. "May my witness be excused?"

"I don't know what you're up to, sir," Marbell said threateningly, "but I'll give you this one chance. Mr. Ellys, please step down."

I could feel Ellys's slimy gaze on me as he stepped off the witness stand.

At the bench I handed over the typed summary. "Your Honor," I said, "Mr. Tillden is not a lawyer and doesn't appreciate the significance of the fact that the People's witness is following a script, albeit one he wrote himself. I'm not saying he's lying, but under the circumstances I believe you should have a copy." I had sabotaged my own case, but it was the right thing to do. Marbell would probably have acquitted Tillden anyway, but this gave her ample reason.

"Even in the U.S. attorney's office," she told me, "I would have done the same thing. Let's resume testimony."

Ellys had his day in court as he recited the remainder of his summary while Tillden looked on, wearing an expression of supreme irony. When the People's case drew to its close, Judge Marbell turned to Tillden. It was three in the afternoon, and she clearly had no desire to waste any more time on Ellys's legal frolic.

"Mr. Tillden," she explained, emphasizing certain words to get her subtext across while retaining the appearance of impartiality on the record—classic judicial double-talk—"the People have rested. That is *all* the evidence they have. I have not reached a *final* decision yet. You *may* testify *if* you believe it to be necessary. The choice is yours."

Tillden got the message.

"Well, Ellys," I said, emerging from the courtroom, "I'm sorry to tell you we lost."

Ellys put on a melodramatic look of sadness. "Why?" he asked. "I told the one-hundred-percent truth."

"Un-huh." I nodded. "But the judge had some doubts about the case. That's what counts."

By early summer I had had a surfeit of petty crime. Some of my classmates, like Alex Barnette—the woman who would have sent pot-smoking college students to jail for a year—retained their initial enthusiasm for the job. To my annoyance, Alex once said that she enjoyed stapling notes to files in the morning. But I wanted to move on to cases that inspired harder work. Even Lewis Sparks, one of the gung-ho Forlini regulars, groaned when he found sixty-five new cases in his mailbox, a record for Bureau 20. Walking back to his office, he consoled himself, "Maybe I'll get lucky and find two or three good cases among the crap."

The attitude of professional skepticism that took hold of most every rookie, and the clumsiness of the overcrowded court system, took their worst toll on honest witnesses, people who came to us looking simply for justice. Late that spring, an elderly gentleman who had been pickpocketed sat opposite me in my office. It was his seventh trip downtown. During our first interview he contradicted himself about where he carried his wallet and when he had first noticed it missing, so I insisted he come in again a week later. He complained that he had already been to the police station, but though an extra trip downtown caused him inconvenience, I didn't want to get taken for a ride. The second interview went better, and I agreed to go forward with the case.

During the last two months, trial had been rescheduled three times. Once the cop was out sick. Another time the defense lawyer was trying a case elsewhere. The third time everyone was ready but all the courtrooms were busy. As we waited for the telephone to ring with news of whether, at last, we would be sent out to trial, I asked the man, who looked exasperated, to go over the facts of the case one more time.

"Listen," he said, "it's not worth it to me to go through with this. I've already missed four mornings of work. This is costing me more than was in the goddamn wallet in the first place."

"I'm sorry," I told him, "but the man you've accused of a crime wants a trial. Try to remember how angry you were when you reported the case to the police. You owe it to the other people he might steal from. You know, at this point I could subpoena you from work and send a cop over to bring you in. I really don't want to do it; I'm just mentioning it. I promise the case will be over soon. Now tell me again: about how many feet from you was the defendant standing when you first saw him?"

"I feel like *I'm* the defendant," he moaned. "Doesn't he at least have to go through these interviews, too?" I explained that a defendant is presumed innocent and has an absolute right not to testify at the trial, but a victim must testify or else there's no case, and I had to be sure the defendant really is guilty. "I know all that," he said, "but it doesn't seem fair that I have to tell my story and get cross-examined in your office *and* on the witness stand, while the guy who took my money can just sit there." To his further displeasure I added that, under both the United States and New York constitutions, I was forbidden even to mention to the jury that the defendant refused to testify. I did not bother to explain that in the AP Parts defense attorneys routinely obtained delays on any conceivable pretext in the hope of wearing down a legitimate witness's desire to follow through.

That day the elderly pickpocket victim and I learned that my subpoena to the police officer hadn't reached headquarters, and therefore we were not ready for trial. Finally, on the fifth adjournment, we were sent out to trial. The defendant pled guilty when he saw the victim enter the courtroom.

Witnesses and victims who can be reached by telephone enjoy the relative luxury of being "on telephone alert"—waiting at home by the phone—but the elderly man whose wallet was stolen had no telephone and worked driving a delivery van, so he came in faithfully and waited. Winning the case didn't seem to make up for the inconveniences he had suffered. Like many victims of crimes, he must have emerged from One Hogan Place feeling twice burned: once by the defendant, once by the system.

NINE

Room 110

The final destination for our cases, a sort of legal grave-yard, is a place I visited only once during my three years in the office: Room 110. Room 110 is located on the first floor of 100 Centre Street, but it could easily have been transplanted from Orwell's Ministry of Love.

In a case I prosecuted against a pickpocket team, two of the defendants had recently been convicted of Jostling—the legal term for attempted pickpocketing. The arresting officer explained that the defendants were graduates of the School of Fourteen Bells, a South American pick-pocket training school that sends its alumni to New York City, where they work in teams and receive weekly sala-ries. The school owed its name to a mannequin outfitted with fourteen bells—one on each pocket. In order to grad-uate, students must be able to reach into every pocket without ringing a bell.

Our files on the closed Jostles couldn't be located, so as a last resort I went to Room 110. Outside the clerk's plex-iglass window, a line of recently convicted misdemean-ants waited to pay fines or ensure that their "closed" cases had in fact been closed. The queue reached down the corridor. I walked to the head of the line, flashed my DA identification card, and was immediately admitted.

Inside, Room 110 was as high-ceilinged as a courtroom,

though considerably more dingy and depressing. Paint was peeling off the walls, and the windows, set well above eye level, were caked with soot. A small army of typists sat in rows, entering data into the court computer system. Around the room, hundreds of thousands of court files stood in uneven piles and spilled over the edges of boxes and carts. Here and there, Legal Aid's blue-backed motions lay atop our white-backed responses.

A clerk steered me to a cart filled with still more dead files. "You'll have to see if you can find what you're looking for in here," he said. "They were closed only last December." Faces with dark, determined expressions crowded around the clerk's window, jealously watching the attentions I received.

I culled through the files in the cart and, by chance, found the closed Jostles. Unfortunately, the file contents had become detached from their folders and, according to the clerk, were now officially lost. All that remained were two sheets of paper listing names and docket numbers. Disappointed but hardly surprised, I thanked the clerk for his help and left. As I elbowed past the waiting line outside, I imagined my reaction had I been made to wait an hour before being informed that my own file was lost.

Room 110, the end of the legal assembly line, seemed to exemplify everything that was wrong with Criminal Court. Each stapled packet of forms, boilerplate motions, and complaints represented a phase of a person's life, one which to that individual was a traumatic event. In Room 110 they became a jumble of stories piled so deeply one upon another that all the human details were lost. They were just dispositions, bodies in the system, trials won, trials lost.

After almost one year in Criminal Court I had become a different person from the rookie who offered sixty days for a farebeat before Judge Friedland. Now I "knew" that Time Served is appropriate: it's only a farebeat: there are thousands of them. A punch in the nose? Give the defendant a break: there are guys out there with guns. Shoplifting is merely an economic crime. We're interested in people's safety, not a few pairs of pants from Saks Fifth Avenue. Besides, the courts and jails are operating above capacity. And who can trust the police—or even one's own witnesses?

I had joined the DA's office hoping to use my discretion wisely, looking for cases worth fighting for. Instead, I was wearing down victims, skeptically questioning every story, and uncertain if in the end I was achieving just results with all my lenient offers and plea-bargains. No wonder certain ADAs joked at Forlini's that prosecutors like me were as bad as soft-headed, bleeding-heart judges. Believing that most defendants are scum who deserve the maximum is easier than dealing with the disquieting fact that every case is laden with ambiguity, and that in prosecuting petty crime you often end up punishing social victims—junkies, prostitutes, delinquents from broken families. But though I remained critical of the hardliners, could I confidently say I was doing a better job?

The only certainty was that no one remained in Criminal Court long enough to see it in perspective. After a relatively short apprenticeship, judges and ADAs moved on to Supreme Court to prosecute felonies, crimes of an entirely different order of magnitude. They seemed to have put Criminal Court out of their minds, referring to it as disdainfully as they referred to the bar exam. My class of rookies began to live for the day when we, too, would climb out of the trenches. A few veteran defenders continued to haunt the halls, awaiting court-appointed cases, but generally these members of the bar were, or had become, third-rate lawyers, depressed and bored by the repetitive grind of eking out a living off farebeaters and drug possessors.

In the meantime, cases continued to flood through the courtrooms and accumulate in our file drawers. One Hundred Centre Street continued to be as fascinating as it was frustrating, and I had learned more about petty crime and low-level criminals than I ever imagined possible, but there was no reference point against which to judge the system and how well it deals out its stock in trade—justice. Are sentences too light? Too heavy? Do token-suckers deserve leniency or are they too far gone to benefit from it? Tonight I arraigned one hundred and fifty defendants. I have one hundred and seventy-five cases in my file drawer. Recidivism is up this year. We lost more cases on speedy trial grounds than last year's rookies. But we *have* more cases. The numbers are numbing.

One Friday afternoon in June, Scott Pryor and I headed back to Bureau 20 after a long, hot day doing the calendar. We talked about some of our outside interests, and Scott mentioned that at home he played the electric guitar over homemade tapes of subway noise. "After coming out of here," he said, "sometimes it's the only thing that makes any sense."

PART II

Madmen and Fugitives

TEN

Special Projects

Every so often and without warning, an ADA a year or two ahead of my class would disappear. But between struggling to contain file drawers swollen with misdemeanors and working the lobster shift, I was too preoccupied to pay much attention to the disappearances. They remained lumped together in my mind with other, still obscure facts of DA life, questions such as the true function of Frauds and Rackets, who chose the members of the Sex Crimes Unit, and why lawyers in the Appeals Bureau never wore neckties or suits. The disappearance mystery was finally dispelled one July afternoon when Mitchel Nelin, my bureau chief, called me into his office and offered me a chance to join the Special Projects Bureau.

Special Projects, he explained, deals with two areas of prosecution rarely encountered in Criminal Court: insanity and extradition. Like other specialized bureaus in the office, Projects is staffed by siphoning off ADAs from the trial bureaus on a rotating basis. If selected, I would spend six months amid madmen and fugitives and return to Bureau 20 in time to join my class when they began to pick up felonies in the spring. Eager for a break from the Criminal Court rounds, I volunteered.

Nelin set up an interview for me, and I went around the office trying to ferret out the lowdown on Projects. No one

seemed to know exactly what took place there, but everyone had an opinion about its founder and chief, Steve
Watts, known as Smokey. A twenty-year member of the
office, Watts had been the top Manhattan homicide prosecutor until he retired in the 1970's to form Special Projects. His reputation for tireless work and dogged investigation was formidable, and everyone agreed that "no one
is sharper than Smokey," but enthusiasm for working in
his five-person bureau was tempered.

One senior assistant peevishly summed up the minus
side: "Watts is a bore." His high murder-conviction rate, it
was rumored, stemmed from his notoriously lackluster
verbal style. Jurors, put to sleep by Watts's endless mono-
tone summations, convicted out of the fear that they had
missed some crucial piece of evidence. As chief of Projects
he was known for answering simple questions from his
assistants with encyclopedic discourses, interspersed with
yawning pauses. His nickname—a reference to his brief
career as a forest ranger—conjured up the image of a
blazing mental fire lost in a distant haze.

At the appointed time I arrived at Watts's office, located
in a backwater area of 80 Centre Street. He greeted me
with a pursed smile that gave me the impression I was
intruding. As he walked around his desk, Watts, a lanky
six-foot-two, accidentally sent a stack of papers sliding
across the floor. A lock of graying hair, worn in the same
schoolboy cut shown in the photos hanging behind his
desk, fell across his face as he bent over and methodically
collected the mess. The famous trial lawyer.

"Well," he began, once the papers had been restacked,
"let me tell you a little about what we do here in Projects." His flat midwestern voice fell and the first in a series
of long pauses ensued. The interview lasted two hours and
reminded me of Mark Twain's remark that if you take out
the word "begat" the Bible is a pamphlet. Without the
pauses, the interview would have been a chat.

Most of Special Projects' psychiatric cases involved
homicides or, in Watts's words, "life-threatening assaults."

Instead of scrambling to keep up with two hundred cases, I would concentrate on eight or ten major offenders, arrange the extradition of fugitives to their home states, and respond to prisoners' requests under the Freedom of Information Law. Pros cases and cocaine possession arrests paled in comparison.

And in spite of the pauses, Smokey's gentle, almost cerebral manner won me over. He was a welcome contrast to some of the overzealous prosecutors in the office, and his enthusiasm for the job seemed mixed with a healthy detachment. There was no egotistical or vindictive edge to his recountings of the Sid Vicious, John Lennon, and CBS murders, cases that had won him a national reputation. When describing a trial, his eyes drifted dreamily over my shoulder to rest on a faded Andrew Wyeth poster hanging across the room. He was simply in love with his work.

At the end of July, I received a note in a tiny penciled scrawl: "Congratulations. You will be joining Special Projects in August. Attached are some cases and a law-review article that you should become familiar with. Steve." It was the first legal reading I had done since training ended last September.

My first task in preparing for Projects was to familiarize myself with the history of the insanity defense.

One of the broadest pillars of the Anglo-American criminal law tradition is the doctrine of *mens rea*—literally, "guilty mind." For most crimes, the accused must be shown to have *intended* to commit the illegal act (acted with a guilty mind) before he or she may be convicted and punished. But if a person is insane at the time, the law deems the criminal incapable of forming "the necessary intent," and thus not guilty (now phrased "not responsible").

The modern insanity defense originated in England. In 1843, Daniel M'Naughten, a Scottish woodcutter, shot at Prime Minister Robert Peel because of Peel's involvement in an elaborate conspiracy with, among others, the

Pope and the Jesuits. The conspiracy was a delusion, but the gun with which M'Naughten mistakenly killed Peel's secretary was real enough, and the mad Scot was tried for murder. The case drew the full attention of the English press and public. At trial, M'Naughten's lawyers put on nine medical experts to show that their client was insane when he fired the fatal shots. The prosecution offered no rebuttal witnesses. Because of the Crown's misfired strategy or incompetence, M'Naughten was found not guilty, and a hue and cry over the manifest injustice of a killer's avoiding the gallows echoed through the halls of Parliament.

After the verdict, Peers and Lords debated the validity of the Scot's acquittal and, in the process, formulated what has come to be known as the M'Naughten Rule. They reasoned that an accused should not be held responsible for his crimes if "a disease of the mind" prevents him from knowing "the nature and quality of his acts" or distinguishing "right from wrong." The M'Naughten Rule has since undergone various reformulations and refinements from case to case (often going undercover by adopting the name of the case in which it was tinkered with), but even in the 1980's its basic principles remained vigorous enough to be successfully employed by another would-be assassin whose marksmanship was as far off target as his thinking: John Hinckley, Jr.

On March 30, 1981, as President Reagan walked with his swarm of aides and Secret Service men outside the Washington Hilton Hotel, John Hinckley burst from a crowd of onlookers, pulled out a .22 pistol, and fired six shots. Three rounds hit bystanders: Press Secretary James Brady, a police officer, and a Secret Service man. One shot ricocheted off a car and struck the president in the chest. At trial, Hinckley's lawyers contended that he should not be held criminally responsible for his actions because delusions compelled him to commit the crime. The government made greater efforts to prove Hinckley's *mens rea* than did M'Naughten's prosecutors, and they spent hundreds of thousands of dollars on psychiatric experts, but the result was no different: the jury found Hinckley not guilty by reason of insanity. National and local newspapers responded with predictable editorial attacks on a legal principle that allows a man to shoot the president on national television and avoid spending the rest of his miserable life in prison.

When I arrived at Special Projects, the M'Naughten and Hinckley cases more or less summed up my understanding of insanity acquittals. With the writers of editorials I shared doubts about the wisdom of turning formerly murderous lunatics over to psychiatrists who might release them once they were deemed recovered. And working in Criminal Court had reinforced my belief that one of the useful functions of our penal system is incapacitation—protecting society from a criminal's future misdeeds. Surely the criminally insane, guilty-minded or not, pose as great a continuing threat to their neighbors as do ordinary offenders.

But there was no point in beginning my apprenticeship under Steve Watts with a load of preconceptions. Eager to start out on a positive note, I set aside my doubts and let Smokey be my guide.

ELEVEN

Kirby Day

Set in the East River opposite 125th Street are two small, rocky islands. Randall's Island, the larger of the two, is dotted with sports fields and parks where I had played football in grade school. After spending a winter cloistered in a Manhattan apartment, its green expanses always felt like lush, open country. Had I not joined Special Projects, Ward's Island would have remained something of a mystery.

Ward's Island is green like Randall's but even rockier and much less flat and inviting. At the southern end, visible from the highway, stand a cluster of regular, rectangular, beige brick buildings: the epitome of institutional architecture. Whenever I crossed the Triborough Bridge from LaGuardia Airport they announced the approach to Manhattan as clearly as the silhouette of the Empire State Building. I had for years mistaken them for the prison on Riker's Island, actually another island farther north in the river. But upon joining Special Projects I learned their true identity: the Manhattan Psychiatric Center, the city's insane asylum.

Ward's Island and MPC are reached either via a narrow footbridge (once painted purple and hot pink at the behest of an aesthetic-minded city official) that arches over the narrow west channel of the river or by a single-lane access ramp that snakes down off the Triborough Bridge to arrive, eventually, at the MPC grounds. During my Special Projects tenure, I frequented the two main ward and hospital buildings known as Dunlop and Kirby.

In mental hygiene parlance, Dunlop is a "nonsecure facility," an open-door asylum. So open is the door, in fact, that a public bus stops directly in front of the Dunlop entryway, and in the afternoon it carries an odd assortment of patients, seated alongside ordinary passengers, into the city for unsupervised field trips. Wall-eyed or stooped, and profoundly preoccupied, the Dunlop patients leave the bus and join the chaos of Manhattan.

The last building on the MPC grounds, surrounded by a twelve-foot, electrically charged fence topped with barbed wire and razor ribbon, monitored by closed-circuit television cameras, its windows covered with thick steel mesh, is Kirby Forensic Psychiatric Center. Kirby is, emphatically, "a secure facility." It houses those criminally insane patients currently considered dangerously mentally ill. *Dangerously mentally ill*—the phrase itself always seemed electrically charged. Upon joining Projects, I pictured jabbering, razor-wielding kooks jumping out of darkened alleyways, straitjacketed loons laughing hysterically in padded cells. Kirby's patients, in fact, represent a certain élite of the already disproportionately violent and neurotic New York City prison population. All have committed extremely violent, perverse crimes, have entered insanity pleas, and now spend their days inside closely monitored wards awaiting the moment when a judge will find them "nondangerous."

On Steve Watts's suggestion I began my induction by joining the deputy chief of Special Projects, Arlen Avnet, and my two fellow assistants, Stan Keller and Bill Markham, on their weekly trip for Kirby Day.

Stan, Bill, and I first met in July, shortly after Steve Watts's congratulatory note arrived in my mailbox. We were all entering our second year in the office, although Stan and Bill had already been in Projects for a few months. Bidding farewell to Bureau 20, I wheeled a push-cart filled with my books and files into our three-man office. Towers of red-jacketed folders marked "Homicide Bureau" teetered precariously in corners, on side tables, and in front of the one soot-covered window. Piles of xeroxes, some bound, others toppling in random directions, covered the shelves. Stan and Bill were at their desks, surrounded by files, reports, notes, and yellow pads. Visible under a pile of still more dog-eared trial folders, another desk waited for me in the corner.

Stan strode across the room and greeted me with a hearty "welcome aboard" handshake. With his tousled sandy hair and good looks he could have been a young congressman from Iowa. Bill was just as All-American-looking, but quieter, almost shy. "Welcome to the land of paper," he said from across the room as I dug out my desk from under the mound of files.

From the first, we all got along well, partly because we were so glad to have escaped from the rookies' rigorous lot, but also because the work itself was engrossing. "Man, I was just itching to get out of Criminal Court," Stan said over our first cup of coffee. "I mean, when my friends outside asked me how work was going I'd tell them the truth. 'I lock up scuzzy people for stupid crimes.' Here at least the people we lock up did something serious."

At eight-thirty in the morning on Kirby Day, Stan, Bill, Arlen and I put our files into shopping bags and walked to a nearby parking lot, where Arlen requisitioned an Olds-mobile sedan from the DA's fleet. It was one of those tropical New York August mornings. Beams of sunlight slanted through the smog and turned the concrete walls of neighboring courthouses orange. People walking to work seemed to move in slow motion, anticipating the oppressive heat from cars, trucks, and buses gridlocked in Foley Square by noon. It was over eighty degrees, with eighty percent humidity, and on the blacktop parking lot it felt like a hundred.

Arlen Avnet, our deputy chief and ten-year member of

the office, was brown-haired, clean-shaven, and slightly overweight. He was also one of the sweatiest people I had ever met, and in the sweltering, polluted heat that morning I had a fine opportunity to observe his prodigious perspiration in full flower. By the time the slow-moving garageman arrived with the keys, Arlen had already sweated through his button-down shirt and stained the back and armpits of his jacket in a Rorschach pattern. What I had thought was some sort of hair tonic I now realized was sweat that oozed from his scalp and ran down his ruddy cheeks.

Arlen, however, was also a good and patient teacher. That morning at the office he had already given me a lecture on the inner workings of Special Projects. None of it was even vaguely familiar. "Don't worry," he said, sensing my perplexity. "Nobody knows about this stuff until they've worked here." Our major function in Projects, he explained, was to follow the continuing fate of defendants who have been found not responsible by reason of insanity. After an insanity plea, people don't just take the subway home from the courtroom. If they're still diagnosed as dangerously mentally ill, which according to Arlen they almost inevitably are, they go to the Manhattan Psychiatric Center. Then, every six months, a group of psychiatrists known as the Hospital Forensics Committee decides whether to release them outright or transfer them to a non-secure hospital. Once a patient has been hospitalized for a certain period, the committee reviews applications only every two years. Questions from the hospital or the patient are resolved once a week in Kirby Court.

While we wended our way up the East River, across the Triborough Bridge, and down the access ramp onto Ward's Island, Arlen continued to delve into specific provisions of the Mental Hygiene Law, the merits of various state psychiatrists, and the atrocious food at Kirby (he had warned me to pack a lunch). Back at ground level, we drove past a stand of towering concrete pylons and along an asphalt field dotted with orange garbage cans. Big white garbage trucks looking like mechanized dinosaurs lumbered about amidst the pylons and glowing orange barrels. "This," Arlen announced, "is New York City's garbageman school. A slalom course for truck drivers." The bizarre landscape seemed an appropriate no-man's-land separating the deranged from the sane.

We crossed another short bridge, continued past a sentry box, and entered MPC. The plain, rectangular buildings rose up before us. A little greenery filled in the spaces, but the entire complex, with its square, brick surfaces baking in the sun, remained forbidding and lonely. The road ended in a parking lot in front of Kirby's electrified fence and grated windows.

Shopping bags in hand, Arlen, Bill, and I filed into a reception area where two guards carrying revolvers scrutinized us from behind a plexiglass window. Arlen announced, "Manhattan DA. Here for Kirby Court." One guard glanced at a clipboard and demanded our ID cards. He then took our bags and nodded to his partner, who, in turn, released the latch to a metal door set flush in the wall.

The door opened into a small cinderblock room containing a metal detector. A plaque on the opposite wall instructed us to place "all metal objects" into a waist-high trap door to our right. Arlen, Stan, and Bill emptied their pockets and silently passed through the metal detector, but though I removed first my metal-rimmed glasses, then my shoes, and finally, in desperation, my jacket, I inevitably triggered the alarm. Eventually, the guards relented —the problem, they said, might be metal fillings in my teeth—and settled for patting me down.

We were then escorted, one at a time, through yet another sealed door into another lobby. Our belongings were returned to us along with red visitors' passes for our lapels, and a floor-to-ceiling door of one-inch steel bars slid shut behind us with a low mechanical hum. Although no other such classic penitentiary features were visible inside

Kirby, the door reminded me that the Kirby patients hadn't "gotten off" on an insanity plea.

The hallway leading to Kirby Court was busy with white-coated psychiatrists and psychiatric social workers going in and out of red, blue, and green doors, and waiting outside elevators to the wards. It seemed like an ordinary hospital, without the pervasive smell of antiseptic.

We walked down dovetailing halls lined with more colorful doors, until we reached the office wing for the hospital administrators and defense lawyers (employees of the Mental Hygiene Legal Service). Circles of middle-aged doctors and young lawyers crowded the main corridor, and the air buzzed with talk about "suicidal ideations," "antisocial personality disorder," and "drug-induced sanity." Arlen, Stan, and Bill sought out doctors for last-minute conversations, but having nothing to contribute, I drank three cups of coffee and wandered around, waiting for court to convene.

The Kirby offices were cheery in their own way. The windows had no gratings and they looked out over a stretch of grass leading to the river. A wooden sign hanging in a chief administrator's room advertised: ANSWERS: FREE. ANSWERS REQUIRING THOUGHT: $1. CORRECT ANSWERS: $5. Kirby, though still as much a prison as a hospital, was hardly the filthy loony bin I had imagined from reading newspaper exposés.

I was watching a barge chug slowly up the river when Stan tapped me on the shoulder and said, "Come on, court starts in five." We headed back down the hallway.

Outside a blue door labeled COURTROOM in stenciled letters, an odd group of people sat on a wooden bench. At one end, a Middle Eastern gent in a suit was speaking to a forlorn-looking man, probably in his forties, who sat doubled over, drawing in his elbows and knees until all four joints met in a single point. "That's Dr. Iban," Arlen whispered to me. "He's one of the Kirby shrinks, and the patient he's talking to is George Corley. I think Corley used to cut up little boys, but I'm not too sure. He's a

Brooklyn case." At the other end of the bench, a smiling, obese woman sat turning her head back and forth like a radar dish. Although she smiled, it was an inward smile, rendered all the more disturbing by her deeply pock-marked face. She looked up, and instinctively I looked away. These two patients, the first I had seen, appeared vividly, *floridly* (in one of the more poetic terms of the psychiatrist's art) psychotic, so much so that I realized almost instantly how little I had appreciated the meaning of the word "insanity." Both the obese woman and Corley had the same intense look in their eyes, as if their unnaturally dark pupils were pulsating in response to a current of confused thoughts.

A court officer announced the morning's calendar call and herded the straggling doctors and attorneys into the courtroom. I joined Arlen and Bill in the front row. Before joining Projects I had seen a variety of courtrooms. There was the Olympian United States Supreme Court room, with its gilded clock suspended above the nine Justices' chairs, the New Hampshire Supreme Court, kept warm during the winter by its colonial fireplace; and the worn and weary rooms at 100 Centre Street. None of these prepared me for Kirby.

We sat in a rectangular room made of cinderblocks and outfitted with as-cheap-as-possible materials: muddy brown linoleum flooring, strips of fluorescent lights, dirty, mangled Venetian blinds, and rows of uncomfortable metal chairs. The windows looked out on the Kirby parking lot. At the far end of the room stood a wooden elementary school desk. Glued to the wall above it, a cardboard sign stated in peeling gold letters, IN GOD WE TRUST.

His Honor, Justice Anton Steenbeck, one of the Civil Supreme Court justices from the Ex-Parte Motion Part who rotated through Kirby each week, sat robeless behind the unimpressive little bench. He was flanked by a jaundiced-looking clerk and a female stenographer bent over her stenographic machine. Justice Steenbeck stared glumly out the window.

Unlike most legal proceedings, there were three attorneys on each Kirby case, one apiece for the patient, the hospital (represented by the New York State Attorney General), and the People. Protocol began as the clerk read down the list of names on the calendar, to which the lawyers either responded, "Ready," or called out some previously agreed-upon adjourned date.

In the growing heat of the day, the monotonous rhythm of call and response, broken by occasional inquiries from His Honor as to "why this case still isn't ready after six months on the calendar," was soporific.

"Louis Stapleton," said the clerk.

"Ready."

"Ready."

"Ready."

"Leona Pye."

"Ten twenty-four."

"Ten twenty-four."

"Ten twenty-four."

The stenographer bent lower and lower over her machine, and I looked up at Arlen, expecting a silent acknowledgment that we were suffering together during this litany. But though he had now sweated through his necktie, Arlen continued patiently to record in his crabbed writing the adjourned date for every case on the calendar, many of which had nothing whatever to do with our office.

The calendar call finally ended, and everyone stood up, stretched, and milled about before beginning the main order of business, the psychiatric hearings. I stood in a corner and discreetly flapped my pants, which were sweat-soaked from sitting on an unforgiving metal chair, and let some air circulate inside my jacket. For a moment I wondered why I had traded the excitement of Criminal Court for this miserable hole of a courtroom with an automaton for a mentor. But I thought of the faces of the patients on the bench outside and reminded myself that

they were *psychotic murderers*. Dealing with their fate
was a serious business.

The clerk called out the first case, "Stanley Quirk," and
we resumed our seats. Two uniformed guards escorted a
slow-moving, pale-faced man to a chair beside Chris
Thornberg, his MHLS defense lawyer. Quirk wore a pair
of weathered khaki pants and a work shirt, and though he
was balding both at the front and in a large spot at the rear
of his head, long strands of wispy gray hair fell from his
scalp in random directions. As soon as the guards released
him, Quirk bent forward over the table and stared at the
judge.

"Mr. Quirk," said Steenbeck in a tone that sounded as
though Quirk's was the last case of a long day, "the court
file indicates that this is the third time your release application has been on the calendar, yet you insist on representing yourself without the aid of a lawyer. Are you *still*
sure you want to proceed alone? I must remind you that
the law is a very difficult subject to learn on your own, and
I won't cut you any slack because you're not a lawyer."

As Quirk opened his mouth to answer, Thornberg cut
him off. "Your Honor," he said, "I've tried to convince Mr.
Quirk that I can be of some assistance to him, but I want
the record to reflect that he has consistently refused my
help in preparing his application for release."

"That's right, Judge," chorused the patient as he bent
nearly horizontally over the counsel table. "I feel that I
can get across to Your Honor why I'm ready to be let out,
better than Mr. Thornberg. After all, Judge, anyone who
was radio man in the Forty-fourth Naval Division, and
underwent shock therapy from the Japanese like I did,
would understand why only I can tell my own story. It's a
matter of personal strength, and I have my motion papers
right here, sir." He handed a ragged stack of handwritten
documents to the court clerk and then saluted His Honor.

"Mr. Quirk," said Steenbeck after a quick scan of the
papers, "I must tell you that the psychiatrists have already
given me a report stating that you're just not ready to deal

with the stresses of living on your own. All I see from your application is that although you're still hearing voices, the voices are now telling you to do only good things, not bad things. Is there any other basis upon which you think I should disregard the doctors' report?"

"Well, Your Honor, in the Forty-fourth Naval Division I underwent shock therapy. That therapy taught me a lot, and you've got to remember that, too, Your Honor. I'm really all right since the voices have been better, telling me to be good and to do good things. Anyway, these lawyers aren't going to help me—all they do is file papers and get delays. For a couple of years I trusted the lawyers, but they never did a darn thing for me. I mean, I'm still here, Your Honor, and the people here, they're not good for me to be around. The longer I have to stay in Kirby, well, I'm just going to get worse, not better. You know, Judge, it all goes back to the Navy, where—"

Quirk lay nearly prone across the table in his effort to persuade the court, but Steenbeck's attention had wandered back to the shafts of sunlight angling in through the window. As if roused from sleep by the memory of an unpleasant errand, His Honor turned and interrupted the patient's increasingly incoherent monologue.

"Sir, I have read your written application, at least cursorily, and I have listened to your oral application. However, I remain of the opinion that, without the aid of a lawyer, it is impossible for me to discern whether you have a colorable basis upon which to request a transfer. The hospital has met its burden of proving that you require further inpatient treatment at a secure facility, and in my opinion you have not overcome their showing. Because you have not had the benefit of an attorney, I am granting you leave to refile an application, but only if it is with the assistance of Mr. Thornberg, who is a very competent attorney." Justice Steenbeck winked at Thornberg as if to say, "Competent compared to this loon." "Now, Mr. Quirk, do you understand?"

Quirk raised his balding head from the table and stared dully. "Yes, Your Honor."

"Call the next case, Mr. Clerk," ordered Steenbeck. "Otherwise we'll be here all day. By the way, isn't there any air conditioning in this room? This heat is intolerable."

"Case of Carolyn Appelsammy, on for hearing."

The same two guards escorted Quirk out of court and minutes later returned with the obese woman whom I had noticed earlier on the bench. She wore a faded sundress that seemed about to split at the seams as she took a seat at the defense table.

I leaned over to Arlen and asked what she had done. "She's the one who cut her two kids up and took a bath in their blood," he said in a tone I would have used to describe a shoplift. "There was also some evidence of anthropophagy—drinking their blood or eating their flesh, I forget which. She's been in various hospitals for at least ten years. I doubt they'll ever let her out after what she did, but we've got to go through the motions just in case the hospital screws up."

As we spoke, the parties entered their appearances into the record.

"Stan Keller, New York County DA's office."

"Chris Thornberg, Mental Hygiene Legal Service, for Ms. Appelsammy."

"Ella Carver, assistant attorney general, for the hospital."

During the ride up, Arlen had coached me to watch for Carver, known to all as Ella. There were ADAs from different boroughs and a full cast of defense lawyers but, with rare exceptions, only one AAG—Ella. She was about fifty, and her seniority alone, ten years more than the most experienced attorney at Kirby, would have made her a dominant force in the courtroom. But Ella's physical appearance—tall, almost sticklike, with large bony hands and cold blue eyes—also helped make her the inevitable center of attention.

"Ms. Carver," asked the court, "is the hospital ready to proceed?"

"Yes, Your Honor," Ella answered in an astonishing voice that was at once a wheeze and a shout. The other lawyers nodded to the clerk.

"Very well," said Steenbeck. "Call your first witness." Ella looked down at a stack of papers and after skimming a few lines announced, "The hospital calls Dr. Henry Selden."

The doors at the rear of the courtroom opened and an elderly man wearing a dark suit walked to the stand, where he was sworn in by the clerk. All parties stipulated to Selden's qualifications as an expert, and Ella began.

"Doctor," said Ella, "when was the first time you examined Ms. Appelsammy?"

"Well, I suppose that would be just after she was admitted to the hospital."

"Doctor, was that Kirby Forensic Psychiatric Center, this hospital?"

"Of course it was this hospital," he replied smartly. "You know I only work at Kirby, Ms. Carver."

"Doctor, what I may know is irrelevant. It's the judge, His Honor, who has to understand this case. Now, when was Ms. Appelsammy first admitted to Kirby?"

"Well, Ms. Carver, I believe it was about five years ago. I don't remember the precise date."

"Doctor," Ella wheezed, "would you please examine the hospital record and tell the court the exact date upon which Ms. Appelsammy was admitted to Kirby?"

"Ms. Carver, if I may say so, what difference does that make? I thought you wanted my expert opinion. She's been here about five years. I think she was admitted in eighty-two or eighty-three."

"Doctor, directing your attention to the hospital record before you, does that document indicate on what date the patient was first admitted to Kirby?"

"I'm sure it does," quipped Selden, "but my professional opinion of Ms. Appelsammy's current mental condition has nothing whatever to do with the date of her admission. Why don't you read the hospital records yourself and just ask me what I think of the patient? I'm a doctor, not a file clerk."

Ella's pinched face darkened. "Judge, would you please instruct the witness to answer the question and keep his commentary to himself?"

"Ms. Carver," Steenbeck said dryly, "an experienced attorney like yourself should be able to elicit this type of basic information from *her own* expert witness. Why don't you try again?"

"Doctor," continued Ella, "would you please examine the hospital record and tell the court on what date the patient was admitted to Kirby?"

People twisted uncomfortably in their seats as Selden, with painful deliberation, flipped one by one through the dog-eared pages of Appelsammy's psychiatric records. Steenbeck wiped the sweat from his face with a handkerchief. Outside, cars in the Kirby parking lot shimmered in the waves of heat.

At last, Selden looked up and said brightly, "I think I have it here. The patient was admitted to Kirby on February 4, 1983, and I first saw her that day." The audience exhaled a collective sigh of relief.

"Thank you," grunted Ella. "Now, Doctor, prior to being admitted to Kirby, was the patient ever hospitalized anywhere else?"

"I'm sure she was at another hospital before coming to Kirby, but I don't know what hospital or when she was admitted there. Frankly, Ms. Carver, it doesn't make one iota of difference as far as my professional opinion of Ms. Appelsammy's mental condition goes. I've seen her regularly for four years and that's the basis upon which I—"

"Doctor," interrupted Ella, "you may not think it's relevant, but you're a psychiatrist, not a lawyer, and I'm telling you that there is a way hearings have to be done. So, simply tell me where the patient was hospitalized before coming under your care."

"Ms. Carver," Selden snapped back, "anybody can read these records, so I don't see why you're asking me about this kind of nonsense."

"Your Honor," Ella said, grinding out each word in her thick city accent as if she were chewing on a piece of Selden himself, "I can't take responsibility for this witness refusing to cooperate. If the doctor would do his job, we wouldn't be having this kind of problem, but he hasn't even familiarized himself with—"

"That's not true," Selden interrupted. "At one point I knew every institution Ms. Appelsammy had been in at every stage of her life, but I can't be expected to carry around that sort of information in my head. Anyway, it's in the record if you need to find it, although I can't see why that would ever be necessary."

"Excuse me, Mr. Witness," said Steenbeck, once more looking longingly out the window. "I think Ms. Carver has a point, so if you don't mind, I'm going to grant a recess during which time the two of you can discuss the questions Ms. Carver needs to ask and then, perhaps, if we are fortunate, we may be able to get beyond the *second* case on today's calendar. One hour."

A murmur went through the audience as Ella and the doctor walked quickly to the rear and out the door. Carolyn Appelsammy, all but ignored during this skirmish, looked up quizzically at Thornberg. I could hear Ella and Dr. Selden arguing outside the courtroom door.

Arlen drew me aside and whispered, "Now you see how Ella operates. She just recites the same set of questions she's asked for the last ten years. But don't underestimate her. She usually gets what she wants."

I began to sympathize with Steenbeck's lack of enthusiasm for Kirby Court. After an hour and a half in this steaming courtroom nothing had been accomplished except postponing Stanley Quirk's next pro se motion and watching Ella prepare her witness on the stand. The aspect of testimony that Selden chafed against is known among lawyers as laying the foundation for an expert opinion. In court, an expert may give an opinion only under two strict conditions: the witness must be an expert and must know the facts of the case. Selden and Ella, I thought, must have been through that simple routine a thousand times before. Certainly Selden's dislike of formalities had its appeal—if you want a psychiatrist's view of a patient, you should take it in whatever form it comes —but why be so defensive about a few background questions? There seemed to be some deeper antagonism at work.

When court reconvened, the case proceeded more smoothly. Selden recited the list of hospitals where Ms. Appelsammy had been treated, complete with dates of admission and release, and he described his own relationship with the patient. He briefly recounted her crimes, which were as grisly as Arlen had said. There was, in fact, "evidence of anthropophagy." Thornberg, the defense attorney, made pages of notes and Carolyn Appelsammy continued to scan her head back and forth, seemingly oblivious of the proceedings that would determine her fate for the next two years. The foundation for an expert opinion finally had been laid, and Ella had reached the crucial issue.

"Doctor, do you have an opinion, to a reasonable degree of psychiatric certainty, as to whether the patient, Ms. Appelsammy, is currently dangerous to herself or to others?"

Selden's testimony was unequivocal. Ms. Appelsammy still experienced psychotic episodes and suffered from a syndrome known as "explosive personality disorder." She had been violent on occasion and had even threatened members of the staff with spoons—the only utensils allowed on the wards. "I have no doubt whatsoever," Selden concluded, "that the best interests of the patient would be served by her continued supervision in a secure facility." Ella sat down.

Stan Keller, my colleague, stood up, said "No questions,

Your Honor," and sat down. I looked over at Arlen. He nodded to himself and continued taking notes.

Thornberg began cross-examination. His object, it appeared, was to discredit Selden's opinion by showing that Appelsammy had been a cooperative and friendly patient on the wards. Selden admitted that the violence he mentioned boiled down to two shouting matches with another psychotic patient over a stolen towel. The spoon incident, on closer examination, was in reality a tug-of-war between a staff member and the patient who was still finishing a bowl of oatmeal.

As Thornberg pressed harder, it came out that Appelsammy maintained a job on the prison grounds, had friends on the wards, voluntarily participated in group therapy, and even reminded the staff when they neglected to give her her daily dose of Thorazine. Thornberg made Selden recite numerous entries in the hospital record stating, "The patient presents no management problem"; "Ms. Appelsammy seemed in a sustained good mood this week"; "Patient showed remorse when describing the murder of her children." There were no documented escape attempts, no violations of ward rules, even her personal grooming had improved.

Throughout the cross-examination, Carolyn Appelsammy occasionally looked up at Thornberg, whom she seemed to like. But despite the patient's evident self-possession and the lack of violence in her recent past, Selden clung to his opinion: "She will be a danger to herself and others if given added freedom. That's my professional psychiatric opinion."

"Doctor," Thornberg said angrily, "are you seriously stating that even though Ms. Appelsammy has been a nearly model patient for the past two years, you believe she would not be able to handle the stresses of a nonsecure facility?"

"That's my opinion. You've heard it already, Mr. Thornberg. She's not ready." Thornberg sat down.

The heat was stifling. I supposed that I was not the only

one in the room with a headache and dry throat. Steenbeck looked out from his diminutive bench. "Court will recess over lunch while I formulate my verdict."

At first, Selden had seemed a persuasive witness. The patient's crime was unspeakable, and her "explosive personality disorder," coupled with "violence on the wards," made the prognosis grim. But after Thornberg's questioning, the case seemed less one-dimensional. Had I spent two years in an asylum, I would probably also have had a few incidents with my dangerously mentally ill fellow patients. And Selden did seem to have exaggerated the severity of Ms. Appelsammy's outbursts. Could one fight with a staff member over a bowl of oatmeal doom a patient to two more years of involuntary hospitalization? On the other hand, what did it mean that Ms. Appelsammy showed "remorse" ? Was it just a passing mood or a profound revelation about her crime? How did she compare with other patients? The doctor had given his "professional opinion," but who was to say that he could predict the future? The crime itself, a frightening, deranged act, cast a shadow over the testimony that made dispassionate analysis difficult.

Arlen, Bill, Stan, and I took our bag lunches to the small visitors' cafeteria. Arlen had been right: the only food available—bologna sandwiches in vending machines—looked distinctly unappetizing. He skimmed the remainder of the calendar and suggested that, after hearing Steenbeck's verdict, I would be better off going back to the office and starting my first assignment than listening to more hearings.

Just as the clerk announced that court was reconvening, Ella came over to our table and Arlen quickly introduced me as "the latest Projectile." The assistant AG shook my hand and asked, "How'd you like that Dr. Selden? Tried to stab me in the back on the goddamn witness stand. I'm telling you, lawyers and psychiatrists don't mix. That's all there is to it. A word to the wise."

Back inside the crowded courtroom, Steenbeck sat

erect behind the schoolboy desk. Ms. Appelsammy, Thornberg, Stan, and Ella all kept their hands folded as His Honor delivered his verdict. "One expert, Doctor Henry Selden, testified," said Steenbeck. "I find his opinion amply supported by the evidence in the patient's file. Cross-examination raised some questions about the patient's progress, but it did not substantially undermine the expert's credibility as to her potential for violence. No witnesses testified on the patient's behalf. The doctor's opinion is hereby adopted by the Court, and the patient shall remain at Kirby Forensic Psychiatric Center for a period of two years."

TWELVE

Doctor, Lawyer, Institutional Man

Back at Projects, four overstuffed red case folders were waiting for me in a pile on my desk. A handwritten note taped to the topmost file said: "Patient: Edgar Plutowski. Most recent crimes: Murder 2; Attempted Robbery. Hospital Forensics Committee recommends transfer to non-secure facility. Read file, then see me. Steve."

Murder 2 is, in New York, the highest-level homicide charge for a victim other than a police officer or a prison guard, "intentionally causing the death of another person." Victims suffer profound emotional and physical scars from assault, robbery, and rape, but murder is the preeminent crime, the final illegal act. The bulk of the file on my desk and the seriousness of the charges were intimidating, especially since the week before I had been writing up farebeats. I had graduated from misdemeanor school and matriculated directly into postgraduate prosecution. I carefully untied the red strings on the jacket labeled "Homicide Bureau."

The files in Plutowski's case had been culled by former members of Projects and were now in no particular order. They seemed an incomprehensible morass of information, except for one envelope labeled "Crime Scene Photos." It held three glossy, eight-by-ten, black-and-white prints that showed, from three different angles, a black man of about forty, lying on a patch of grass, mouth open, eyes blank. At first I found the photographs a little disappointing. There were no gaping wounds in the body or pools of blood. One angle showed what looked like blood on the victim's sport coat, but it might have been a grease stain. If you didn't know he had been murdered, you might have thought he was daydreaming. But knowing that the man in the picture was dead—or, as I soon found out, stabbed to death—transformed the otherwise unremarkable image into an object of fascination. I wondered what the photos in Carolyn Appelsammy's case looked like.

The remainder of Plutowski's file documented a criminal history stretching back thirty years. There were reports of numerous juvenile offenses, and a mass of paperwork from his homicide and attempted robbery cases: felony complaints, indictments, an autopsy report, motion papers, court transcripts, briefs on appeal, and judicial opinions. The three other folders held reams of xeroxed juvenile home records, detention center records, prison records, and the most recent entries in the Kirby hospital chart—hundreds of badly copied, handwritten pages.

That afternoon, Stan returned to the office and found me muddling through the files making pages of notes about events that occurred in 1956. "Who cares if your patient was violent when he was nine," he said, "if you don't know what his current diagnosis is? Start with the present and work backwards." The advice sounded reasonable, so I fished through the files and pulled out the Hospital Forensics Committee's most recent report on Plutowski, written and signed one week ago by Shirley Reiser, Plutowski's treating psychiatrist.

Reiser's report began with a brief summary of the patient's history, and on the last page it stated her diagnosis: "Chronic schizophrenia, undifferentiated type," with "antisocial personality disorder." The schizophrenia was "currently in remission."

The gist of Reiser's conclusion was clear enough:

Plutowski was "nondangerous to himself or others" and therefore ready to be transferred to a nonsecure facility, but I had no notion of how to assess its validity. Reiser and the members of the Hospital Forensics Committee were professionals with MDs and years of experience in the field. How was a lawyer supposed to evaluate their conclusions? Stan's sole contribution to Carolyn Appelsammy's hearing, "No questions, Your Honor," didn't steer me in any particular direction. And although Justice Steenbeck had sentenced the woman to two more years at Kirby, I assumed that in some cases we were supposed to take a more active role.

Feeling too confused to return to the psychiatric records, I went to see Smokey the following morning. "Basically," he said, "we are the only ones who know the whole story about the case. You've seen how Ella operates. Do you think she reads the reports to decide if they're reasonable? She's there to do whatever the hospital recommends." Smokey paused as his eyes wandered over to the Wyeth poster. "As for the doctors, I want you to form your own opinion, but Arlen and I have become somewhat pessimistic about the quality of work to expect from them. Not that they don't care about their patients, but they don't seem to care about the facts." He gave me an enigmatic little smile, and another pause ensued. "It's understandable. They try to see the world from their patient's point of view. Your job is to read the records and ensure that their opinions make sense."

Smokey went on to explain that I should start by providing "the doctors" (a phrase that referred collectively to the entire Kirby staff) with a complete dossier on Plutowski's criminal history. But I had to proceed with caution. Years ago, he warned, Kirby defense lawyers claimed that we were guilty of witness-tampering because we talked to the doctors before hearings. "Before sending anything to the hospital," Smokey said, "ask the treating psychiatrists whether they might find objective data about a patient's prior crimes useful for diagnosis and treatment. If they say yes, which they always do, you can argue, 'Hey, the doctors asked to see our files, so I obliged them.'"

After the meeting I telephoned Dr. Reiser at the Kirby wards and obtained an "invitation" to discuss Plutowski's criminal history. Eventually I steered the discussion around to why Reiser believed her patient should be transferred to an open-door facility. In her wobbly voice, Reiser, who was among the oldest psychiatrists at Kirby, explained that Plutowski had been a "model patient" during his last two years at Kirby, had had "few fights with other patients," was generally cooperative, and responded well to drug therapy. "In short, young man," she said, "Mr. Plutowski presents no management problem."

"But Doctor," I said, "don't you think the murder case says a lot about Plutowski's potential for violence?"

"What do you mean?" she asked.

"Well, it seems to me that if a person has cold-bloodedly murdered a stranger, even eight years ago, some violent tendencies must remain, however you classify them in psychiatric terms."

"Oh," she said, "you mean the murder he talks about?"

"I suppose so," I replied uneasily. "I mean the one where a man in the park asked him to have sex, and a few minutes later Plutowski came back and stabbed him to death with a knife."

"That's right, the murder where Plutowski says **he** turned himself over to the police."

"Yes, where he killed Tennie Pauling."

"Just a moment," the doctor's feeble voice now sounded more forceful. "You mean he *actually* killed somebody?"

A wave of disbelief rose up from the base of my skull. Police perjury in ECAB had been bad enough, but this bordered on the surreal.

"Yes, Doctor," I said, trying to remain calm. "A body was found, an autopsy report prepared, and a full investigation pursued. The works. Your patient even made a confession to the police the day after the crime."

"All the time I thought he just made the whole story up to impress me," said Dr. Reiser. "Well, it's certainly fortunate you telephoned. Tell me something more about the crime, if you don't mind." Reiser didn't seem at all embarrassed by her mistake. If anything, I sensed she was slightly amused by the surprise.

I summarized the details of Plutowski's murder and robbery cases and then asked Reiser whether this new information would change her recommendation. "I just don't know," she said, "but what you've told me certainly makes a difference."

I pictured Plutowski as he walks into his weekly therapy session. "Doc, I didn't mean to kill that man." Reiser looks up from her notes to reply, "Now, now, you don't have to make up grandiose stories about yourself for my sake. Tell me, how are you feeling today?" Yet what was even worse, perhaps, than Reiser's ignorance of the most important events in her patient's life was that she was Plutowski's treating psychiatrist, *the expert.* Cases hinged on expert opinions. I was beginning to understand what Smokey meant by "making sense."

It took three days to read through all the daily entries in the hospital chart, decipher the sloppily written prison records, and assemble a rough chronology of Plutowski's life. After the frantic pace of Criminal Court, the opportunity to prepare a case thoroughly seemed a luxury. By the end of my immersion in the files, I felt that I had come to know Plutowski, or "Pluto," as he was known on the wards. His life story was a series of tragedies strung end to end, from his earliest years up to the present.

Plutowski grew up an only child. His parents separated when he was six, the same year he started school. He was reportedly a poor student who had trouble concentrating and "learned very little." Teachers attributed his academic problems to "hyperactivity." By the time he had turned eleven, Plutowski was already angry and restless— staying out nights, throwing objects at family members, and fighting. The incidents reached a new peak of intensity when he lit a fire at a neighbor's doorstep. Throwing up their hands at this incorrigible child, the Plutowskis agreed to their son's psychiatric hospitalization. That was in 1958.

Later that same year, for "therapeutic" reasons, Plutowski was transferred to a "special school" in the country, an institution along reform school lines. The change of atmosphere did little to settle the child, and the doctors, for lack of a more effective treatment, prescribed tranquilizers. Despite this "therapy," Plutowski became more violent. He threw furniture at employees and other patients and threatened people with knives.

After seven years at the special school, Plutowski's behavior deteriorated until the staff felt it had no choice but to have him incarcerated. He was eighteen years old. The change, not surprisingly, only exacerbated his violence. During the next two years in a correctional institution, Plutowski violated at least twenty disciplinary rules, remained "assaultive and aggressive," and made "suicidal threats." He spent 150 days in "seclusion" (the euphemism for solitary confinement), a corrective measure that might drive even a psychiatrist mad.

At twenty, Plutowski was relocated to a state mental institution, where he was diagnosed as "mentally retarded." More disciplinary violations and periods of seclusion followed. Occupational therapy failed and Plutowski rotated from one ward to another, unable to adjust to any job for more than a couple of days. One doctor noted that Plutowski "admitted homosexual activity." I wondered what he expected from a physically healthy twenty-year-old deprived of female company since puberty.

In addition to growing ever more restless and aggressive, Plutowski began to take his anger out on himself. One summer, according to the records, he swallowed "128 metal hooks" and "some glass."

The pattern of maladjustment and violence finally broke when Plutowski was transferred to a specialized state hospital. For reasons none of his treating physicians understood or bothered to explain, Plutowski fared so well that he was granted privileges, including a brief home visit. That winter he was transferred to a nonsecure ward and by the spring he had left the state hospital to live with his father.

But Plutowski's improvement was short-lived. Within two months of his release, he attempted suicide—an overdose of Thorazine—and was readmitted to a secure psychiatric ward. Two months later, he "eloped" (the Mental Hygiene professional's euphemism for "escaped") only to reappear, nine days later, at the Twenty-sixth Precinct in Manhattan. According to the police reports, he walked in "somewhat dazed" and confessed to stabbing a man in a park. The police "verified" the confession and arrested Plutowski for murder. After lengthy negotiations with the DA's office, Plutowski pled guilty to Manslaughter and received a relatively lenient sentence: zero to seven years. The only information in the file about Plutowski's intervening jail term was that after three years he was released on parole.

Once out, Plutowski again attempted suicide and was again placed in a secure psychiatric ward, where he remained for two more years. According to one doctor's note, he confessed to murdering a woman but later retracted the confession. The second murder was never investigated. Otherwise, Plutowski behaved as a model patient—he even held a job cleaning floors—and was eventually released. About a month later, however, he was rearrested. In this, his last and most recent criminal act, he tried to rob a subway token booth clerk using his finger pressed inside a jacket to imitate a gun. A police officer intervened, and during the struggle Plutowski severely bit the officer's hand.

This time Plutowski pled Not Responsible by Reason of Insanity and was sentenced to Kirby, where he had spent the last four years. Someone not familiar with his past might have thought his behavior on the wards humorous. Whether assigned to the laundry, the garden, or the commissary, Plutowski, now nicknamed Pluto, habitually abandoned his job on the pretext that he was "needed somewhere else." He tried to sell watches, obtained from some unknown source, to his psychiatrist and offered judo lessons at a modest rate.

On another occasion, Pluto had tried to steal keys from security guards in order to elope. Soon after, he was caught stealing money from staff members and fellow patients. Confronted with the thefts, he insisted that his victims were deeply in debt to him and the stealing was, therefore, justified. When his defense was exposed as false, Pluto reacted so violently that he required restraint in a "camisole" (another euphemism, this one for a strait-jacket). Three times during the past four years, the Hospital Forensics Committee turned down Pluto's request for a transfer to a nonsecure facility. This year, with his detention once more due for review, the committee voted for a transfer to Dunlop.

Reading this history, I was struck by one of Pluto's more candid comments, made during a therapy session only a month before the committee's vote. Dr. Reiser had asked Pluto what he would do if released. Pluto answered, "There's nothing I can do out there. I can't get a job and I don't know how to live on my own yet. I mean, yeah, I might have to steal just to survive."

Pluto was right. Without the supportive structures of a mental hospital or a prison he had always been driven, by turns, to robbery, suicide, or homicide. Since age eleven he had moved from one institution to another, having his clothes washed, being treated by staff doctors, and given meals and a warm place to sleep. And even within the familiar confines of Kirby, he stole property and "acted out." He may no longer have been suicidal, but in spite of his psychiatric progress he remained violent and criminally inclined: in a word, dangerous. The idea of Edgar Plutowski sitting among the Dunlop patients who rode the bus into Manhattan on unsupervised trips was chilling.

The camisole incident had happened only a few months ago. Once more, it was time to see Steve Watts.

As usual, I found Smokey settled comfortably behind the mountain of paperwork that covered his desk. He motioned for me to have a seat, and as I related Plutowski's case history Smokey nodded at each unhappy turn. He had seen many such patients before. Institutional men, he called them, people whose entire consciousness spread just beyond the cinderblock walls of Kirby and other like facilities. Their situations are truly tragic. Lost souls who will either pine away inside a prison cell or hospital ward, or else be released, only to commit more crimes. Smokey suggested I continue talking to Dr. Reiser —Pluto should stay at Kirby.

After a month, Pluto's case appeared on the Kirby calendar. With some coaxing, Reiser had re-evaluated Pluto's prognosis, and the Forensics Committee now advocated that Pluto remain in Kirby for another two years. I received a number of angry phone calls from Pluto's defense lawyer.

The hearing on Kirby Day went smoothly, especially since Ella Carver, the powerful, voluble assistant attorney general, had the privilege of examining Reiser first. After she finished, there was nothing left for me to do. Repeating Stan Keller's performance in the Appelsammy case, I stood up, said, "No questions, Your Honor," and sat down.

Pluto was present throughout the hearing, and after Reiser offered her damning conclusions he chose to testify. Sitting on the witness stand he exuded a charming, boyish warmth. His body was soft and chubby and he had a large, friendly face. But in his eyes was the dark whirling look I recognized from other patients.

"Your Honor," Pluto said, "you know, it's not right for me to spend so much time inside a place like Kirby. I'm still a young man and, like, my friends are out jammin' to the raps on the radio. You know, summers go by, year after year, and I just sit inside watchin' TV, not seein' no friends, and takin' all them drugs they give me here. Your

Honor, ma'am, I heard Doc Reiser, and I agree I still got plenty of problems to, like, go through in therapy and such, but stayin' at Kirby ain't gonna give me no chance to get it together. Judge," he said lowering his voice, "please, ma'am, give me a chance. I won't disappoint you. I mean, Doc Reiser was gonna recommend a transfer but then she just changed her mind. I'm just askin' for a chance."

Justice Shirley Parnell, a tall, silver-haired woman, listened carefully. It was a pleasure to appear before a respectful, intelligent judge and I saw from her expression that she was moved by Pluto's speech. Nevertheless, she turned to Pluto, who sat next to her in the witness chair, and in her formal, almost patrician manner said, "Mr. Plutowski, you've heard the doctor's testimony. I assure you that I feel sorry you have spent so much time here at this institution, but the doctor's opinion is clear. You simply are not ready to handle the freedom of a nonsecure facility. Now, please step down and join your lawyer."

Pluto slumped in the chair. His round face looked suddenly drawn and elongated. Parnell's remarks accurately summed up the situation, but I still winced as she explained to the man pleading with her that he was not ready to cope with the outside world. I comforted myself with the vague reassurance that Kirby was a far more humane environment than most prisons, and certainly more nurturing than the street; that I, we, the State, had won, and that I had done the right thing. But the victory could hardly be called sweet and Plutowski's situation haunted me for weeks.

During the following months at Projects, as the territory where law and psychiatry overlap became more familiar to me, I found that, in one respect at least, criminal lawyers and psychiatrists, whatever their abilities, perform similar tasks: both attempt to analyze and explain an individual's antisocial behavior. Our differing methodologies, however, generated friction in almost every case. As Ella

Carver had said to me at Kirby, "Lawyers and psychiatrists don't mix."

In the privacy of our offices in Projects, ADAs studied the factual evidence gathered by police and provided by witnesses (a category that includes doctors, nurses, and social workers). In court we offered our conclusions to a judge, and success was measured in terms of the ability to persuade that we were correct. Psychiatrists, by contrast, based their diagnoses largely on the tales told by patients and their behavior on the wards. They listened to dreams, fantasies, memories, and associations, and from that vast sea of information they tried to form coherent explanations. A patient's acceptance of a theory, and positive change in behavior, are the psychiatrist's ultimate judge and jury. In Projects, we had little or no interest in the quality of a defendant's relationship with family members; and in Kirby, psychiatrists never sent out investigators to gather other versions of important events in their patients' lives. Smokey and Arlen considered psychiatry too unscientific and subjective; psychiatrists complained that the law oversimplified complexities. The legal process, perhaps of necessity, tended to reduce the subtleties of psychiatric art to a series of either/or propositions, and psychiatrists resented it.

Pluto's case was no exception. Dr. Reiser considered Pluto's schizophrenia "in remission," by which she meant that the patient showed no overt signs of psychosis. Under prevailing psychiatric theory, schizophrenics are never cured in the sense that one recovers from a cold or the measles. Doctors speak of the illness as being either in remission—meaning that no symptoms are observable—or "florid."

During the hearing, however, we bent the terms into unrecognizable shapes. Pluto's defense attorney argued that since Pluto was "in remission" he was no longer mentally ill. Ella Carver undermined this conclusion by having Reiser "admit" that the patient's schizophrenia could become florid again without significant warning and that, therefore, Pluto would never be "cured." In rebuttal, Pluto's attorney had the doctor explain that patients frequently remain in schizophrenic remission for years and lead a wholly normal existence without a relapse. As far as I could tell, this intellectual ping-pong succeeded only in annoying Reiser and the judge, but it was business as usual on Kirby Day.

Pluto, in remission or not, would probably never be fit to live on his own. It was a fact that had seemed evident from the outset. In a small town three hundred years ago, there might have been many Plutos—village idiots or eccentrics—who were either taken on as a communal burden or locked away in inhumane "hospitals." Now the burden had been assumed by the state, and in this case it looked as if it would last Pluto's lifetime. His treatment in jails and mental institutions had culminated in the creation of a person not of this world. He had become an institutional man.

THIRTEEN

Fugitives

One morning in October a three-page telex message arrived in my mailbox. Lieutenant Arnold Davis of the Montana State Police was desperately looking for "one Stephen Aldrich," who he said was wanted in five states. According to the telex, most of Aldrich's crimes involved his estranged wife, whom he had kidnapped twice and continued to harass as she moved from state to state trying to escape his unwelcome attentions. Lt. Davis listed the reasons he thought high bail appropriate:

> It appears from Aldrich's performance that as long as he is free he is not going to allow . . . his wife to live a normal life and walk the streets a free person. . . . We have had to keep moving her around from place to place. . . . He is a very resourceful subject, capable of obtaining any information he needs to commit fraud and . . . harass anyone connected with the victim. A few of his favorite means are to notify the post office of a change of address for your mail. He has post office boxes in Montana as well as answering machines all over the country. Before you are aware, he has your mail and is looking for information.
>
> Another favorite is obtaining telephone bills. . . . From the bills he can obtain phone numbers called

from the long distance company. He has used this method to locate his wife . . .

He also obtained my [Lt. Davis's] bill. He called the phone company and told them to send my September bill to his brother's address. From the long distance numbers on my bill he found out that I had been in California and what hotel I had stayed at. He called the hotel and requested a copy of my bill. I had used my Mastercard and the bill contained the card number. He used the number to wire himself money three times, totalling $1,000.00.

I have been informed by special agents investigating him that because Aldrich does not have a permanent address and uses different aliases and social security numbers, he has easily beaten the system and can go on doing so . . .

Attached to the telex were a xeroxed photo of Aldrich—hair combed back, holding two juggling pins, and wearing a tuxedo—and a letter from his wife. She included her own reasons for high bail:

I cannot begin to express just how manipulative and deviant a personality Stephen Aldrich is. . . . Chronic violence is a part of a regular program of manipulation. It is coupled with a denial of sleep, proper diet, and almost complete cutoff from the outside world. For example, I was not "permitted" to read magazines, watch television, or look at friends we might pass on the street. To do so would precipitate a severe beating. . . . The violence several times led to loss of consciousness, as his specialties included choking until blackout, hitting repeatedly on the head, and, once, attempted drowning . . .

Of course, violence is only a part of his personality. He stole constantly, exulting in the thrill of having outwitted his victim, society in general, and the police . . .

I feel very strongly that he must be removed from the streets, as he is almost certainly a clinical psychopath.

The telexes were date-stamped two days ago. Apparently they had traveled from one bureau to another before finding their way to Special Projects. Our computers showed that Aldrich had been arrested in Manhattan for a farebeat two days ago. I grabbed my jacket and ran to arraignment court.

Down in AR-1, I went into our files, but Aldrich's case had already been heard. The court clerk's notes from lobster arraignments showed that the judge had set a hundred dollars' bail at four A.M. I checked with Corrections and found that Aldrich had promptly posted the money. He was, as the police are fond of saying, in the wind.

Even after twelve months in the DA's office, I had had no experience with fleeing felons. I pictured a fugitive from justice as a sweaty-faced desperado traveling across state lines at night and accompanied by a sexy blonde picked up at a truck stop. Most of the fugitives I encountered in Smokey's office, however, weren't exactly captured on the run. Usually, they had been arrested in New York City on some unrelated petty charge—farebeat or drug possession—when a name and fingerprint check led to the discovery that an apparently ordinary misdemeanant was in fact a wanted person.

But names and descriptions often underwent creative transformations in the hands of the sleepy police officers working the telex machines, and there were times when it took so long to confirm whether in fact we had the right Joseph Brown—or was it Joseph Browne, or Josef Braun? —that many fugitives slipped through Criminal Court. I then performed the unpleasant duty of notifying out-of-state authorities that we had missed our chance. This task was never more unpleasant than in Stephen Aldrich's case.

Even when we did identify a captive criminal in time to

reach arraignment court, it was not sufficient for me simply to inform a sister state's police force and, like the mounties, have them get their man. The United States Supreme Court, Congress, and the Constitution itself have paved the fugitive's road home with paper, forms, and technicalities, a process known as extradition. Criminals may not be shipped across state lines, like choice fruit, without a prosecutor in the "asylum state" giving a court some good reason to send a prisoner off to another jurisdiction, the "demanding state." The local DA may be put to some trouble, but that is better, so the constitutional analysis goes, than mistakenly sending an unwilling person around the country.

The good reason required for extradition comes in the form of the most aesthetically pleasing of all legal documents: a governor's warrant. These poster-sized warrants are decorated with magisterial seals, ribbons, and flamboyant signatures, and are accompanied by a thick packet of affidavits testifying to the facts of the fugitive's crime and establishing his identity. Marching into court with one of these prepossessing mandates, I felt like a Roman messenger bearing great tidings from Caesar himself.

During nine months at Special Projects, I extradited hundreds of prisoners to almost every state in the union. Most tended to be minor criminals, much less glamorous and inventive than Stephen Aldrich. Three or four times a week a New Jersey parolee ran afoul of the law in New York, and a county sheriff from across the Hudson River would come to pick him up. Almost none of the Jersey fugitives ever demanded a governor's warrant. They signed waivers of extradition in front of a judge and were driven back through the Holland Tunnel to a Jersey courthouse.

More remote states would pay for extradition—flying two officers to New York City and back—only in serious cases. In one instance, an armed robber had escaped from a one-room jail in a remote Arkansas town. After the jail break, he tied the local sheriff to a tree, handcuffed him with his own cuffs, and stole his pistol. About a week later, the escapee was arrested in Manhattan for cocaine possession, a fugitive warrant dropped, and I called Arkansas to give the sheriff the good news. He wasn't in, so I left a message.

That afternoon, I received a call from a husky-voiced man with an almost incomprehensible drawl. "This the Maan-hattan Dee Yay?" he asked. "Mah nayme i' Shurff Burton Sims uh Holville, Ark'nsar. Son, ah'm. 'spected up yo'r way nex wik. Ah jes got a li'l prolum hur. Nah, ah'm lookin' at a map of the fi' buruz: whij one is Maan-hattan?"

I explained that Manhattan was the long, thin one and wondered if he would ever find his way at all. Despite my doubts, the balding, heavy-set sheriff, who looked as if he operated speed traps on the outskirts of Holtsville, appeared in court days later, accompanied by his slender deputy. Their prisoner-to-be, a smirking, muscular young man, signed a waiver of extradition. Sheriff Sims identified himself on the record, and His Honor, one of the more ill-tempered judges in Supreme Court, then looked over at Sims's deputy and asked, "Who the hell is this?"

"Your Honor, sir," the deputy's voice cracked, "I am Harold Meacum."

"Mr. Meacum, what is your position with the Arkansas Police Department?" asked the judge.

"Chief of food services—and deputy, sir."

Even His Honor smiled as the prisoner was released to the overweight sheriff and his cook. It could only be a matter of time before the next escape.

Whenever a state offered to fly an armed escort to Manhattan to "rendite" a fugitive, our governor's office almost always agreed to honor the request. It was a matter of comity. Absent some hideous error, the warrant was issued and we handed over the defendant. Every few weeks, a patrolman from New Mexico or Alaska arrived in my office, delighted at the opportunity to do a little sightseeing before flying home handcuffed to a murderer or a rapist.

Only twice during my term at Projects did a demanding state seem too demanding. Both cases were initiated by a newly elected, iron-willed Virginia governor whose election agenda included the return of all fugitives. Some zealous members of his staff apparently discovered that two warrants for fugitives in New York City had long gone neglected, and they determined to remedy the situation.

One fugitive, Terrence Black, had been caught breaking into a service station in Alexandria thirty-five years ago. Black went to trial, lost, and was sentenced to a year. Just before he completed his prison term, the Virginia Corrections Department discovered that Black fell within a repeat offender statute requiring that he serve not one year but ten. Black had a predictably outraged and despairing reaction. Out of the blue, he owed nine more years for *the same crime*. A few weeks later, while on a work-release program, he escaped and fled to New York. During his next thirty-four years in the city, Black was arrested only three times, and always on a charge of Disorderly Conduct. All the while, he held a regular job and kept a telephone number listed under his own name. Acting on a request from the Virginia police, the NYPD arrested Black at work and brought him to 100 Centre Street.

The other fugitive belonged to Bill Markham, the more soft-spoken of my Projects officemates. Bill's fleeing felon was wanted on a fifteen-year-old Virginia robbery charge. Like Black, he was living in New York City and was easily found by the police: he was the priest at a Brooklyn church.

Bill and I considered both of Virginia's extradition requests outrageous, but I saw no legal reason to refuse extradition. Bill, however, concocted a novel theory to stall the proceedings. Our governor could deny the extradition request, Bill said with a wry smile, because Virginia had not made good-faith efforts to find the men earlier. In essence, the Virginia authorities have waived their right to extradite. It was a clever argument, probably sound, and our governor's office chose to stand by it.

But, motivated by some perverse sense of duty, Virginia persevered and a four-month volley of phone calls and letters ensued. Long after I left Special Projects, their governor's office tracked me down at Bureau 20 to ask about the status of Black's case. I announced, with regret, that the responsibility had passed to a new member of Projects.

Serious criminals, fugitives in the Hollywood sense, came our way only rarely. One afternoon Arlen handed me a telex from the Wisconsin police. The Madison authorities were requesting the extradition of "one Rita Baker, wanted for escape." The telex, however, did not include any facts to support the charge. Escape from where, on what charges? Had Wisconsin recently elected a new governor?

When I called the Madison central detectives' office and mentioned Baker's name, I was connected to the chief of detectives. Baker's crime, it turned out, had nothing to do with escape. On the outskirts of a wealthy suburb of Madison, a divorced man and his daughter had rented a two-bedroom house. With them was a Jamaican woman who worked as their maid and cook, Rita Baker. A few weeks after the family's arrival, neighbors called the police complaining that people had "stopped coming in or out of the house" and that "funny smells" crept out from beneath the doors. The police broke in and found the blue-faced bodies of father and daughter lying in the living room. A half-eaten dinner, lightly covered with mold, sat on the dining room table. The police searched the attic and pried open a few trunks. Inside the last trunk the officers found more than a million dollars in cash and an ounce of cocaine. The maid was gone.

A full-scale investigation began. Of the evidence gathered, most telling were the telephone company records of incoming and outgoing telephone calls, known as MUDs and LUDs. From tracing the numbers, two intersecting dramas emerged. One series of calls linked the house to a ring of high-level cocaine dealers in New York who were suspected of smuggling drugs into the country via a Jamaican connection. Another series led to the father's former wife, whom he had continued to visit. Witnesses who knew the people said that the maid was in fact the husband's live-in lover. The medical examiner's report concluded that father and daughter died from ingesting a mixture of cocaine and oven cleaner. Large amounts of the concoction had also turned up in the food.

The detectives speculated that Baker and her employer-lover had been importing substantial quantities of cocaine into Wisconsin. In the meantime, the man had probably taken up again with his former wife. Upon discovering his infidelity, the jealous maid-lover poisoned him and his daughter, by giving them a taste of their own medicine. After the murders, she left the state, perhaps hoping to return to Jamaica with the help of her New York associates.

Baker might have succeeded had she not been caught loitering around known drug sellers in a police Pressure Point area on the Lower East Side. Anyone arrested in a Pressure Point zone, no matter how minor the offense, must be taken downtown and booked. When Baker's case reached arraignments, I was ready. The judge set bail at $100,000, she signed a waiver of extradition, and within days she returned to Wisconsin facing a double homicide indictment.

Joseph Lombardo, my first and only mobster, earned me some temporary fame within the office. Lombardo worked within a network of shady business associates in Florida who were suspected of masterminding what are known in the underworld as "bust-outs," a businessman's con game running into the hundreds of thousands of dollars. Lombardo and his cronies had allegedly set up a number of fictitious retail businesses through which they established a credit rating. Relying on the bogus rating, Lombardo ordered huge stocks of goods for sale in his supposed business. Once the goods arrived, Lombardo shipped the merchandise out of state and sold it on the black market. Then he skipped town without paying the creditors.

At the behest of the Florida Department of Probation, Lombardo was arrested for parole violation on a prior case —basically a pretext to bring Lombardo in and investigate his network of bust-out operations. But Lombardo's business scams never came to the attention of the arraignment judge: the sole charge before His Honor was Lombardo's failure to pay $500 restitution to a Florida creditor in a three-year-old case. Lombardo assured the judge that he didn't owe anybody a cent, and that if released on his own recognizance he would clear the whole thing up. The day after Lombardo's arraignment, I received a note from the rookie ADA who had arraigned Lombardo. He summarized Lombardo's promises to the court and signed off, "Believe it or not, the judge bought the story."

Embarrassed at once more having to deliver some bad news to a sister law enforcement agency, I telephoned Detective Caesar Tronka, the detective who had alerted the New York authorities to Lombardo's presence in Manhattan. Before I had a chance to tell him about Lombardo scamming the arraignment judge, Tronka asked, "What did he try to pull in court?"

"Detective," I said, "how did you know he would try to pull anything?"

"Listen, Mr. DA, the mug's a professional wiseguy; he learned it from his father, whom I locked up fifteen years ago. I'm telling you he's a real actor. In the precinct, as we were bringing Mr. Lombardo in a few years ago, he faked a heart attack right in front of the sergeant. He did a beautiful job, but he couldn't fool EMS; they said the guy was a fake. So, with a crook like that, you figure he'd never waste an opportunity."

I told Tronka about Lombardo's promises to the judge at arraignments. "That's okay, Counselor," he said, "it's just one more slimeball in the wind."

After speaking to Tronka I called the Florida Department of Probation to check on whether Lombardo actually owed restitution. Lombardo's probation officer, like Detective Tronka, showed no surprise that Lombardo had talked his way out of court.

"Of course he owes restitution," the officer said. "In fact, he never made a single payment. If the judge down here has half a mind to, he can whack Lombardo for three years. But don't feel bad," he reassured me. "He's a smoothie; everyone believes him."

The judge in Manhattan arraignment court had set a short date for Lombardo's next court appearance—one week—but I assumed my mobster would already be on the next plane headed anywhere but Florida. A week later, I received a phone call from a judge's clerk ordering me to get downstairs forthwith: Lombardo was in court.

When I arrived, the hallway outside the courtroom was crawling with its usual ant farm of activity. A harried-looking man with a red face and a pinstripe suit pushed through the crowd, handed me his card, and announced that he had been retained by Lombardo. While being jostled amid the usual press of junkies, hookers, farebeaters, and lawyers, I told Lombardo's counsel that I knew his client had lied to the arraignment judge in order to avoid being kept in on bail, that I intended to expose his fraud to the court, and that I wanted him held until a governor's warrant arrived from Florida. The lawyer mumbled, "Thanks," shook my hand, and quickly disappeared into the recesses of the hallway.

Inside the courtroom a court officer announced, "Joseph Lombardo, fugitive matter, docket number 7No87453." The lawyer with whom I had spoken in the halls stepped to the defense table next to his client. Given Lombardo's profession, I had expected to see a slick-looking Italian of the Don Corleone variety. Instead, the short,

Rough Justice

paunchy, and sloppily dressed Lombardo looked the epitome of a "regular guy"—certainly not well to do, and somewhat dull-eyed.

I started to explain why the court should hold Lombardo without bail, but the judge cut me off before I had even begun to gather my usual head of prosecutorial steam. Any change in the defendant's bail status would have to be made in Supreme Court, nine floors above. His Honor ordered us all forthwith to Justice Waxman's part, where I could see about locking up my mobster.

The defense lawyer, Lombardo, Lombardo's very pregnant wife, and I left the courtroom simultaneously and headed for the elevators. Riding in an elevator car with a fugitive whom I wanted to extradite into the clutches of Florida law enforcement wasn't wise, but chaperoning Lombardo seemed the only way to prevent his escape, since he was free without bail. If he ran I could at least yell for help.

As we rode up I tried not to look at Lombardo, but I heard him behind me breathing heavily. He must really dread the thought of going back to jail, I thought. All of a sudden, Lombardo started gasping for breath. I turned around and noticed his lips trembling and saliva foaming at the corners of his mouth. The elevator stopped at seven, and when the doors opened he hit the floor face first, with a thud. His wife screamed, "Oh my God, you're killing him!" and three court officers sprang into action. One officer held back the elevator doors while the two others dragged Lombardo, now writhing furiously, into the hallway. He seemed to be in the throes of a grand mal epileptic seizure. As we waited for EMS to arrive, a crowd gathered around to watch Lombardo, who now had started to bleed from the mouth. His wife alternately sobbed and muttered in my direction, "You're killing him."

Seeing Lombardo on the floor, I recalled Detective Tronka's tale of the feigned heart attack, but given the bloody, headlong fall in the elevator, I hesitated to call

Lombardo's bluff. A lawsuit for withholding medical attention from an epileptic would not exactly improve my reputation. I instructed the court officers not to let EMS take Lombardo out of the building and then ran for the nearest telephone.

Tronka answered after one ring. He described the phony heart attack at the police precinct: heavy breathing followed by a dive to the floor. Lombardo was up to his usual tricks.

Back in the hallway outside the elevators a growing circle of ADAs, lawyers, and court officers stood gaping at the writhing, bleeding Lombardo. EMS personnel had just started to check his vital signs. His wife continued to sob; she glared at me when I pushed to the front of the crowd. I pulled aside the paramedic team leader and quietly asked if there was anything unusual about this particular seizure.

"You know," he said, "this guy really doesn't have anywhere near the pulse rate or breathing pattern he should have for a grand mal seizure."

Armed with this admittedly swift medical opinion, I asked EMS to stand back and leave the defendant alone. The wife once more lapsed into moaning: "You're killing him." As we watched, Lombardo's grimacing and wheezing subsided as mysteriously as they had come on. Groggily he pulled himself up on his feet. Then, like an animal that unexpectedly turns on its master, Lombardo bellowed, "No, you won't get me!" and charged in my direction. He moved slowly, like a short, clumsy bear, and I easily ducked his attempted tackle. Behind me, however, was a window. Lombardo grabbed the sash, but before he could open it four court officers threw him face first to the floor. Two of the strongest men forced his hands into handcuffs behind his back while a female officer stood over him.

When Lombardo cried out, "Let me go, let me go, I won't try to escape, I promise," the female officer jammed her black-booted foot squarely into Lombardo's crotch.

"You feel where my foot is?" she shouted. "Feel it? One more word out of you and I'll put you out of commission. Understand?" Lombardo promptly quieted down and allowed the officers to chain his ankles and lift him to his feet.

Justice Carl Waxman was conducting his calendar in the relative peace and quiet of his elegant Supreme Court courtroom when I burst in with news of my emergency bail application. Within minutes, Lombardo, still wearing handcuffs and leg chains, was hustled to the defense table by two court officers. His crying wife took up her post in the first row of gallery seats and I began explaining to the court how the man who now stood manacled before him was wanted in Florida for parole violation, had lied to the arraignment judge, had faked a heart attack and an epileptic seizure, and moments ago had lunged at me in an attempted escape.

"Well, sir," said Waxman with a half-concealed sneer to defense counsel, "what does your client have to say about all of this? And let me caution you, every moment you speak takes away time from my calendar."

"Judge," answered the red-faced lawyer, now grown even redder as he rose to defend his client, "to the best of my knowledge Mr. Lombardo suffers from the tragedy of epilepsy, and clearly, the stress of these proceedings, as well as hearing the outrageous allegations by the district attorney's office, has triggered a seizure. A simple medical examination will show the DA's characterization of the episode in the hallway as 'fraudulent' to be utterly baseless. Therefore, Your Honor, I'm asking you to keep Mr. Lombardo out of the system so he can seek appropriate medical care and straighten out his differences with the Florida Department of Probation. It would be unfair to penalize a man who has come back to court voluntarily for a disease which is out of his control."

"Is that *all* you have to say, Counselor?" asked Waxman.

"Yes, Your Honor."

"Well then," His Honor continued in an ominously

cheerful tone, "there are a number of excellent physicians at Riker's Island, and I'll be very interested to read their report on your client's condition. Remand Mr. Lombardo, please." Waxman offered an icy smile, the guards took charge of the body, and Lombardo moved haltingly toward a door behind the prisoner's bench. As he disappeared into the holding pens he looked over his shoulder and shouted, "You can't do this to me. Today's my son's birthday."

FOURTEEN

The Morning Mail

A few times a week Special Projects received certified letters from two of the largest prisons in New York State, located, poetically enough, in the towns of Stormville and Fishkill. The letters contained prisoners' pro se motions asking either for return of lost bail money or for information from their case files under the Freedom of Information Act. The motion papers usually were written in longhand by the prisoners under the guidance of a jailhouse lawyer (a fellow prisoner who had become familiar with legal terms and forms), were riddled with incomprehensible legal jargon, and raised every conceivable argument. Steve Watts, methodical to a fault, insisted that Stan, Bill, and I respond to even the most farfetched points. The motions piled up, unanswered, on the corners of our desks until the last possible moment.

The ostensible purpose of imposing bail is to give a defendant a financial incentive to return to court. If the defendant fails to show up, he forfeits the money. Under the New York Criminal Procedure Law, forfeited bail can be returned, but only in "exceptional circumstances." That limitation, however, proved to be no deterrent for prisoners with time on their hands.

Stories of sudden illnesses, trips to South America to attend funerals of uncles and aunts, absentmindedness ("I forgot the right date"), and being incarcerated elsewhere ("I was in jail in Brooklyn, so I couldn't possibly have come to court") were the norm. Like police officers' dropsy stories, they were just variations on a tired old theme. Most prisoners didn't even try to document the exceptional circumstances that kept them away from court. The name of the doctor who supposedly treated them, the dates of the funeral for the deceased relative, or the charges in another jurisdiction were strangely absent from the lengthy motion papers. The stories, we all realized, were bald-faced lies: most defendants returned to court only after being arrested on new charges months later. Yet even from inside the walls of the institutions where they served time, prisoners were not above committing fraud on the court. From a prisoner's point of view, I imagined, trying to recoup one's financial losses, even on the flimsiest of pretexts, might seem somehow just. The government had won the case; why shouldn't the loser at least get his or her bail money back? Prisoners often wrote, "The State has suffered no prejudice since the defendant ultimately pled guilty and was sentenced." If I had become cynical about honesty during the past year in Criminal Court, reading bail remission motions ensured that I wouldn't forget my hard-learned lessons.

Still, prisoners were entitled to a fair hearing, and for truly deserving prisoners I willingly searched out a justification for returning bail. Tyrone Biggins, arrested for the gunpoint robbery of a liquor store, was one of the exceptional cases. Before the most recent stick-up, Tyrone had already jumped bail on two other Manhattan felonies. Given his abysmal track record, the judge at arraignments set bail at $10,000. It seemed unlikely that Tyrone would walk away from this one. But in an occurrence rare by 100 Centre Street standards, Tyrone's mother intervened on his behalf. Family members more often than not gave up on "black sheep" who got arrested too many times. If relatives came to court at all it was to give moral support, not money. Ms. Biggins, however, put up her entire life savings so her boy could fight his case from outside Riker's.

Tyrone made it to his first two court appearances, but when a firm trial date was set, he skipped out. Like most bail jumpers, Tyrone was soon rearrested on yet another robbery, and now, facing four felonies, he pled guilty and threw himself on the mercy of the court. The judge gave him five to ten in Stormville. But in the meantime Ms. Biggins's $10,000 bail had been forfeited.

From the bail remission papers I learned that, in addition to being a mother whose faith in her son knew no bounds, Ms. Biggins barely spoke English, suffered from arthritis, supported her immigrant grandmother by scrubbing floors, and was now thrust into abject poverty all because of her desire to do the right thing by Tyrone. I argued to Smokey that if all these heartrending details could be verified, we should agree to the return of the money. Looking dreamily out his window, he agreed. "After all," he said, "Tyrone committed the crimes, not his mother."

Two weeks later, a bent-over old woman with calloused hands and a warm smile came to my office. She brought along her tax returns, her savings passbook, some hospital records, and family photos. Under a hardship exception to the general rule against remissions, Tyrone's mother got her savings back.

New York's Freedom of Information Law (FOIL) provided another creative outlet for legally inclined prisoners, but like the bail remission statute it was subject to frequent abuse. During the course of a trial, defendants are always provided with reams of information about the prosecution's case: statements of witnesses, police reports, transcripts of hearings, photographs. As I knew from Criminal Court, failure to turn every scrap of paperwork over to the defense can result in an "automatic mistrial." Nevertheless, convicted prisoners requested copies of any and every thing they felt might assist them in preparing their appeals. One man asked me to send him the gun he had used to commit murder.

The appellate process figured only distantly in the scheme of things for members of the trial bureaus, but for prisoners it was the last hope. The possibility that judges reviewing a trial transcript might overturn their convictions provided a powerful incentive for legal work. Although I refused to relay sensitive information such as the home addresses and telephone numbers of the People's key witnesses, I otherwise liberally granted FOIL requests—perhaps too liberally. In my first responses to Stormville and Fishkill prisoners, I ended my letters with, "If you need further assistance, please contact me." Within weeks, I received a number of requests from other prisoners. My name seemed to have become associated with unusually prompt and generous provision of information.

Bail-remission motions and FOILs, while certainly the least significant side of the daily routine at Special Projects, offered a view into the lives and thoughts of prisoners, a part of the justice system rarely seen by ADAs. These verbose, histrionic motions suggested idle hours weighing on men and women who carefully followed all the legal formalities except one—telling the truth. Given their exposure to the legal system—the two-minute arraignments, pressured guilty pleas, and boilerplate Legal Aid motions—it was, perhaps, not surprising that they often elevated form over substance or tried to take advantage of the system. They seemed to have carried over into prison the notion of life as a game of risk. On the streets, they had "won" for a time. In court, the state took round two. Now they looked for a law, a case, a fact that some judge might be willing to acknowledge. You might get your money back; you might even get a new trial. In all this filing and shuffling the crimes themselves seemed to have been long forgotten. Formalities, excuses, and farfetched arguments were all that was left over and all that the convicts had to cling to.

FIFTEEN

Sammy Magno

In June, Kate and I were taking the Metroliner to Boston for a vacation at her family's house on Cape Cod. While we waited on the Pennsylvania Station platform and watched the silver passenger cars rumble past, I noticed a familiar figure amid the crowd, a short, hairy man wearing a torn T-shirt and carrying an attaché case. Before I could connect a name to the fleeting image, he disappeared into the sea of jostling bodies.

Inside the first car passengers noisily clambered for seats, so Kate and I headed toward the rear of the train, looking for a quiet spot to sit together. On my right, a few cars down, the man appeared again, this time jabbering to a young woman. A sign on his briefcase said, SAMSON'S.

"Katie," I said as we settled ourselves down in an empty section of the train, "guess who's sitting two cars back? Sammy Magno."

"Oh, come on," she said. "I thought he was sent back to Kirby."

We spent the first half of the train ride looking apprehensively over our shoulders, fearing that Sammy might pay us a visit.

Sammy Magno had entered my life the previous November, at a time when Projects had fallen into flux. After ten years, Arlen Avnet, our deputy chief, had left prosecuting to join a private law firm, and an office-wide party was thrown in his honor. There was the usual ribbing and toasting late into the night and the next morning half of the DA's office were fighting nasty hangovers.

Arlen's departure thrust Stan, Bill, and me into positions of greater responsibility, all the more so, in fact, since Smokey was busy interviewing new deputy chiefs and recruiting a permanent staff for Projects. Every two weeks one of us drove the blue DA Oldsmobile up the East River and through the sanitation training grounds to handle cases at the mental hospitals on our own. Extraditions, governor's warrants, and bail remissions were as much a part of our daily lives as the complaint room had once been, and I even grew accustomed to receiving letters from patients with such headings as "The Negro Bible," or beginning, "Dear Mr. Morgenthau, How are you feeling today? Well I hope." We handled each other's cases, covered court appearances, and independently responded to escapes from Kirby or the capture of a fugitive. The telephone rang so often with news of yet another crisis that we started flipping coins to see who would answer.

One afternoon, alone in the office, I picked up a call from Tom Makepeace, assistant director of the West Side Psychiatric Clinic: "I thought I'd see if you had been notified that Sammy Magno failed to appear for his last two appointments."

"Who's Sammy Magnum?" I asked.

"Magno," he said. "This last September some judge released him on condition that he attend therapy sessions, and we're supposed to notify your office if he misses more than two appointments in a row. He was in on an attempted murder. But there's something else." Makepeace paused. "I think he was arrested in Queens or somewhere this week."

"You *think* he was arrested?" I asked. "What do you think he did?"

"I heard something about hitting a neighbor's door with a machete. We got a call from the police that Sammy had been in custody, but they let him go before anyone realized he was a mental patient. I believe the calls came in on Monday or Tuesday." It was now Thursday afternoon.

"Excuse me, Mr. Makepeace, but why the hell did you wait two days to let us know that a mental patient is loose on the streets of New York carrying a machete? He might kill somebody!"

"First of all," he replied defensively, "the cops took away the machete. And second, we tried to get Sammy to come in for his lithium treatment. We even called his girlfriend, Ruth Quill, but she hadn't seen him." I told Makepeace to wait by the phone while I pulled our file.

Sammy's original crime was deranged and brutal—typical Special Projects material. In November, almost one year ago to the day, he had gone to his grandmother's apartment in the West Sixties and asked to borrow money. She refused, and an argument ensued. By his own admission, Sammy pummeled her with a sneaker until she lay crumpled in a bloody heap, just as Raskolnikov had done with the old woman pawnbroker. The grandmother survived, however, and turned Sammy's name over to the police. On the night of his arrest, Sammy explained to a detective that "he had to kill" his grandmother because "she was Lilith and made the walls bleed." After months of psychiatric examinations and reports, Justice Simon Wilde found Sammy to have been suffering from bipolar mood disorder—the modern term for manic depressive psychosis—and therefore "not responsible" for trying to murder his grandmother. Wilde released Sammy on condition that he regularly attend the West Side Clinic and take lithium.

I called the clinic and relayed the news to Makepeace.

"Now I'm worried," he said. "The last time Sammy showed up for his therapy, he was on a real manic high. And he tried to kill his grandmother right about this same time last November. After the trauma of being arrested

n this new case, he could go back to finish her off! What
hould we do?"

Smokey was out of the office until Monday, and Bill and
Stan were both at Kirby. No one had trained me to orga-
nize a manhunt for a murderous lunatic in New York City,
but I couldn't very well ask Makepeace to phone back
after the weekend, when my boss would be in. I told him
to alert the local precinct and then wait by the phone.

Rechecking our files and putting Sammy's name into
the court computer, I discovered that the grandmother,
shortly after recovering from the sneaker attack, left New
York for her native Minnesota: one potential catastrophe
avoided. I also found out, embarrassingly enough, that
Sammy's arrest for the machete attack had been in Manhattan, not Queens. Under Justice Wilde's order, we had
the right to return Sammy to a mental hospital for evalua-
tion if his mental condition deteriorated—"decompen-
sated," in psychiatric parlance. The machete incident was
ample evidence of decompensation, but no one in arraignments had noticed that Sammy Magno was a mental
patient subject to a judicial order. We had had him and
lost him, rendering us doubly responsible if he got into
any more trouble with the machete over the weekend.

The prosecutor on the machete case, Betsy Shoreham,
worked a few doors down the hall from me. I knew Betsy
from riding the elevator to work in the morning. Two
years ahead of me and well into felonies, she already had a
reputation as one of the toughest young ADAs. I found her
at her desk shuffling through a stack of new complaints
and asked if any of them involved Sammy Magno.

"Oh, you mean the nut who tried to whack holes in his
neighbor's door with a machete?" she said.

"I suppose so," I answered. "I just got a call about him
from a mental clinic. What's the story on your case?"

"Well, the police responded to his address the day before yesterday and found him there hacking at the door
and threatening to kill the guy inside. The officers eventually calmed him down and recovered the machete. At the

precinct he gave his name as 'The Clorox Kid,' but his rap
sheet says his real name is Magno. Anyway, the case
sounded more like criminal 'mis' and misdemeanor weapons possession, so I didn't ask for bail, and I doubt I'll
indict him. He didn't even cut anybody. Why do you want
to know about him?"

I gave her a quick summary of Sammy's criminal history, but Betsy still seemed uninterested. Because Sammy
hadn't actually killed somebody, she saw no reason to take
the machete case seriously. Sammy was going to be my
responsibility. Before leaving her office, I asked whether
Sammy had said anything else to the police.

"Oh, yeah," she said, now staring distractedly out into
the hallway. "He said he had a license from the FBI to
break into the apartment because the guy inside was a
crack dealer. He also said the arrest made no difference
because he had another machete at home. What a jerk!"

Back at Projects I tried calling the clinic, but Makepeace had left for the day. At a loss, I alerted sergeants,
lieutenants, and detectives in each police precinct where
Sammy had been arrested, spoke to doctors at Kirby, left a
message for the director of the Department of Mental
Hygiene, and attempted to reach Smokey at home. After
an hour on the phone, I tried to put the case out of my
mind by reading the morning mail.

The first letter was from a Kirby patient named Franklin McGraw Davis. In primitive, angular handwriting Davis began: "I am King and author of King Author court of
Arabian galloping horseman of quick drawn swords name
Quick Draw McGraw and a prisoner in a mental institution under acquittal law 330.20. Do you really believe i
committed a crime? Did you really think for one moment
that i committed a crime? Did you? I mean did you really
think that i Franklin McGraw Davis murdered someone? . . ." He rambled on, ending: "i should be free to
leave the courtroom when i arrive there in January or
February. because no crime took place. All i did was pick

up a wrench and beat F. Sims on the head with it and he fell back and retained himself and refrained himself."

Davis's letter only worsened my anxiety. It conjured up the specter of Sammy Magno wandering the streets in a psychotic stupor, trying to "refrain" some innocent stranger. I reread Shoreham's file, looking for clues. Among other things, I found that Sammy had given the police the name, address, and phone number of his girl-friend, Ruth Quill. Ruth lived across from a drug rehabili-ation center in one of the worst sections of Alphabet City, but still she was worth a try. I dialed the number, fully expecting one of Sammy's fellow psychotics to greet me with "Go away" or "Huh?" or a hang-up, but Ruth an-swered, and to my surprise, she greeted me coherently.

I didn't want to let on that I was desperately searching for someone to help me lock Sammy in a padded Kirby cell, so I told Ruth that I was "looking for Mr. Magno." My ruse, apparently, was not too subtle.

"Are you from the Police Department?" she asked.

"No," I said, embarrassed at my own duplicity, "I'm from the DA's office."

"Well, I'm glad somebody called," she said. "Sammy's terribly loony these days, and, my God, when he's not taking his lithium he's terrifying. That's why I called the police the other day."

"You called the police about the machete incident?" I asked.

"Did I? He woke up everybody in the building over it. Banging away at Felipe's door, screaming that he was going to kill him because he had been walking into his apartment and stealing things."

"Had he been burglarizing Sammy's apartment?"

"Of course not, but when Sammy gets high he imagines all sorts of things. He thinks Felipe walks *through* the walls. Sammy told me he hides under tables and watches him. He's got to get some help."

When I explained to Ruth that all I wanted was to get Sammy into treatment at a hospital called Kirby, she agreed that if Sammy came home she would walk him over to the clinic, where we could do whatever was necessary. I left work that evening hoping Sammy's name would not greet me from the front page of tomorrow's *Daily News*.

The next morning I called the clinic. Makepeace, sounding delighted, explained that Ruth had taken Sammy in hand and convinced him to let the police take him to the hospital.

"Where is he now?" I asked, almost as an afterthought. Makepeace didn't know. "What do you mean you don't know where he is?" I asked.

"Well," he said, "it's the Police Department's responsibility. Usually, when they arrest an EDP [Emotionally Disturbed Person], they take him to the Bellevue Psych Ward. Why don't you try calling over there?"

I called Bellevue, and after being switched from floor to floor I was connected to the ward administrator. "Sammy Magno?" said the listless voice. "Let's see. Oh, yes. It seems we owe your office an apology. Mr. Magno was brought here last night by the police. We had him restrained on a stretcher because he was quite upset upon arrival. But apparently members of the staff left him unattended, and when they returned he had released himself. The next thing anyone knew he was gone."

I wondered how I would put this latest turn of events to Smokey when he returned on Monday. Then Ruth Quill called to ask why Sammy was now sitting in his apartment instead of in a ward at Bellevue. "I tried to help you," she complained, "but if this happens again Sammy's going to lose faith in me completely and you'll be on your own. He was ready to go to the hospital, but after they abandoned him on a stretcher in a hallway, he slipped out and walked home."

Ruth must have thought of me the way I thought of Tom Makepeace, placating and somewhat inept, but she kindly agreed to help us yet again. At the end of the day Sammy, carrying a toothbrush and a change of clothes, returned to the clinic. The police, however, refused to take Sammy to Ward's Island, and the Kirby security staff said it was too late to come to Manhattan.

Sammy seemed to lead a charmed existence. He beat his grandmother into unconsciousness, got arrested on three occasions, and was tied to a stretcher in a psychiatric ward, yet remained immune to incarceration. But this time I was determined. After a few irate telephone calls to Kirby, three white-suited psychiatric prison guards arrived at the clinic and drove Sammy out to Ward's Island. Sammy's charm, I thought, had finally expired.

The following Monday, I learned better. Steve Watts explained that patients who violate court orders, even as glaringly as Sammy, can't simply be whisked away to a locked psychiatric ward. Three months ago, Justice Wilde had found Sammy suitable for outpatient treatment and had released him, albeit under strict conditions. Just because he had since violated most of Wilde's order didn't mean he needed long-term recommitment. To keep him in, Smokey said, I needed to know more.

Under the circumstances, Ruth Quill seemed the most promising lead, so I went back to the police file for her number and dialed it.

"Samson's Escorts," said a sultry female voice.

"Excuse me," I said. "Wrong number."

I redialed, again heard "Samson's Escorts" in a seductive tone, and again excused myself. I checked the file and discovered that I had dialed a number Sammy had told the police was his own. That Sammy gave an escort-service number as his home telephone seemed farfetched, but he was, after all, certifiably insane, and the subject, even if a mistake, was too interesting not to pursue.

Once more the voice on the phone purred, "Samson's Escorts."

"Hi," I said. "Is Sammy Magno there?"

"I'm sorry. Sammy's not here right now, but can I help you?"

"Yes, I'm an old friend of Sammy's and he gave me this

number to call in case I came through the city. Got any idea where I can get hold of him?"

"Sure, hon," she said. "He's at 437-5591."

I thanked her and hung up, perplexed. She had given me the number of the Kirby wards. After waiting a discreet interval, I called back and explained that I had tried to reach Sammy but kept getting some psychiatric hospital.

"That's right," she said. "Sammy's been doing a bit too much, uh, stuff lately, so he's going to get some rest. But he says that there's no problem and he'll be better in a week or two."

"Too much coke, huh?" I prompted. "Sounds like the same old Sammy. By the way, what does he do at this number? I mean, is he working for you?"

"No, silly," she laughed. "We work for him. He owns the business."

"Is that right?" I asked. "How much do you charge?"

"Well, for a young lady to come visit your apartment it's one hundred and fifty dollars for the hour. Are you interested, hon?"

"Not tonight, thanks. But I will try to reach Sammy at the hospital, just to give him my regards."

One snowy evening a week after my Samson's Escorts discovery, Ruth Quill arrived at Special Projects. Steve Watts caught a brief glimpse of my informant in her threadbare pea coat and blue jeans as she entered my office. He later asked me, "Who's that flake you were interviewing?" Ruth did look the worse for wear, but she turned out to be both intelligent and eager to help. She opened with an unexpected revelation—she and Sammy had been married. I asked her to tell me the whole story.

"I first met Sammy in California in '67," she said. "He owned a used clothing store in San Francisco called Skinside Out. We were both flower children, taking LSD, smoking dope, the whole Aquarian trip. We moved in together and had Alicia, who's sixteen, and later our son,

Atom, who's thirteen. But after a few too many years of Sammy's craziness, I took the kids with me to Mexico."

According to Ruth, Sammy's mother had left her husband and kept Sammy with her while she worked as a cocktail waitress–prostitute in Connecticut. Sammy apparently saw "everything that went on." When he turned thirteen, he moved in with a string of gay men who kept him as their "boy." Then he started up one business after another, some of them "on the shady side." "Once he even tried to burn down a store for insurance purposes."

I asked if she had ever heard of Samson's Escorts.

"Oh, God, you know about *that*?" Ruth said with disgust. "To tell you the truth, I was hoping not to get into it. But sure, Sammy's been into prostitution for years. In fact, the other day our daughter Alicia was down in Sammy's apartment and he had one of his girls over. Sammy was singing the praises of prostitution to her, and my God, she's his own child—although he also tells her not to lose her virginity until she turns eighteen. Sammy has a strong purist streak. Some weeks he pumps himself full of vitamins and eats only vegetables and bottled water. Once I cooked a steak on his stove and he blew up at me, saying that now he couldn't eat anything cooked there for days! Of course, a month later, he was staying up for four days in a row freebasing coke."

When she finally broke up with Sammy, Ruth said, she took Atom and Alicia and went to live with friends in New Hope, Pennsylvania. "One day, Sammy appeared at the door and said he wanted to see the kids. He was so high his eyes were about to pop out of his head, but I let him hang around just to talk. After a while, he got wound up over moving the whole family out west somewhere, and ranting and raving about pioneering in covered wagons.

"The next thing I knew, he took off all his clothes and started dancing naked around the house flailing this huge kitchen knife. I told him to put it down, but he wouldn't listen. Of course, the knife slipped and gave him an ugly cut in the foot. I bandaged him up as best I could and then

kicked him out. Sammy got pretty upset at having to
leave, especially with his cut foot and all, but I had to think
of the children. Later that night, the New Hope police
called. They found Sammy barefoot, pushing a shopping
cart through town. At two in the morning I went to the
police station, handed Sammy some bus money, and said
good-bye. That was the last we saw of each other for a
while."

Ruth said that other DAs had called about Sammy in the
past, but at the time she didn't want "those creepy kind of
people messing around" in her life. "But now, God knows,
I can't seem to help him much anymore," she said, "so
maybe you can do him some good after all." Trying not to
appear too creepy myself, I explained that my concern
was to get Sammy the help he needed, not just to lock him
up in Kirby and feed him sedatives. Ruth seemed encouraged. I asked her if she considered Sammy dangerous.

"Well," she said wearily, "I may as well tell you the
whole miserable story. About a year ago, I decided to
move back to New York to take wordprocessing classes.
Next thing I know, one of Sammy's neighbors gets ten
years for dealing crack and Sammy wangles me the lease.
So that's where Alicia, Atom, and I live—right under
Sammy. And let me tell you, I get to hear the kooky stuff
that goes on up there. About three months ago, just after
the court business over his grandmother, Sammy went
way off the deep end. In the middle of the night I heard
these crashes coming from his apartment. I went upstairs
and yelled, 'Sammy, what on earth is going on in there?'
He came to the door, bathed in sweat and covered with
scratches. Then he invited me inside.

"First, I had to be debugged by this special machine
before I could walk all the way in. The machine was just
an old computer with a screen that flickered. But I agreed
to stand in front of the stupid thing because by this time it
was clear how far gone Sammy was and I suspected he
might even be suicidal. Then I looked around and knew
that Sammy had gone stark raving mad. It looked as if he

had been throwing chairs and tables at the walls all night long and then stacking up the remains in the center of the room. There were even a few blackened sticks in a corner where he had lit some weird kind of funeral pyre. Worst of all was the machete. The walls had these huge gouges where he had been hacking away.

"That night Sammy told me he was appointed by God to protect the world from demons and he had been doing battle against powerful forces. That's what all the noise was about. After talking with some of the neighbors, I called the hospital. The next day, an emergency medical team came to our building and Sammy met them at his door stark naked except for a hunting knife. But Sammy's no fool, even if he's crazy. When he understood that these people could take him back to the hospital, he got dressed, and a minute later, as calm as could be, he explained that of course he was taking his lithium: 'You can go back to work. Everything's under control.' And they believed him!

"Since then, things have gotten worse. He keeps our son Atom in his apartment for hours while he raves about his supernatural delusions and throws furniture around. Once Sammy smashed a mirror on the floor because he got lost in it or some such nonsense, and he made Atom walk barefoot over the broken glass because 'Atom is Jesus and he won't be hurt.' Sammy almost pulled a similar maneuver with an electric fan, but I caught him before he went too far.

"It's just gotten so out of hand that now I'm willing to try to get him some kind of help, even if it means putting him in an institution. If you can just force him to keep taking his lithium he'll calm down enormously. I know he will. Then he can deal with the coke and the girls and his whole messed-up life."

By the time she finished her bizarre tale, Ruth was teary-eyed and distraught, and I was having trouble assembling my impressions. There was always a temptation to assume the worst about defendants, since the racier the case, the more incentive to work on it, and the more worthwhile the task of locking someone up. But Ruth had been married to Sammy, and continued to live one floor below him—facts that didn't speak too well for her reliability. She might be a bit crazy herself, or out to seek revenge for any number of obscure reasons.

"You know," she said just before she left, "I don't see why they let Sammy out after his last case, but you probably have some idea. At least I hope you do."

The next morning I told Steve Watts the entire Sammy Magno saga—from child abuse to arson to drug addiction to attempted murder. Even Smokey, the veteran homicide prosecutor, was impressed enough to hook me up with my first detective: Henry Bandrowicz, a member of the Investigations Bureau and one of Steve's longtime associates.

Henry arrived at Projects that afternoon. He was in his fifties and had a gentle, boyish smile and a melancholy wateriness in his eyes. There was also an undercurrent of toughness in his attitude, an impression reinforced by his broad shoulders, his trademark black raincoat, and the small automatic pistol he wore tucked under his vest. He looked somewhere between an ex-cop and a hit man.

I had hoped to accompany Henry into some of Sammy's seamier haunts and learn firsthand about detective work, but the DA's office had a longstanding policy against prosecutors going "into the field," that is, anywhere but their offices or court. Detective work is done by detectives, not rookie lawyers. While Henry was out and about, I was to remain at my desk reading reports and interviewing the occasional witness. I sketched out the Sammy Magno situation and Henry quietly said, "Okay. I know what to do."

Staying at the office was just as well: Sammy's summary hospitalization had created a stir throughout the Mental Hygiene defense lawyers' community, and as I was leaving that evening, a messenger handed me an Application for a Writ of Habeas Corpus demanding Sammy's immediate release. Terms like "unconstitutional," "violation of due process," and "illegal detention" stood out from the lists of current legal citations. This was no boilerplate motion.

Sammy's defense lawyer, Clare Dacey, and I met in Simon Wilde's courtroom the following morning. At that moment, His Honor was embroiled in the pretrial phases of a highly publicized case against two henchmen hired to "inch" a man for giving information to the police. "Inching" was a form of punishment used by Jamaican drug dealers that involved the systematic hacking of arms and legs, inch by inch. Young and nattily dressed, Wilde sat at his bench surrounded by a noisy crowd of lawyers. He motioned for Clare and me to approach and the circle of lawyers parted. From behind his aviator glasses and beneath his blow-dried hair, he announced that Sammy's application could not be considered for three weeks. The crowd of lawyers closed around the bench again before Clare had any chance to object. Wilde, I gathered, had had enough of Sammy Magno.

Leaving the courtroom, I recognized a court officer with whom I had worked in Criminal Court. He asked me what I was up to and I told him about some of the more sensational details of Sammy's case. "You talking about the nut who beat his grandma with a sneaker?" he asked.

"Yeah," I said. "You wouldn't believe some of the wild things this guy has been up to. We've got him back in Kirby temporarily, but His Honor wants to hear argument on Writ for Habe."

"Funny you say, 'wild,' Counselor," he said, "because last year I was in court during the hearings in that case, and every day this guy came and sat in the audience. Before they'd take the perp back into the pens, he'd shake Sammy's hand like they was old buddies. Anyway, one of the guards says to me, 'I recognize that guy from somewhere.' All of a sudden it hits both of us that he's Bobby Layzer, the porn star. He's been in dozens of porn flicks.

I'm telling you, the guy is hung like a goddamn Wiener schnitzel!"

A week later, Henry the detective resurfaced, still wearing the same black raincoat. Henry had managed to track down a number of Sammy's unsavory connections, including the infamous Bobby Layzer. Bobby, who claimed to have retired from the Wiener schnitzel business, wouldn't come downtown to talk with me, but Henry nevertheless weaseled some information out of him. Bobby admitted cofounding Samson's Escorts with Sammy; in fact, it was Bobby's idea to place an escort ad in the Yellow Pages. Besides the call-girl ring, Bobby said Sammy made money watching the door at Bobby's own private orgies for cocaine dealers and hookers. But they had recently broken off business relations, he said, because Sammy wasn't honest: "Not that he cheated me. Sammy just wouldn't admit he was a low-level pimp. He'd say, 'I'm not a pimp, I'm a player.'"

The Bobby Layzer connection also led Henry to Natasha Freely, a pornographic actress who was Bobby's wife and costar. On our promise of anonymity, Natasha agreed to come downtown. Naturally, I was amused at the prospect. Many of my colleagues had had cases involving call-girls and strippers (one of whom came to the office wearing a raincoat buttoned up over what she called her "working clothes"), but Natasha was my first porn queen.

She came to my office one afternoon, accompanied by Henry's black figure. I had expected a lithe, buxom trollop in sleazy clothing, but instead, Tash, as she liked to be called, was a middle-aged woman of average build who wore her mousy brown hair parted in the middle and pulled behind the ears. Nevertheless, as she settled herself in a chair opposite my desk, angling her legs and chest to their best advantage, I saw vestiges of her former allure. Stan and Bill had learned about the interview and managed to be present, eavesdropping from their desks.

I introduced myself and thanked Tash for coming downtown.

"That's all right," she said, looking around at Henry, Stan, Bill, and me. "I like attention from men."

"Now, Ms. Freely," I said, "please give me your full name. I need it to run a check on your background."

With a sigh, she complied. "Okay, it's Natasha Alexandra Barohovitch."

"What a lovely name" said Stan, leaning over his desk with a lecherous grin.

She turned to Stan, the handsome, all-American-looking DA, and said, "Yes, it is a lovely name, isn't it?" I gave Stan as stern a look as I could muster, and moved on.

Natasha, I quickly understood, took her role as a film star seriously. The episodes with Sammy that she recalled were dated not by year, but according to the film she happened to be working on at the time. "We first met while I was working as Bobby's costar in *Layzer Gun,*" she said. "But I never noticed his weird behavior until two years later. *The Natasha Freely Story* had just been released and Sammy ran up to my apartment to tell me that I was a goddess. I laughed, but he was serious. A *real* goddess. He started going on about people from outer space and how I was the only pure female besides Ruth who could save the earth.

"I told Sammy he should go sleep it off, but then he pulled a knife and made me walk all over the neighborhood with him while he talked about demons and this woman named Lilith. He didn't hurt me, so I just let the whole thing drop. Besides, Sammy was always saying how much he loved me. Especially after he saw *Shy Dove*, where I played an Indian princess. He tried to go to bed with me a few times, but I told him he was too crazy to handle—although he was probably a good lover."

After an hour of this sort of conversation, I realized that while Natasha was delighted to be the center of attention, she knew very little about Sammy. Still, the knife incident, which could be interpreted as an attempted kidnapping, showed that Sammy had been dangerously psychotic years before he attacked his grandmother.

"Ruth can tell you more about Sammy than anybody," Natasha said as I put away my notes. "She was going to come down here with me today, but she had to go see her probation officer."

"Probation officer? Are you sure?" Henry and I exchanged glances. We had run Ruth's rap sheet and it was clean.

"Oops," Natasha said. "Maybe I shouldn't have said anything. I guess the cat's out of the bag now." This was the first of the bad news.

The legal aspect of the case, however, was already in full swing. I had finished a twenty-page brief defending the constitutionality of the Mental Hygiene Law as well as Sammy's summary hospitalization. Justice Wilde summarily denied the Application for a Writ of Habeas Corpus, but ruled that Sammy was entitled to a hearing to determine his dangerousness at the soonest possible date. Clare Dacey and Ella Carver, the assistant attorney general who dominated Kirby, both wanted Sammy's case heard in Kirby court, but Smokey was adamant that it not be relegated to the Ward's Island backwaters. Supreme Court justices, he said, were much tougher-minded. Making a rare court appearance, Smokey argued that since Wilde had originally drafted the condition of Sammy's release order, he must decide whether the order had been violated. His Honor, not surprisingly, agreed and set the case down for the following week.

The next time Henry came hulking down the Special Projects hallway, he was accompanied by a contrite Ruth Quill. "Okay," Ruth said as I closed the door. "I should have told you that I was on probation, but I thought you'd never believe me if you knew." Before going to New Hope, it turned out, Ruth had spent three years in Mexico living with a group of people who were smuggling grass into the United States. "That was all right with me, I admit," Ruth said, "but when Uzi machine guns started showing up in the house, I had had enough. Unfortunately, the police already had my name on file, and when I tried to cross over the border they arrested me for conspiracy to smuggle narcotics. I spent three years in a Mexican jail, and I'd probably still be there if it weren't for the prisoner exchange program. That's why I don't have a U.S. criminal record."

Henry called Ruth's probation officer and found that this time she was telling the truth. Ruth agreed to atone for her breach of faith by leading us to two more potential witnesses—Sammy's crack dealer and a Haitian plumber—and she and Henry disappeared down the Projects hallway.

With a hearing now definitely in sight, I began assembling psychiatric evidence. At one time or another during the last year, Sammy had been examined by a dozen experts, all of whom had differing views on his need for recommitment.

John Kuhn, a respected private psychiatrist, had first seen Sammy during the grandmother-beating proceedings. Although appointed by Justice Wilde only to render an expert opinion, Kuhn continued to see Sammy in his midtown office. He liked Sammy and considered him in some respects a pet project. He joked about Sammy's delusions and downplayed his potential for violence: "Once he's on lithium, he's more or less normal. If you met him you'd think he was odd, but there's no way he's dangerous. And from a professional standpoint his problems are much more interesting than most of my clientele's. Granted, if he stops taking lithium and does cocaine he'll snap, but he assures me he's taking care of himself."

At the opposite end of the professional-opinion scale was Sanford Edwards, a crusty old doctor who worked at the West Side Clinic and clearly had it in for Sammy. Edwards sounded like he had been at the clinic for too many years: "Sammy's a manipulative son of a bitch, I tell you. When that jackass judge let him out the first time I was ready to retire. Once, Sammy came into my office in a wild manic fit. He burst in like a dervish and started throwing my files all over the goddamn floor. The minute

Security appeared, though, he pulled himself together. He's a slippery eel, I tell you, and he knows how to control himself when it's to his advantage. The problem is, he's only too ready to let himself go back to running the call-girl operation and smoking cocaine. For any manic patient, taking cocaine is like pouring gasoline on a fire; with Sammy all hell breaks loose. When he gets high, you better believe he's dangerous, and I'd be only too happy to testify about it."

Another psychiatrist at the clinic shared Edwards's doubts about Sammy: "I remember that in September Sammy came in for a check on his lithium level, which is a very important and delicate part of therapy. Sammy had nearly lethal levels of the drug in his system. We all assumed that he hadn't been taking the drug and that at the last minute took a massive dose to try and fool us."

Sammy's current psychiatrist at Kirby was more optimistic about his prognosis, though for reasons that sounded peculiar to me: "Well, it's true cocaine will send Sammy off into a manic episode, but the stuff you buy on the street contains only a very small part that's pure cocaine. It's hard to know if Sammy could even find high-quality drugs. Besides, he's stabilized on lithium. You wouldn't believe the change that's come over him. He's a different person."

Everyone agreed, however, that if Sammy continued to neglect his medication and do cocaine, he would be sufficiently dangerous to require involuntary commitment. Even John Kuhn conceded the point. Sammy was among those rare patients who, though insane at the time of their crimes, can become reasonably sane simply by taking one drug and avoiding others. The doctors referred to the condition as "drug-induced sanity." It was a neat legal loophole that reduced the case to one fundamental question: could Sammy Magno be trusted to avoid cocaine and take his lithium?

After listening to Sammy Magno stories for months, one thing about the case seemed obvious: Sammy was indeed a slippery eel. The machete incident was the least of his transgressions. He had violated nearly every clause of Wilde's order, indulged in drugs and violence, suffered delusions, and neglected his therapy. Whenever it was to his advantage, Sammy could pull himself together, but left to his own devices he indulged to a dangerous degree. With the evidence I had accumulated, winning the hearing seemed a foregone conclusion. I only worried that Wilde might become so enraged at the flagrant disregard of his own order that he would pour down his wrath, commit an error, and be reversed on appeal.

Two days before the hearing, Henry returned from the field emptyhanded. Sammy's crack dealer, Felipe Haskell, was also the man on whose door Sammy had been pounding with a machete months ago. When Ruth and Henry went to speak with him about testifying, they found his apartment boarded up by the police. The day before Henry's visit, some of the locals had beaten down Felipe's door and shot him six times in the abdomen. When the police showed up, they found Felipe bleeding next to a few hundred vials of crack. Felipe was currently under indictment for dealing narcotics and was convalescing in a hospital. As a witness to Sammy's drug-related violence, he was a dead end.

The Haitian plumber wasn't much better. Called in by other tenants to repair some stopped-up toilets, the plumber traced the stoppage to Sammy's apartment. He dismantled Sammy's toilet and found two dolls' heads, one stuck through with pins, the other disfigured with cigarette burns. A second plumber had to be called in to finish the job, tenants said, because the superstitious Haitian refused to touch the dolls, thinking they were evil. No one in the building, however, could locate the name of either plumber.

Between doing the paperwork, reading Henry's reports, interviewing witnesses and psychiatrists, and explaining my every move to Steve Watts, Sammy's case had required daily attention since I picked up Makepeace's first phone call. I knew the evidence inside out. Whenever I dropped off a letter with Karen, the bureau's lone, valiant secretary, she looked up and said, "Sammy, right?"

"Sammy Magno," I explained, "isn't a case, it's a way of life."

"Why don't you just marry the guy?" she laughed.

The hearing began the day after Wilde's notorious "inching" case concluded. The trial had lasted longer than predicted, and by the time we began Sammy had been in Kirby for three months. Clare Dacey and I met outside Wilde's locked courtroom that morning for last-minute negotiations. Despite some setbacks, Smokey and I were convinced that with Ruth, Makepeace, Tash, Dr. Edwards, and even Atom, if necessary, we still had a powerful case. Clare tipped her hand and said that Sammy would agree to six more months in Kirby if we would dispense with the hearing. Seeing that even Clare knew her case was a loser, I refused.

At the last minute Ella Carver had been removed from Sammy's case. Clare and I agreed that Ella's absence indicated some division of opinion within the hospital bureaucracy, a surmise reinforced by Herman Weintraub, Ella's substitute. This was another bad omen. In a nervous, grandmotherly voice, Weintraub prated on and on about technical points of dubious validity and marginal interest. He was worse than useless, and the AG's office knew it. When Clare and I spotted him heading gawkily toward the courtroom, we hid in a corner.

Clare again seized the opportunity to try and sell me on a six-month compromise for Sammy, but she was interrupted by a quavering voice from behind my back: "Excuse me, Clare, but I have to talk to you *right now*." I turned around, ready to fend off an interruption from Weintraub, but instead found myself inches from a dumpy, dark-haired man with an intense look in his eyes, a look I recognized from other patients at Kirby. He was flanked by two white-suited psychiatric guards. This was the man to whom I had been "married" for the last three months.

Sammy looked smilingly at Clare, but the deep creases in his sunken cheeks and across his forehead made even his smile appear worried. He had tried to shave but had missed a few sections of his chin and neck. There were worn patches in his wide-lapeled, double-breasted suit and stains on his half-unbuttoned shirt. With his hair slicked back he looked like a moth-eaten Chicago gangster of the twenties.

"Listen, Sammy," said Clare as she caught hold of his arm. "I'm talking to the DA about your case. Do you think you could wait a minute?" Assuming that I was the last person Sammy wanted to meet at that moment, I turned away from the charmed circle of attorney and client.

"This is the DA?" he asked excitedly. Clare explained to Sammy that since I was in fact the prosecutor, he should keep quiet. But instead of recoiling from me as from one of his imaginary demonic foes, Sammy extended his hand. "Listen," he said. "I want you to know I don't hold any grudge against you for what you've done. I just want to shake to show there's no hard feelings."

Reluctantly I reached out. Sammy grabbed hold and started pumping my hand with enthusiasm. "Anyway," he continued, "even if I don't appreciate the way you got me back in the hospital, I know it's for everyone's good. I'm telling you that I really will keep it together if you guys let me back out. Sure, I run Samson's and all that, but so what? I haven't hurt anyone, and I won't hurt anyone, either. I give you my word. Don't answer me, though. I just want you to know I respect you for doing what you think is the right thing, and—"

"Sammy," Clare interrupted, "let's talk later. I'll tell the DA everything you want, but right now we've got to take care of some legal details. Okay?" Sammy finally let go but continued talking. "Sure, no problem. I understand. Listen, I just want you to know that I respect what you're doing, however things turn out."

Once more Sammy thrust out his hand, but this time I pretended not to notice. Turning my back, I mumbled, "Pleased to meet you."

Clare whispered to me, "I tried to talk him out of wearing that outfit, but he said he wanted to look his best for Judge Wilde. He told me he saved the getup from a place he used to own called Skinside Out." Once again, the disturbing revelation: *This guy really is out of his mind.*

The hearing began at ten, and Wilde, well known for maintaining strict control over his courtroom, wasted no time in taking the upper hand. "The way I see this case," he said, "it's simple, and I don't want to spend a lot of time on it. The only issues are whether Mr. Magno violated my order, and if he did, whether that means he's dangerous. I don't want to rehash all the evidence I heard the last time he was in this courtroom. Is that clear?" Weintraub, Clare, and I nodded in unison. I hoped Wilde's attitude signaled his disgust with Magno and a desire to send him to Kirby for as long as possible as soon as possible.

"Good," he continued, "and I gather everyone agrees that Mr. Magno *did* violate my order. Ms. Dacey, you're not going to argue that your client adhered to it, are you?"

"Well, Judge, I should be given an—"

"Ms. Dacey, do you have *one witness* who can testify that the West Side Clinic's records are incorrect?"

"Well, Your Honor, not exactly. Our position is—"

"Of course not," Wilde plowed forward. "So the only people I need to hear from are the psychiatrists, isn't that correct?"

"Judge," I said, "the People intend to call a number of lay witnesses who have firsthand evidence relevant to Mr. Magno's dangerousness. They include the patient's ex-wife, who—"

"Mr. Prosecutor," His Honor cut in, "lay witnesses are of no use to the court in determining a delicate psychiatric issue. You should know that. I'm not going to waste my time by listening to a bunch of useless testimony that I am in no position to interpret. Do I make myself understood?"

"But Your Honor, if I could just summarize the testimony for the court as an offer of proof, I'm sure you would agree that it *is* relevant to the issue at hand."

"Excuse me," said Wilde. "Psychiatrists *only*. Call the first doctor." Ruth, Tash, Henry, Makepeace, and all of Henry's work instantly evaporated.

Sanford Edwards, a psychiatrist at the West Side Clinic, took the stand and, under my questioning, delivered a crotchety account of Sammy's conduct. He described Sammy's failure to take lithium, the effects of cocaine on a manic-depressive, and Sammy's wild conduct at the clinic. "There's no doubt in my mind," Edwards said, "that Mr. Magno would require an enormous amount of therapy before I'd ever call him safe enough to let out of a secure setting."

Wilde, however, remained critical. Twice he interrupted to ask, "Is the patient dangerous when on lithium?" Both times Edwards answered, "If he could be trusted to take his lithium, he wouldn't be dangerous. But he won't take it unless he's hospitalized." Wilde grumbled in response.

By three that Friday afternoon, it was clear we would have to reconvene on Monday. Wilde began to declare a recess, but Clare Dacey pulled out a new Application for a Writ of Habeas Corpus. Sammy had already been involuntarily committed for three months to the day, Clare argued, and because the Mental Hygiene Law states that an individual may not be hospitalized involuntarily for more than three months without a hearing, Sammy was entitled to immediate release. I vociferously opposed the writ on all sorts of grounds: the hearing was already in progress, hence we had met the statute's time limit; the delay was due to the court's schedule; and Clare herself had added to the delay by bringing her previous Application for a Writ months ago. Weintraub sat next to me, staring at a yellow pad covered with notes.

Looking sternly at the defendant, Justice Wilde said, "Mr. Magno, please rise." Sammy stood up, his hands trembling on the table. "Sir," Wilde said, "I am granting your application and releasing you today." Even Clare seemed surprised.

"Thank you, Your Honor," Sammy blurted out. "I promise I'll—"

"Just listen," Wilde snapped. "Don't talk. I am putting one condition on your release. You must check in to the West Side Clinic every morning for a urine test. The clinic will measure your lithium levels and check for the presence of any illegal drugs, specifically cocaine. If you don't follow my conditions, I warn you now, you'll regret it."

"Thank you, Judge," said Sammy. "I really will—"

"Just listen. Don't talk," Wilde repeated. "Court is adjourned."

Feeling that Sammy's conditional release was a premonition of how Wilde viewed the evidence thus far, I left the courtroom dismayed. If Edwards, my most forceful medical witness, hadn't persuaded Wilde, nobody would. All weekend I imagined Sammy Magno walking the streets, planning the revival of Samson's Escorts, his next cocaine binge, and all sorts of weird demonic rituals involving his son. It occurred to me, with stomach-churning force, that keeping Sammy's case in Wilde's courtroom had quite probably destroyed any chance of winning. Sammy remained in the hands of the very judge who considered him suitable for release immediately after he bludgeoned his grandmother. The DA's office was now in the embarrassing position of asking the judge to admit he had made a mistake by releasing Sammy in the first place.

Adding to my already unsettled state of mind, Ruth Quill called me from her bathtub on Saturday night wanting to know when she would testify. She sounded drunk and got incensed when I explained that Justice Wilde had forbidden me to call any lay witnesses. On Sunday morning a Kirby psychiatrist called to complain that since he hadn't gotten to testify Friday, he had half a mind not to come in at all. Later, Smokey called just to see how things were going. I told him that unless my intuition was completely off, Wilde would be re-releasing Sammy under the same order. All night I kept wondering what I had done wrong.

Monday morning I came to work ready for the denouement of my association with Sammy Magno, Ruth Quill, Henry, Natasha Freely, and the host of peripherals who had become as much a part of my working world as the receptionists and secretaries on my floor. As I sat behind my desk wistfully contemplating my dog-eared red trial folder packed with psychiatric reports, police reports, statements from witnesses, notes, and other litigation paraphernalia—evidence which, it now seemed, would amount to nothing—the phone rang.

A psychiatrist from the clinic asked if I had heard the news.

"What news?" I asked, fearing that Sammy had gone berserk and killed someone.

"Sammy checked in this morning as ordered by the judge."

"Right," I said glumly. "Was he taking his lithium?"

"Oh, he was taking his lithium, all right," said the doctor, "but along with a healthy dose of cocaine."

Half an hour later, I walked into court carrying a slip of paper that bore the details of Sammy's latest transgression. Not only had he violated the terms of his release under the habeas writ, but, worse still, he had done so at a time when he *knew* he would be discovered. It was a clear sign that Sammy wanted to be kept in an institution. When Wilde assumed the bench that morning, I stood up and, with the excitement of someone who announces that he is holding the winning Lotto number, delivered a full account of Sammy's breach of faith with the court.

During closing arguments that afternoon, Wilde interrupted my lurid descriptions of Sammy's nocturnal, drug-inspired madness to ask, "Mr. DA, can the State really predict whether the patient here will in fact take cocaine if he is released?" It was difficult to know how to answer a question that seemed to have been rendered self-evident.

"Well, Your Honor," I said, "Mr. Magno has certainly shown his propensity in that regard, a propensity confirmed by the events of this last weekend."

"Excuse me," Wilde pushed on, "but you certainly can't be asking me to place a person in the hospital on the basis of what he or she might do *in the future*?"

"Yes, I am, Judge," I said flatly. "That's the purpose of committing people who are dangerously mentally ill."

"Not in my opinion," said Wilde.

Sometime before reaching New Haven, I went to the dining car for a bag of potato chips. As I stood in line a voice called out from behind me, "Hey, Mr. DA!" Yes, I thought, the people you prosecute go on living, even when you're on vacation.

I turned around, resigned. "Hi, Sammy. How's life on the outside? You being good?"

"Sure," he said, putting a hand on my shoulder. "You know I'm a son of a bitch. Anyway, you did a hell of a job, and I want you to know I don't hold any grudge against you."

I pointed to an infected cut on his hand. "How'd you hurt yourself?"

"That?" he said with a grin. "I got it sort of accidentally on purpose. Listen," he suddenly lit up, "I want to buy you a bottle of champagne. *Right now*. I mean, the case is over."

I explained that my wife was waiting two cars down, so I couldn't stop to celebrate this unexpected reunion.

"Come on," he said. "You tried your best, but I'm one smart motherfucker. And you know something?" he whispered. "They should've fucking locked me up."

SIXTEEN

Second Thoughts

In a city populated by so many of the world's wealthy and famous, it was inevitable that at least one cameo case would come to every ADA. My moment arrived when Smokey came into my office one afternoon and asked if I would mind taking on an extra project. I was still busy with Sammy Magno, among other cases, but judging from Smokey's demeanor I took the request to be a polite order. Half an hour later, I was proudly talking about my new assignment: the Andy Warhol death investigation.

The facts surrounding Warhol's death were indeed curious. For about the last year of his life, Warhol had been suffering from gallbladder disorders. When a variety of homeopathic remedies failed to cure the condition, Warhol, who had an almost paranoid distrust of doctors, reluctantly entered New York Hospital for surgery on what had developed into a gangrenous condition. He came through the operation well and immediately afterward was taken to recover in a private room, attended by private nurses on duty around the clock. Sometime during the night one of the nurses noticed that "the patient had stopped breathing," and dialed the hospital emergency code. When the resuscitation team arrived, they found Warhol already dead.

Shortly after the autopsy the medical examiner's office

referred the case to our office and Steve Watts headed up the investigation. In its autopsy report the ME concluded that Warhol had died of "arrhythmia," an unedifying diagnosis meaning roughly that Warhol's heart had stopped. The reason his heart stopped, however, remained unknown.

Warhol's death seemed to be merely an unfortunate act of fate until Smokey began to interview members of the team who had responded to the emergency code. Everyone was surprised to learn that when the team arrived Warhol's body was, in the words of one team member, "cold and getting stiff." By measuring the amount of blood that had sunk to the lowest points of the corpse, it was eventually determined that Warhol had died between two and three hours before the nurse sounded the code. The nurse's whereabouts that night were never decisively accounted for.

We subpoenaed Warhol's hospital chart and found more evidence of negligence. At regular intervals during the evening, one of the nurses had written, "Pulse ok, temp ok." Steve pointed out that these notes probably meant she hadn't actually measured Warhol's vital signs at all. "A pulse is a number," he said, "not 'ok.'" But even assuming the worst—that the chart was falsified and the nurse hadn't paid any attention to Warhol—we still had to prove that the nurse's failure to watch over Warhol had *caused* his death. To this end, we sought opinions from Harvard, Columbia, and Stanford medical school professors. "His heart stopped; that's why he died," said one highly respected cardiologist. "I noticed in the chart that his intake of fluids was much greater than the outflow," said another professor, "but that's the only unusual sign anywhere. He could have died without any indication that a nurse would notice."

In the end we were left with a folder full of suspicions and little concrete evidence. The circumstances, highly irregular though they were, did not justify criminal charges, and three weeks after it had begun, the investigation folded. The only accusations ever seriously contemplated were Criminally Negligent Homicide and Reckless Endangerment—negligence "evincing a depraved indifference to human life" or creating "a grave risk of death." Even with those charges, however, we needed to prove beyond a reasonable doubt that the nurse's inattention had caused Warhol's death. Our final meeting with members of the "front office" was devoted to drafting a press release announcing that no indictments were forthcoming.

Despite its inconclusive result, the red-herring Warhol investigation did cement a couple of my longstanding beliefs. First, the wealthy and famous received disproportionate attention from law enforcement. How many obscure people died under egregiously negligent medical care without getting full-dress treatment from the DA's office? And, second, Warhol's shock of white hair was a wig.

Shortly after the Warhol matter, Smokey made another important announcement. Special Projects would soon have a permanent staff of ADAs, and to ease the transition I would remain in the bureau through April—three months more than I had originally bargained for. As it turned out, my last months under Steve Watts were dominated by a series of major psychiatric cases that, like Sammy Magno's, raised many questions in my mind about the handling of the criminally insane.

Among the most difficult was the case of Tanya and Katia Soklov, a mother and daughter who had emigrated from the Soviet Union along with Katia's maternal grandparents. All four lived together in a two-room apartment on the Lower East Side. Tanya worked as a cashier at a store to support her elderly invalid parents, and Katia had enrolled at NYU. One fall, the Soklovs' neighbors became suspicious when they noticed bad smells coming from the apartment. Photographs taken upon the Police Department's entry showed the repellent images of both grandparents, bloated and blue-faced, lying naked in the Soklov's horribly disheveled living room.

When Tanya and Katia were arrested and questioned, they independently claimed that the murders were in fact a Jewish death ritual carried out with the grandparents' full consent. Tanya said she received instructions for the ritual from her deceased brother, who visited her every night in her dreams. "When the time was right," she said, both grandparents lay on the floor while mother and daughter "tied bath towels around their necks and pulled." Psychiatrists called in on this sensational case came up with an equally sensational diagnosis: a rare form of lunacy called "shared paranoid delusional disorder," or *folie à deux.*

When I started work on the case, Katia Soklov had applied for a transfer to a nonsecure facility after only one year in Kirby. From her first day on the wards, Katia had been extremely well adjusted. She spent hours reading or knitting, and she socialized only with the staff. But when she began therapy, she gave the doctors an entirely new explanation of the crime. She said she feared that KGB agents were following and plotting to kill her. Eventually, she said, she realized her grandparents were involved in the conspiracy, and so, with the help of her mother, she strangled them.

Katia's new story was as paranoid and deluded as the first, but her levelheaded behavior on the wards and the abrupt change in her explanation looked suspicious, especially in light of what I found in our files. The medical examiner's autopsy report noted that in addition to strangulation marks, both grandparents had suffered broken bones and numerous bruises. Neighbors had told the police that on the night of the murders, they heard banging and fighting in the Soklovs' apartment. The death-ritual scenario appeared increasingly implausible and cold-blooded, violent murder the much more likely story.

Perhaps because of the wildly exotic nature of their confessions, both mother and daughter had been found "not responsible by reason of insanity" and sent to Kirby. But whatever the reason, I came to the chilling conclusion that Katia had fooled the doctors and was, in all likelihood, quite sane—at least by legal standards. When I voiced my suspicions to the Kirby psychiatrists and Katia's defense lawyer, they admitted that they too had suspected as much. She had beaten the system.

Katia's case presented a poignant ethical dilemma. If she wasn't crazy, I had no basis for trying to keep her in the hospital. But since I believed she had connived her way out of a murder conviction, I felt that she should stay in Kirby as a second-best form of punishment. The law, however, left us no choice. Reluctantly we consented to her transfer to a nonsecure facility. In fact, Katia should probably have been released outright: she was dangerous, but not mentally ill.

One of the last Special Projects murder cases I handled involved a teenager named Cecilia Rodríguez. Cecilia's case, like Katia Soklov's, underscored some of the limitations of the justice system in dealing with the criminally insane. Cecilia grew up in a broken home in Harlem. Her father left the family when she was eight and Cecilia spent the next several years at the mercy of a neglectful and occasionally sadistic mother. During that time, the mother entertained a series of boyfriends who often took a more than paternal interest in Cecilia. Mrs. Rodríguez apparently encouraged her daughter's sexual abuse at their hands. On top of it all, the mother was also an alcoholic and a heroin addict. Whenever she was drunk or high, she mercilessly heaped verbal and physical abuse on her pretty young daughter. From the start, Cecilia didn't have a chance for a normal life.

By the time she was sixteen she had taken to leaving the house for days on end to fend for herself rather than live under a regime of abuse. After spending three days on the streets one February, Cecilia returned home particularly depressed. Her boyfriend had dropped her and she was out of money. Her mother, as usual, greeted her with scorn. Neighbors who were interviewed later reported hearing Mrs. Rodríguez calling Cecilia a bitch and a whore.

At about eight o'clock that evening Mrs. Rodríguez went to her bedroom and telephoned a relative. By her own admission, Cecilia took a steak knife from the kitchen, entered her mother's bedroom, and began slashing. Mrs. Rodríguez dropped the phone in mid-conversation and ran out the front door, pursued by her daughter. Running down the front steps, Mrs. Rodríguez tripped, and while she lay helpless on her face on the sidewalk, Cecilia drove the knife up to the handle into her back. Within minutes the police arrived and arrested Cecilia for murder.

Later that night, she was interviewed on videotape by an ADA. Preparing for a hearing a year later, I watched the tape to learn something "firsthand" about the patient. From her first listless answer, Cecilia seemed strangely absent. In psychiatric terms, she lacked affect. She neither smiled nor sulked, her eyes were glazed over, and her voice was frighteningly strong yet monotonal.

"Why did you do it?" the interviewer asked.

"They killed my father." Cecilia's voice registered not even a trace of emotion.

"Who killed your father?" the interviewer asked. The father was known to be alive and well in Puerto Rico.

"My mother and her boyfriend."

"How do you know?"

"I saw them do it. They pushed him off a roof and he died."

"Where did you see it?"

"A man told me. I didn't see it myself."

"I thought you said you saw them kill your father."

"No. A man, my friend, told me."

"Who? Do you know where he lives? What's his name?"

"No. But I see him sometimes, out on the street. He said

he saw them push my father off a roof. He saw them kill him."

During the initial prosecution, our office fought vigorously against letting Cecilia off on a "not responsible" plea, but when all the psychiatrists who interviewed her agreed that Cecilia suffered from "paranoid schizophrenia" coupled with "explosive personality disorder," there seemed no point in taking the case to a jury. Standing before Justice Richard Byers, Cecilia was found not responsible for her mother's murder by reason of mental disease or defect. Byers, however, found Cecilia sufficiently dangerous to rule that she be hospitalized at Kirby.

Twelve months later we received Cecilia's petition for a transfer to a nonsecure facility. Hers was another problem case, though for reasons quite different from Katia Soklov's. I felt sorry for Cecilia, and, more important, thought that murdering her mother, however brutal a crime, was an extreme but understandable reaction to years of psychological and physical abuse. Cecilia had no other recorded violent episodes; the killing appeared to be an isolated incident not likely to be repeated. On the wards, however, Cecilia had been both introverted and unresponsive to therapy. With the homicide only one year in the past, the doctors opposed her transfer to a nonsecure ward.

It was an unfortunate reality that the law made no distinction between the mentally ill who murdered their mothers, husbands, or relatives by whom they have been abused, and those who randomly attacked. Why deny Cecilia a chance for living where the windows and doors have no bars and are never locked? She was a member of a class of patients sufficiently large that some setting could have been provided as an alternative to living among serial killers at Kirby, who might all too closely resemble abusive family members. But, as in many cases, my hands were tied.

* * *

As the end of my nine-month Special Projects tenure approached, I began to long again for trial courtrooms. Smokey had been an inspiration, and the cases were as interesting as any I would be likely to handle for years, but a decision about the defendant's responsibility had already been reached, an approach to investigating the crime had been taken, and I had to live with the results. My role was somewhat after the fact, and Projects seemed a "second-line" bureau. I wanted to be on the front lines, interviewing witnesses, gathering evidence, taking control of cases from the start. Sitting at my desk for eight or ten hours a day reading dusty files and contemplating inhumane acts, I felt I had peered deeply enough into the turbulent waters of twisted minds.

One psychotic man murdered a prostitute in a hotel room, partially dismembered her body, and cut her heart out of her chest. Across the hotel wall he wrote, in blood, "I done it cause my love left me." The crime-scene photos remained burned into my memory. I regretted ever having seen them.

A budding SoHo artist was dining with his girlfriend at his agent's apartment. The artist and the girlfriend went into the next room and started arguing. When the agent heard screams, she went in and found her client hacking at the young woman with a large knife. The agent ran to the phone and called 911. A tape of the call was in the file.

"Police emergency," said the receptionist.

"Help, please," said the agent. "There's a man killing a woman with a knife in the next room. Send somebody over."

"Name, please."

She gave her name.

"Address."

The agent complied.

"Phone number."

"What difference does it make? He's *killing* her. Send somebody right away." Her voice quavered with terror.

"Lady," said the receptionist just before hanging up, "if

you want to be an actress, go to Hollywood." In the file I found a *New York Post* clipping with the headline A LIFE-OR-DEATH CALL TO COPS MET BY ABUSE.

Purvis James was a meek-looking patient who, before reaching age nineteen, had stabbed two strangers to death. One victim had asked Purvis for a cigarette in Central Park. The other was a friend who, Purvis said, looked at him the wrong way. Purvis had been in Kirby only a year but insisted on contesting the Hospital Forensics Committee's decision finding him dangerous. One week before the hearing he tried to strangle a nurse, but fellow patients pulled him off just as she began to turn blue.

A psychotic woman dropped her baby from a twelfth-floor window because a voice told her the child was from bad seed. When I spoke with the woman's psychiatrist I mentioned my surprise that the child had survived the fall and suffered only a ruptured spleen. The doctor wasn't impressed. He said that infants often survived such falls. I wondered, How often?

But apart from having to subsist on a diet of gore, there were deeper reasons for my discontent with the work at Projects. One complaint was purely practical. During ten months of litigating dangerousness hearings, I put on witnesses only in cases in which the hospital doctors could be convinced to go along with our conclusions. Financial restraints, I was told, prevented us from hiring independent psychiatrists for all but the most illustrious criminals, and so I tried a number of cases solely by cross-examining the patient's doctors. In the hands of a masterly trial attorney like Steve Watts, the technique worked, but I was by no means skilled enough to pull off that kind of legal tour de force with any regularity.

After I lost one hearing involving a woman who had attempted to kill her brother by stabbing him with a screwdriver, the judge cornered me in the Kirby hallway. "How does your office expect to be taken seriously," he asked, "when you won't shell out the money to have the patient examined by an independent psychiatrist?" He had a point.

More frustrating than the lack of funds for hiring psychiatrists, or the occasionally troubling outcomes of cases like those of Cecilia Rodríguez and Katia Soklov, was the fact that I had begun to see the insanity defense itself as a proposition that did not fit comfortably into the larger scheme of criminal law. The rationale for insanity acquittals is that the criminally insane act at the mercy of mental forces beyond their control and are therefore not capable of freely choosing to avoid criminal conduct. Advocates of the defense find it morally unjustifiable to punish someone for a crime born of mental disease rather than a guilty mind; in essence, they trace the crime to its root psychological cause. Hence, in New York State, insanity acquitees are said to have been *not responsible* for their crimes.

In cases involving acutely psychotic individuals, the reasoning carries a great deal of force. Every criminal-law class includes the parable of a man who shoots another person whom he sees as a tree. In that case, there can be no interpretation of the shooter's mental state to show that he intended to kill anybody. A tree-shooter, obviously, should not be held liable for the intentional killing of another person. But such cases were, in my experience, extremely rare.

The Kirby inmates whom I prosecuted included a particular class of the criminally insane. They were not patients whose psychoses rendered them unable to participate in the legal process, men and women who didn't understand the function of a judge or a lawyer. Those sorry cases languished in mental hospitals until they could grasp the outlines of courtroom procedure—if ever. "My" defendants suffered from mental illnesses that compelled them to commit crimes but did not rob them of the ability to understand what they were doing at the time, or to grasp the proceedings that determined their fate. The murderers knew they were murdering; the maimers knew they were maiming. Most knew it was illegal, and all understood the events in court.

In this sense I had trouble distinguishing the Kirby patients from many other "sane" defendants who came through Criminal Court. Many of the petty thieves, token-suckers, and low-level drug dealers I had prosecuted came from disadvantaged or broken homes. They were predominately black or Hispanic and poor, and had begun life at the bottom of the social ladder. Was a purse-snatcher whose father left home when he was three, whose mother took more interest in a crack habit than in her children, and whose friends all had rap sheets any more "responsible" for his crime than Cecilia Rodríguez? Cecilia had been driven to murder her mother through psychological forces beyond her control, but at the time of her crime she knew she was murdering and that it was illegal to do so. Many purse-snatchers were driven to crime by social forces equally beyond their control. Both offenders needed rehabilitation, both deserved punishment, yet one class went into hospitals, the other into prisons.

Over the years, a great deal of scholarship and study has gone into the difficult moral question of how to deal with the insane murderer, the mad rapist. But the solutions offered under the current state of the law seem still to need a great deal of refinement, if not outright reform. Too many cases slip into gray areas where the law falls short of what is necessary to achieve a just result.

Perhaps insanity acquitees could be sentenced to the same periods of incarceration as sane people who commit similar crimes (with the possibility of continued hospitalization if they remain mentally ill), but serve the time in a mental hospital. If they recover before the minimum period expires, they can be transferred to an ordinary prison or placed on probation. Defendants like Sammy Magno or Katia Soklov, who avoided appropriate punishment, might thus be rerouted through the prison system. Their fates would no longer turn solely on the predictions of doctors whose opinions—however valid—did not fit comfortably into the legal process.

Driving back from Kirby with Steve Watts one afternoon, I broached the subject and explained my reservations. Smokey, who usually waxed loquacious on legal topics, responded with uncharacteristic brevity. "I believe in the insanity defense," he said, "because it's the right thing to do. End of story."

PART III

Felons

SEVENTEEN

Second Honeymoon

During my last months in Projects I occasionally returned to Bureau 20 and visited Ida, my former trial-prep assistant, in her haremlike cubicle. As we listened to the radio on spring afternoons, she kept me up to date on bureau gossip. Within the same month, two ADAs had divorced their husbands after carrying on affairs within the bureau. These amorous doings caused much clicking of tongues and led to 20 being known as the Peyton Place Bureau.

There was other news closer to home. Annette, my rookie officemate who suffered insomnia whenever she worked nights, had gained notoriety for unconditionally refusing to work the lobster shift after the new class of rookies arrived. She insisted, with good reason, that the office had promised us only one year of misdemeanors and night work. Now, without even an apology, our move to felonies had been postponed until spring—extending the Criminal Court gamut by three months. I thought Annette would be fired for her outright insubordination, but in a Solomonic move the front office transferred her to appeals.

Scott Pryor, who had once confided to me that he feared becoming hardened by the job, had failed the bar examination for the third time and under office policy was obliged to leave. This was cause for general mourning, since Scott, kind and soft-spoken, was among the best-liked members of our class. I was still in 20 when he flunked for the second time. He bore up under the strain of studying and simultaneously holding down a job, but there was no mistaking his drawn, depressed expression as he sat at his desk plowing through exam notes. His third failure seemed too cruel a blow, and everyone stopped by to offer condolences when he cleared out his desk. Scott looked as if he had been crying, but he remained dry-eyed as we shook hands and said good-bye.

Scott's, Annette's, and my departure had decimated our class in 20. With only five rookies left out of the original eight, caseloads blossomed to three hundred apiece, and even Alex Barnette, who had once said she enjoyed stapling notes to cases in the morning, began to complain. Whenever I stopped in to visit my remaining colleagues, they were hunched over their desks like dull-eyed automatons. Their files collected in drifts.

The incoming class of rookies might have eased the load, but John Patton, who had recently replaced Mitchel Nelin as bureau chief, believed that if misdemeanors were spread evenly between the first and second years, Criminal Court would run more smoothly. Putting his scheme into practice, Patton postponed our move to felonies for a few months. He was thus responsible, indirectly, for Annette's departure. Discontent ran high. Jim Bronson said, "We've been swindled." It seemed just as well that I had stayed on in Projects.

Eventually, however, the "new rookies" took over Criminal Court, I returned from Projects, and we began to prosecute felonies. After being steeped in Criminal Court and Special Projects, it felt almost like making partner in a law firm. There was no anonymous distribution of cases, no legal assembly line, no Kirby court. Felony assistants handled every facet of their cases, from ECAB through trial. Caseloads dropped from two hundred trivial matters to twenty-five serious ones, trials were conducted before justices of the Supreme Court and juries of twelve in well-appointed courtrooms, investigations involved more than a few phone calls, and we were given larger offices.

Our promotion also inspired a new sense of responsibility. The potential for repercussions if an indictment lacked vital legal language, or if we delayed too long going to the grand jury, was enormous. Already a colleague in a neighboring bureau had had her name besmirched in a frontpage *Daily News* article. One afternoon an irate judge had subjected her to an impromptu harangue for moving too slowly in a razor-slash case. Like all of us, she had grown accustomed to a sometimes antagonistic relationship with judges, so she gave his tirade little thought. She woke the next morning to a twenty-five-point banner headline: JUDGE RIPS ASS'T D.A. Her name was plastered all over the front page in a highly unflattering context. When I passed her in the hallway a few days later I gave her my support—she really had been handed a bum rap. Everyone in the office was being sympathetic, she said, but her wounds still looked fresh. Our roles as responsible public officials hit home.

I also became aware of other sets of invisible, ubiquitous eyes and ears besides the media. Our superiors, members of the front office whose judgments intruded more and more on our freedom of action—Robert Morgenthau, Jim Stark (chief of the trial bureaus), John Patton—somehow kept tabs on every move in the felony arena. Between them, they read every complaint, preapproved every plea bargain, and received daily reports on trials in progress. The cases I wrote up in ECAB reappeared in my mailbox days later bearing little notes: "No GJ" (no grand jury); "Investigate further"; "Reduce." The front office replaced Dave Ames as Big Brother.

But my colleagues and I were repaid for taking on new responsibilities in a currency unavailable to misdemeanor assistants: time to prepare. Like most felony ADAs, we wrote up only five or ten cases a shift, of which perhaps three merited grand jury action. The rest were reduced to misdemeanors and foisted on rookies, or dismissed. With trials and hearings still months away, there was time to telephone police officers, interview witnesses, do legal research. We watched rookies scurry about, growing paler and more distraught as their workload mounted and ours diminished. And as the mad press of Criminal Court faded, it even took on the rosy, nostalgic hue of apprenticeship. Sure it was miserable, but we had survived. Sitting in our new, larger offices, or idly thumbing through the *New York Law Journal,* we all enjoyed second honeymoons with work.

We also began to blend into the larger community of felony assistants and to take our places as full-fledged members of the office. There were veterans whose cases routinely made the papers—Greg Waples was trying Bernhard Goetz, Linda Fairstein took on Robert Chambers—and fifth-year ADAs going out on homicide call. Every week John Patton chaired a meeting of the thirty felony prosecutors in Bureau 20. True to form, Patton spent as much time discussing baseball scores, the DA's basketball team, and poker debts as he did official matters. It was a sign that we were on our own. Moving upstairs— as our promotion was called—meant coming of age.

The New York Penal Code defines a felony as any offense punishable by more than one year in prison or a thousand-dollar fine, but the term has always carried more weight than the code's clinical definition implies. In feudal common law, "felony" denoted any crime punishable by forfeiting one's land, one's title, or even one's life. In an era when land and aristocratic privilege numbered among life's most valued attainments, the levy of such heavy penalties was appropriate only for especially grave offenses, those involving significant moral turpitude.

The graver implications of felony offenses, and the stigma upon those who commit them, carried over into our lives at 100 Centre Street. For my class, assault now meant a stab in the back rather than a punch in the nose;

larceny, forging fifty thousand dollars worth of checks instead of shoplifting pantyhose. Victims of these crimes suffered serious physical, emotional, or financial injury and took a passionate interest in how we dealt with the people we accused. Robbery victims were terrified of riding alone in elevators; assault victims went to plastic surgeons. They all wanted to see just punishment meted out.

And the defendants had far more to lose. Felonies were ranked in ascending order of seriousness—from E through A—and each level carried preset minimum and maximum sentences that increased with the number of a defendant's prior felony convictions. Within months I was discussing whether to ask for 12½ to 25 after trial or reduce the charge so a defendant would do "only" 4 to 8. It was a giant step from haggling halfheartedly over whether a farebeater should get Time Served or five days. Cops, too, took their felony collars seriously: they showed up on time, kept reasonably accurate paperwork, brought unwilling witnesses downtown, and wore ties and jackets to court.

We began with grand jury training.

Though I had been an ADA for more than a year and a half, the only fact I knew for certain about grand jury practice was a backdrop that threw all the other details into relief: *grand jury proceedings are secret.* Unless ordered by a judge, anything said in the grand jury, even the outcome of the jury's vote, cannot legally be repeated to anyone outside the office. The secrecy was so well maintained, even among prosecutors, that I still had no better idea of how the grand jury functioned than I had when I arrived for fingerprinting at the start of my rookie year. Newspaper editorials and scholarly articles called it either "the tool of the prosecutor" or "a shield between public and overzealous law enforcement." It seemed a fuzzy combination of Star Chamber and Quaker prayer meeting.

Initiation into the mysteries of the grand jury began with a week-long series of lectures bearing such soporific titles as "Pleadings" and "Pleadings, Cont'd," a rite of passage through what looked to be trial by boredom. But as it turned out, grand jury work was fraught with pitfalls we would be expected to recognize and avoid on our own.

In *Lost Illusions,* the classic novel of a young writer's foray into the corrupting Parisian literary scene, Balzac takes the reader on a detour through French bankruptcy law. He begins the digression in a chapter entitled "A Free Lecture on Dishonoured Bills for Those Unable to Meet Them":

> Let us look into the matter. Even a lengthy disquisition will seem too brief. Ninety percent of our readers will find the following details as appetizing as the spiciest news-item. They will offer new proof of this axiom: there is nothing about which people are more ignorant than that which they ought to know: the workings of the law!

The following exegesis on the grand jury system may not rise to Balzacian heights of eloquence, but I believe the subject matter, which appears in the headlines of newspapers every day, has an edge over French debtor-creditor law in the breadth of its appeal.

Under New York law, indictment by a grand jury is the first critical phase of a felony prosecution. Son of Sam may be caught redhanded by the police, and the DA may file a complaint against him in Criminal Court, but the only way he can be brought to trial is via the grand jury. Technically, an indictment is a written accusation, a piece of paper stating that the grand jury has accused a person of certain crimes. But on a more immediate level, the filing of an indictment in court informs a defendant, and the rest of the world, that the state thinks it has enough evidence to convict the person at trial. It is an act that ruins careers and reputations. In jurisdictions still practicing capital punishment, indictment sounds the accused's death knell.

A New York County grand jury is composed of between sixteen and twenty-three Manhattan residents drawn roughly from the same pool of people called to ordinary jury duty. Every month a group of about two hundred citizens arrives at 80 Centre Street. From a cramped waiting room on the first floor they are herded over to 100 Centre Street, where a Supreme Court justice instructs them on the law and then divides the group into six panels: four "A.M. grand juries" and two "P.M. grand juries." During their one-month term, panels hear cases in the grand jury rooms on the ninth floor of One Hogan Place.

The physical set-up of the grand jury bears little resemblance to a trial courtroom. The rooms themselves are oak-walled and high-ceilinged, with tall windows; they are closed by thick, soundproof doors, and outfitted with blackboards. From semicircular rows of seats, the jurors look down over a table and two chairs—one for the witness, one for the stenographer. Prosecutors ask questions from a perch behind the highest row of seats at the rear of the room, and each witness testifies from "center stage," like a patient with an exotic disease exhibited at a medical seminar. Grand jurors themselves may then raise their hands and whisper their own questions to the prosecutor. If the question is legally permissible the prosecutor will say, "A grand juror would like to know . . ." and the witness must answer. When the question is improper, the ADA simply states so, and there the matter ends. Except to testify on their own behalf, defendants have no right to be present, and there is no judge keeping watch to ensure that the proceedings are fair. It is the DA's show, from overture to finale.

Yet in spite of the formal dissimilarities, a grand jury presentation approximates a trial. One by one, prosecutors bring their felony cases before the panels. Witnesses testify, physical evidence is introduced, and the ADA instructs the jurors on the law. At the conclusion, the doors close and the panel votes whether the defendant should be charged with some or all of the crimes suggested by the state. If a simple majority of grand jurors decide that the accused probably committed a felony, an indictment will be drafted by the DA's office and filed in court. The indictment is, in a sense, the grand jury's verdict.

From a prosecutor's point of view, many presentations have a sense of special urgency owing to a procedural hurdle known as "One-Eighty-Eighty Day." Whenever a judge sets bail on an accused felon, Criminal Procedure Law Section 180.80 gives the DA's office 144 hours, including Saturdays and Sundays (when no grand jury is sitting), to indict. If the People miss the deadline, the defendant must be released, no matter how high the bail, no matter how strong the proof of guilt. The state remains free to indict later, but in the meantime the defendant will be out of jail, possibly committing more crimes or riding the next bus out of town.

Near the end of the grand jury training course we got down to daily practice. For some reason, I thought that grand juries heard all the evidence in every case, more evidence than even trial juries. Six days—144 hours— therefore sounded like an absurdly tight schedule for obtaining an indictment. Federal grand jury investigations, I knew, lasted months and resulted in lengthy reports, letters, and barrages of subpoenas. Things were a little different in Manhattan.

"Remember," said the chief of the Trial Division, "grand jury time is limited. Every year we file more than eleven thousand indictments. Some of our cases involve complex fraud, political corruption, or homicide based on an intricate string of circumstantial evidence. But if your case is typical, keep it short. Besides, witnesses' memories invariably change over time, and the less a person says on the record, the harder it is to impeach him with trivial inconsistencies later on. Jurors often fall for cheap shots like, 'Isn't it true, Officer, that in the grand jury you stated that it was *five minutes* before you arrived at the scene, but today you're saying that it was *half an hour*?' So, try to get it over with in ten or fifteen minutes."

The vocabulary of grand jury practice alone was daunting. "Getting it over with" in ten minutes seemed impossible. But having learned to arraign a hundred defendants a night in AR-1, interview thirty cops in one ECAB shift, and reduce cases to one-liners, I suspended disbelief. At a bureau meeting welcoming my class of rookies into the "major leagues," John Patton once again distinguished himself with reassuring advice. "It's really true." His blue eyes opened wide in a show of sincerity as he repeated an old prosecutorial saw. "By the end of the term you can indict a ham sandwich."

EIGHTEEN

Runaway Train

In April my name appeared on the weekly felony intake schedule: eight to four in ECAB. It was a much-anticipated moment. During the shift I picked up six cases: a two-defendant robbery, a car theft leading to a high-speed auto chase, a residential burglary, the illegal possession of a loaded .357 magnum, and two chain snatches. When the papers came back from arraignment court, I found that most of my defendants already had felony convictions, making them Predicate Felony Offenders. The man with the .357 magnum had two previous "violent felonies." Under the law he was a Mandatory Persistent Violent Felon. If convicted on my case, he faced a *minimum* sentence of six years to life—serving six years before becoming eligible for lifetime parole.

The two-defendant robbery, however, was my most pressing case. The previous midnight a middle-aged lawyer had been set upon in front of the Marriott Marquis Hotel in Times Square by a pack of more than a dozen teenagers who were cruising the area and leaving a wake of smashed windows and bloodied faces. The group pummeled the lawyer, knocked him down, and then dragged him along the sidewalk for ten yards. During the attack, his pockets were sliced open with a razor blade and his wallet taken.

Two plainclothes cops from the Street Crime Unit, patroling the neighborhood in a police car disguised as a taxi, picked up a radio run about the robbery and seconds later saw a couple of teenagers running down the block. The officers followed. Just after the kids turned a corner, they traded jackets—a classic ploy to avoid identification. The officers moved in and questioned the kids. "I told you we shouldn't've tried to take him," said the taller one. "Shut up," said his accomplice. "We're not talking. We want lawyers." The officers put the two suspects into their taxi-cruiser and returned to the Marriott lobby. Bleeding and bruised but still coherent, the victim identified the boys in the rear seat of the "taxi" as members of the gang who had attacked him.

To Police Officer Robert Smith the crime was a typical wolf-pack robbery: teams of kids rampaging through midtown, pillaging anyone in their path, were commonplace. To me, working felony ECAB in April, it was a major event: the first case to send me to the grand jury. The defendants, Lamont Jackson and Artis Sledge, aged fourteen and sixteen, both had rap sheets. One had stabbed a woman in an elevator in Brooklyn a month earlier; the other had a misdemeanor knife conviction. Their cases could have been sent to Family Court, but, given the ruthlessness of the crime, John Patton and I decided to keep the matter in Supreme Court. The kids might be young, but they were asking to be treated like adults.

The arraignment judge set $1,000 bail on each defendant—a sum that their lawyers said neither boy would be able to raise—leaving me six days in which to arrange interviews, pull together potential witnesses, and present the case to the grand jury. If I missed the deadline I would still be free to indict, but in the meantime Jackson and Sledge would be out and about, possibly committing other crimes or going into hiding.

The victim, Andrew Sussmann, a well-to-do business lawyer, looked shaken when he came to my office. There were two large scrapes on his forehead and his neck was in a brace. When he described the attack, his face hardened and his voice rose. Even after I warned him that trial might be months down the road, he said he was determined to follow through.

Sussmann vividly recounted being thrown to the ground by the largest of the gang and then set upon by the others. "There were about twelve of the kids," he said, "like a horrible swarm of flies. I lay on my stomach and tried to protect my face while they beat me nearly senseless. Then the whole group dragged me along the sidewalk while someone cut open the pockets of my new Banana Republic safari jacket and took my wallet. After that, they ran off. When the cops came back around in the taxi, I had no trouble recognizing the kids in the backseat. They were right in the front row of the gang."

Sussmann then handed me the jacket, pants, and boots he had worn on the night of the crime. The pants and jacket were in tatters and, in a few places, bloodstained. The toes of his boots were shredded from being scraped along the pavement. I began to pick up a bit of Sussmann's anger: Sledge and Jackson deserved hard time.

Nevertheless, the case had problems. When pressed, Sussmann said he was "pretty sure" the taller of the two kids had struck him with a fist and the shorter one had raised a hand, but neither had gone into his pockets. Sussmann added that he never saw exactly who stole his wallet. This admission spoke well for his forthrightness, but it only exacerbated the legal problems. There is nothing illegal about standing near someone who, in turn, commits a crime. To be found guilty of being an "accomplice," you must act "in concert" with the criminal—be present with the intent to aid or abet. Mere morbid curiosity will not suffice.

What were Jackson and Sledge actually doing during the brief, chaotic encounter in front of the Marriott? Robbing Sussmann? Helping others rob Sussmann? Or just maliciously enjoying a show at the expense of some rich sucker? It wasn't hard to imagine a good defense lawyer creating a reasonable doubt in closing argument after trial: *The People have offered no proof that the defendants cut the victim's pockets. No wallet was found on either of them, no razor blades to cut pockets. The only evidence is that one of the two hit the man, but the witness isn't sure which one did it. What kind of half-witted case has the State brought? Ladies and gentlemen, this is at best a petty assault by one of my clients and a baseless charge against the other.*

Sussmann's testimony, his mangled clothes, and Sledge's statement ("I told you we shouldn't've tried to take him") would have to convince a jury of twelve beyond a reasonable doubt that these two kids were in on the crime. One-eighty-eighty day was approaching, and Jackson and Sledge would be released from jail unless they were indicted. This time John Patton wasn't much help. "You spoke to the victim," he said tersely. "If you believe he's reliable, go ahead and indict. But remember, Sledge's statement might be suppressed at a hearing."

I could have waited, let the kids be released outright— quite possibly never to be heard from again—and tried to develop the case a bit more. Maybe I could find a witness at the Marriott or even a passerby. But though the case was hardly a "lock," I was certain that Sussmann had been robbed and that the kids were guilty. They should be indicted promptly, problems or not.

Patton briefly ran over the grand jury process with me: Have Sussmann give a sketch of what happened, what the people who attacked him looked like, and whether he later saw them in the custody of the police; then ask Officer Smith to describe arresting two male teenagers, speaking to the victim, and giving him an opportunity to see the defendants. Read the grand jury the robbery law and then let them vote.

Straightforward as this script sounded at first, Patton reminded me about one not-so-obvious legal snag: the *Trowbridge* rule against bolstering identification testimony. Under that judge-made law, the victim can testify

that he or she identified the defendants while they were
in police custody, but the officer is absolutely forbidden to
mention that "the victim told me those were the guys
who robbed me." This restriction is supposed to prevent a
victim's identification from being artificially bolstered by
anyone who didn't actually see the crime take place. The
identification is an event involving only the identifier—so
goes the logic—and thus only the identifier should be
allowed to testify about that significant, and ultimately
subjective, moment.

I walked Sussmann and Officer Smith across the street
to One Hogan Place. By the time we arrived at the grand
jury rooms on the ninth floor, the waiting room for witnesses was packed. I had promised Sussmann that he
would be out of the building by noon, but looking around
at the little old women with bandaged arms and legs,
distraught families, and indignant businesspeople like my
own witness, it was clear we were in for a long wait.

Smith spotted one of his buddies and instantly got into a
heated discussion about a fellow officer who won a gold
shield because he had a "hook" in the department. Sussmann, who seemed to accept the situation as part of "the
gritty reality of criminal law," began reading a dog-eared
copy of *Newsweek* he had found on one of the benches. I
went to put my grand jury slip (a form listing the name of
the case and the charges) up on the warden's desk.

Grand jury wardens, like court clerks, live their professional lives for the sole purpose of ensuring that proper
procedures are followed in their bailiwicks. They call
lunch and coffee breaks, keep track of grand jury slips,
and ensure that a minimum number of jurors—a quorum
—have arrived for work. For reasons that might someday
be explained in a study of the anthropology of civil ser-
vants, both wardens and clerks tend to be wisecracking
cynics who like nothing better than to haze fledgling lawyers and ogle female witnesses.

Herc, a career warden who knew every ADA by name,
was a short, swarthy, assiduously clean-shaven man who

waxed his head. That morning he sat joking with one of the grand jury reporters, a heavily made-up woman wearing a skirt slit up the side. On top of a pile of grand jury slips for this morning's cases, a copy of *Car and Driver* lay open to a Porsche centerfold.

"Heilbroner," he said, "you going to be long? We got a runaway train in number three, so I don't want you holding up everybody else." Grand juries that asked too many questions of the witnesses, demanded exegeses on arcane points of law, and took forever (that is, more than three minutes) to vote an indictment were known as runaway trains. ADAs, I had heard, emerged from these anomalous sessions in a sweat. Worst of all, runaway trains meant delays for everyone.

I put my slip on Herc's table, told him I had a straight-ahead Rob 2, two witnesses, and rejoined Sussmann. Off and on during the next hour Sussmann and I rehearsed his testimony. I had been warned that witnesses coming before the grand jury always testify at excessive length. The crime is fresh in their minds, and the grand jury is the first official body before whom they will have appeared. Understandably, they want to ensure that the defendant gets indicted.

But Sussmann proved especially loquacious. He was a lawyer, and, true to form, he wanted to squeeze every detail he thought relevant into his testimony. "I was coming from a business meeting that began right at eight o'clock," he said. "Things went longer than expected—someone had made a serious error in the P and L sheets that needed straightening out—and so we broke up about eleven-thirty. I remember I had on my Banana Republic safari jacket and pants and a pair of Bally boots. They were all new, and the whole outfit cost me probably four hundred dollars."

"Excuse me, Mr. Sussmann," I interrupted, "but the grand jury doesn't need to know about your meeting or your clothes. Just tell them about the robbery. You can go into all the details if the case ever goes to trial."

"But aren't they going to wonder what I was doing there at that hour?" he asked. "And it also seems sensible to me that they should know my clothes were brand new and were ruined during the attack."

"Honestly, Mr. Sussmann, it makes no difference from a legal point of view. Please just give them the facts of the crime."

Eventually, Herc's voice rose over the hubbub: "Heil-broner, you ready on Sledge and Jackson? Go to number two."

I stepped into grand jury room number two, thanking fate that I had missed being hit by a runaway train my first time out. Inside, jurors were smoking cigarettes, reading magazines, talking, and laughing. They seemed to be enjoying the job. When I walked to the front of the room to introduce myself, they fell silent and all twenty-three heads looked up to see what kind of case I had brought them. The court reporter in the slit skirt crossed her legs, adjusted her steno machine, and nodded for me to begin.

I wasn't half as nervous as I had anticipated. The sight of crossword puzzles and cigarettes lying around the room took the edge off the high seriousness that dominates a trial court. There was no judge keeping watch, and I was the only person in the room wearing a tie.

"Members of the grand jury, good morning," I said. Almost in unison, they answered back, "Good morning."

"Today," I continued, "you will be hearing evidence in the case of *The People of the State of New York against Artis Sledge and Lamont Jackson.* There will be two charges for your consideration: one count of Robbery in the Second Degree as to each defendant. And you will be hearing from two witnesses: Andrew Sussmann and Police Officer Robert Smith. I now call Andrew Sussmann."

I picked up my notes, went to the soundproof door set in the rear wall, leaned through, and, over the din of conversations outside, called, "Andrew Sussmann." Whether in the grand jury, ECAB, or court, ADAs were always yelling. It was a professional liability I had forgotten about while poring over psychiatric files in the quiet of Special Projects.

Sussmann, looking a little paler and somehow smaller than he had just moments ago, walked in, stood next to the stenographer, and raised his right hand while the grand jury foreperson administered the oath. I went to my perch at the rear of the room.

"Do you solemnly swear," said the foreperson, "that the testimony you are about to give the grand jury on the complaint of the People of the State of New York against Artis Sledge and Lamont Jackson shall be the truth, the whole truth, and nothing but the truth so help you God?"

"I do." Sussmann sat down.

In full jury trials, the witness still places a hand on the Bible during the swearing-in. In the grand jury he or she promises to be truthful "so help me God." In either setting, jurors are instructed to evaluate credibility and decide who is lying and who is honest. I wondered which would be more daunting to a determined perjurer: the prospect of eternal damnation or doing three years in Stormville Prison for lying under oath? Perhaps witnesses should be required to swear that they testify under penalty of perjury, a class E felony, and place a hand on the Penal Code.

We began, as always, with pedigree. Sussmann gave his name, his profession, and the date of the crime.

"Now, Mr. Sussmann," I asked, "please tell the members of the grand jury what happened to you in front of the Marriott Hotel that evening."

"Well," he said, "I had been in a business meeting that started right at eight o'clock. The whole thing lasted longer than I expected, since someone had messed up the P and L sheets, and I think we got out at eleven-thirty. Anyway, that evening I was wearing my new Banana Republic safari jacket and pants and a pair of Bally boots. The outfit cost at least four hundred dollars and . . ."

"Mr. Sussmann," I interrupted, "just tell the members

of the grand jury about what happened in front of the Marriott Hotel, please." So much for the rehearsal.

As he described being thrown to the sidewalk, beaten, kicked, and robbed, Sussmann looked intently at the jurors, who cast meaningful glances back and exchanged excited whispers among themselves. The voyeur's thrill is a part of every criminal case, and I took this jury's murmurs as a signal that they believed Sussmann. He ended by recounting how, fifteen minutes after the attack, he saw the two boys who robbed him in the backseat of a taxicab next to some police officers. "I was feeling pretty dazed, and my Banana Republic safari jacket was a mess, but I'm sure the taller one hit me and the shorter one raised his fist."

I looked around the room and noticed that one of the grand jurors, a man in a plaid shirt, had his hand raised. Sussmann looked up at me worriedly and I scanned my notes, wondering what I had left out. I went over to the juror and let him whisper his question into my ear.

"Mr. Sussmann," I said, "a grand juror would like to know whether you ever got your wallet back."

"No," he answered with a smile.

After Sussmann finished, I called Police Officer Robert Smith to the stand. From my experiences in criminal court I knew that placing a member of the New York City Police Department before the public can be a source of either tremendous pride or humiliation. Already I had tried cases in which the officer's attitude on the witness stand was so arrogant and his policework so incompetent that, in closing argument, I had to ask jurors not to hold the officer's behavior against the victim.

"Write a letter to the police commissioner," I pleaded, "but don't vent your anger by releasing a guilty man." Sometimes the argument worked.

An officer like Smith, however, lent dignity to the grim process of handcuffing and interrogation. Smith was in impressive physical condition—arms like thighs, thighs like hams—and his handsome face and brown eyes soft-

ened the toughness of his physique. He looked both gentle
and formidable.

Smith was also something of a hero. That morning, as
we walked across the street to One Hogan Place, he complained about a leg injury he said was acting up and I
asked how he had gotten hurt. A few years back, Smith
said, he had been assigned to patrol the Port Authority
Bus Terminal on night tour. One morning he followed a
grizzled old man up to the men's room door since "the old
coot looked a likely robbery target." While Smith waited
outside, a wild-eyed youth suddenly burst through the
bathroom doorway and ran off down the corridors. Inside
the men's room Smith found the old man lying on the
floor. "He robbed me," he said, "and he had a gun." Smith
gave chase but lost the robber in the maze of platform
entrances and exits.

Half an hour later, back near the men's room, Smith
found the same thief skulking about, in all likelihood looking for another victim. Coming up behind him, Smith
asked if he would answer a few questions. The robber
wheeled about and delivered a kick that severely frac-
tured and lacerated Smith's shin. In a heroic act that
earned him a Police Department citation—Smith pointed
to a ribbon underneath his shield—he grabbed the robber
and, as he began to black out from the pain, placed his gun
to the man's head. When support police arrived at the
scene, Smith was bleeding profusely, semiconscious, but
still holding the perpetrator.

Smith's demeanor on the stand was as impressive in its
own way as his heroism. He never resorted to the cop's
lingo of "perps" and "collars," language that without fail
alienated jurors, and his thoroughgoing professionalism
cleared the air of any cobwebby notions about police misconduct or corruption that might have hung in the jurors'
minds. When he reached the *Trowbridge* bolstering issue,
Smith delicately skirted the matter, just as we had discussed. "I brought the two defendants around to the
scene of the crime. Mr. Sussmann had an opportunity to

see them as they sat in the rear of the taxi." He finished without raising a single question.

My last task was to charge the grand jury on the law of robbery. Theoretically, both defendants had committed a number of crimes—larceny, assault, even disorderly conduct. But in this case the only sensible decision was to charge the most serious illegal act: Robbery in the Second Degree, "forcibly stealing property" from the victim while "aided by another person actually present" at the scene. I read the statute for Rob 2 and left the room. Compared to the high formality of a trial court, the entire process had been surprisingly relaxed and oddly intimate.

Barely thirty seconds later a buzzer sounded. Herc put down his copy of *Car and Driver* and went inside to get the verdict. "No problems," he said as he handed me the grand jury slip, now bearing a red check beside each of the charges. I had successfully navigated my way through the straits of *Trowbridge* and hearsay without running aground: a two-defendant indictment for a Class C felony. Sledge and Jackson never had any more of a chance than Sussmann had had the night they laid into him. And all under fifteen minutes.

NINETEEN

Detective Work:
Hot Paper

Part of our new jobs as felony prosecutors involved investigating cases, not just making a few phone calls, but following up on every lead until we hit a dead end or went to trial. By most objective measures, my first foray into detective work was a failure: I didn't break any witnesses or obtain a single indictment. But the investigation nevertheless led me into a perplexing matrix of illegal activity.

One August afternoon a woman from the Transit Police came into my ECAB cubicle unannounced. She had a slightly bemused expression. "Counselor," she said over the noise of officers traipsing up and down the corridors and rookies conducting farebeat interviews, "this case is a little over my head, could you give me a hand? I think it's a felony, but there's something weird here." Things were slow—I had been writing up pros cases and farebeats, since the felony basket was empty—so I asked her to have a seat.

"Well," she said, "I was on my lunch break near Times Square when the manager of a B. Dalton bookstore comes running out onto the sidewalk calling, 'Police! Police!' He pulls me inside, where a security guard is holding the perp, a Steven Peel. The manager and cashier said the guy came in, browsed around, and then asked to cash a hundred-dollar American Express traveler's check.

"The cashier said she called AmEx, found out the check was stolen, and asked Peel to wait. She must have tipped him off because he got nervous and started to back out the door. The security guard told him to stay put, but, next thing anybody knows, Peel knocks over an entire shelf of books and tries to bolt for the street. The manager and the guard held him but he put up a hell of a fight. Both guys got punched in the face. Anyway, when the manager called me in, they had Peel up against a wall."

"Officer," I said, "I hate to tell you, but that's not even a felony. You've got two minor Assaults and Criminal Mischief, maybe Uttering a Forged Instrument."

"Hold on, Counselor," she said, "that's only the beginning. After I arrested Peel, I found a bunch of peculiar stuff in his wallet. First of all, there were three more stolen hundred-dollar American Express checks, all from the same series as the check he tried to pass off. He also had a stack of credit cards on him—an airline credit card, a passkey card, some kind of law firm ID, a Chase Bank check-cashing card, and a Mastercard. They were all in the name of this guy Theodore Collins, whoever he is. I tried calling him on the phone but no one picked up. I also found three stolen telephone credit card numbers on a piece of paper in Peel's wallet."

The case was certainly a felony, but nonetheless I sighed. A paper case: credit cards, telephone numbers, and American Express checks. The most time-consuming and least exciting of all felonies. For the next week I would be calling AT&T security, the card owner, the bank. A grand jury presentation would take hours, not counting interviewing all the prospective witnesses. Why couldn't she have brought me a nice bloody assault or a vicious robbery?

"Well, Officer, you seem to have all of the facts straight. What do you need my help for?" I asked, hoping to write up this dog of a case in ten minutes and move on.

"The first problem," she said, "is that the American Express checks weren't ever issued to anybody. Second, the owner of the cards never reported them stolen. And third, I don't know if possessing a stolen telephone credit card number is a felony."

I was tempted to ask her to straighten out these difficulties herself. If she took long enough, the case could be foisted on some other unsuspecting prosecutor in a later shift. But in ECAB we generally adhered to an honor system: once you touch a case, it's yours. I began my investigation by dialing AT&T security from my bolted-down telephone.

Within an hour I had amassed enough information to charge Peel with a host of misdemeanors and one low-level felony. Given the amount of suspicious material he had had in his wallet, the actual charges appeared lightweight. But Theodore Collins, the owner of the cards, still wasn't answering his phone, and you can't charge a person with possessing stolen credit cards unless the owner tells you they're stolen. Without Collins, the strongest felony counts were pure speculation, at least in a court of law.

Just as the complaint came back from typing I received a call.

"ADA Heilbroner?" asked a husky voice. "This is Agent Ebert of the Federal Bureau of Investigation. I understand you're writing up a Mr. Steven Peel for possession of stolen American Express checks and some hot paper." How did these guys get their information?

I explained to Ebert that the checks weren't listed under any name with AmEx, so I had held off on those charges, which in any event were misdemeanors. "For all I know, Agent Ebert, they're found property. But we got him on some stolen telephone credit card numbers that should be enough to hold him until we hear from the owner of the credit cards. Don't worry, though. No judge in his right mind would let this guy go without some bail."

"You know," Ebert continued, "our agency thinks Peel regularly peddles stolen paper out of an Off-Track Betting office in the area. We've been watching it for months.

Those AmEx checks, for instance—they're stolen, all right: right out of an air shipment that landed in Newark last month. At least seven hundred thousand dollars worth were taken, and they've been turning up all along the East Coast. Our agency would like very much to have a word or two with your Mr. Peel."

I apologetically explained to Ebert that for the moment we were stymied. After his arrest Peel had demanded a lawyer, and under state law we were forbidden to question him further about the AmEx theft or anything else. We would have to wait until after the arraignment. Ebert and I agreed to reconnoiter. In the meantime I sent a note to AR-1 requesting at least $5,000 bail on Peel.

The next morning I reached Theodore Collins at his law firm. "Yeah," he said, "I know the cards you're talking about. I've had them for over two years. In fact, I still have 'em in my desk." I told Collins he must be mistaken. The cards were sitting inside the property clerk's vault.

"I don't know whose cards you've got," he said, "but I'm telling you I've got mine right here in my desk. Come to think of it, though, there is something that happened about six months ago. My car was broken into and a brief-case full of my receipts was stolen. I never got the case back or anything inside it. Maybe the guy used the receipts to make a bunch of phony cards."

This sounded plausible enough, especially since Collins himself seemed above suspicion, and the possibility of forgery accounted for the cards never being reported as stolen. I called security at Chase to let them know that some bogus cards had turned up.

Chase, however, viewed the matter more gravely. Aaron Stevens, chief of security, asked me if the Master-Card had a hologram. I had only a Xerox copy of the card, but from the copy I could make out the Chase hologram insignia.

"Jesus," said Stevens, "we thought that no one would ever put in the time and money to forge our holograms.

This is serious business. Get that card and I'll be over at your office tomorrow to check it out."

The situation was a little bewildering. Was Steven Peel a low-level dealer in hot paper or part of a burgeoning ring of high-class thieves with inside connections at American Express? I hoped I was about to spearhead the prosecution of the new hologram technoforgers.

Stevens arrived at my office an hour early. He was accompanied by two more of Chase's private investigators, one of whom carried a small black box. Verifying the card's authenticity, he explained, involved running it through a slot in the black box that read the electronic code on the back. I had expected something a little more technically impressive.

"Couldn't someone forge the electronic code as well?" I asked.

"Nope," said Stevens. I assumed he knew his business, so I watched quietly as the investigators ran the card through the slot three times. When they announced that the card was genuine Stevens looked relieved. Though I was glad for Chase, I was a little disappointed that the case had lost some of its glamour. I asked if perhaps Collins had ordered a second card.

"Nope," Stevens repeated, looking at the print-out of Collins's accounts. "No second card. It's the real thing, all right. But Collins's check-cashing card isn't valid any longer. It was canceled three months ago."

"Canceled?" I asked. "By whom?"

"By us. Eight hundred bucks' worth of bad checks were cashed against the card. Collins refused to pay up, so we canceled the card. According to the records, this good-for-nothing still owes us the money."

After the Chase investigators left, my first impulse was to bring Collins downtown, by subpoena if necessary, and confront him with the facts. But because he was beginning to look more like a defendant and less like a victim, I had to proceed with care. Once more I went to John Patton for advice.

Patton took Peel's case, now metamorphosing into Collins's case, seriously: it was not a matter that inspired his usual off-handed jokes. Instead, he took me to see Jim Stark, the chief of the Trial Division, number two in the DA hierarchy. Stark, whom I had met on only a few formal occasions, had a formidable reputation, rather like Smokey—chief of Special Projects—without the pauses. The meeting was brief but illuminating. I described Steven Peel's arrest and the paper trails leading to the AmEx theft, the telephone credit card numbers, and Theodore Collins. When I mentioned that Collins had said receipts were stolen from his car, Stark laughed. "He's a crook," he said.

"What do you mean?" I asked, feeling my thunder about Collins being a deadbeat slipping away.

"Jim," Patton joined in, flashing his disarming smile, "I thought *I* was cynical. This is way over the edge. I guess that's what comes of being head of the Trial Division. No one's innocent."

"He's a crook," said Stark more seriously. "Check him out. I bet he'll be indicted one of these days."

Checking Collins out began with what Stark called the basics: rap sheet, current and former addresses, employment history, and Kronos check. Kronos was a company that provided financial data about a person's debts, assets, and the like. How they got their information remained a mystery to me; all I knew was that it would be at least a week before their report came back. In the meantime I returned to the ostensible focus of the case: Steven Peel.

Forty-eight hours had passed since I wrote up the case, and I decided to go down to arraignment court and find out if my $5,000 bail request had been granted. A tired-looking rookie told me that he had requested bail on my case earlier in the day but the judge nevertheless released Peel on his own recognizance. It was a turn of events unfortunately all too common in Criminal Court. Judges, sensing weaknesses in a particular case, frequently released serious offenders on minimal bail or none. Steven

Peel's release, however, seemed egregious. How could any judge be so irresponsible as to let a violent forger and fence walk out of Criminal Court? It was obvious Peel would never come back.

When the file arrived in my mailbox, the picture at least became clearer. According to his rap sheet, Steven Peel was a thirty-four-year-old black male who lived in Newark and had never been arrested for anything. Given the facts of the case, the sheet had to be wrong. Hot credit cards, recently stolen AmEx checks, and bootlegged AT&T numbers do not find their way into the wallets of men who have never seen the inside of a holding cell. And Newark was the site of the $700,000 AmEx theft. It crossed my mind that even the name Steven Peel had a hollow ring. He had probably been arrested a dozen times and on each trip through the system given the cops a different alias. It was a trick of the trade that often worked. Albany, with its overburdened NYSID computer system, and not the arraignment judge, was to blame. Still, I didn't look forward to explaining the whole thing to the FBI. My case was a shambles and Peel was in the wind. I spent the better part of the afternoon pacing my office and drinking coffee.

Days later, the information on Theodore Collins, Esquire, arrived in my mailbox. The long, flimsy printed Kronos sheets confirmed that Collins was, in fact, a licensed attorney, and that a year ago, at age forty-one, he had left one law firm and joined another. Collins had also switched residences three times during the same period, moving into progressively smaller apartments and less exclusive neighborhoods.

Collins's finances lent the events a still darker cast: he owed a total of $75,000 to five separate lending institutions. The amount of the debt was not unusual, but the fact that it was split among five banks was indeed odd. And, in addition to that, he had stiffed Chase for eight hundred bucks.

I called Collins at home and he greeted me with a distinctly unenthusiastic response—hardly what one would expect from a witness whose credit and identification cards had been recovered from the clutches of a forger. I explained, in an intentionally vague manner, that some problems had arisen with the cards.

"Let me get back to you," he said abruptly, and before I could protest, he hung up.

At the end of the day, Collins called back. "I'm so sorry," he said, now the picture of a contrite witness. "I looked for the cards in my desk, where I always keep them, and they're gone. I don't know where they went. That thief you caught, he must have gotten them somehow, but I have no idea where from."

Collins was not a senile old man who mislays his wallet three times a day. It had been more than a week since I told him about the cards. He must have looked for them in the interim. And still there was no mention of the canceled check-cashing card or the debts.

"Well, Mr. Collins," I said, finding a pretext to bring him downtown, "could you come into my office and identify the cards? At this point I'd like to make sure they're yours."

Collins said he had to leave the city for two weeks the following morning but would call me as soon as he got back. I had no legal hold on him and I felt reasonably sure that the police could find him if necessary, so I agreed to postpone our meeting. Besides, the case against Collins thus far depended strictly upon conjecture and suspicion. Though Collins was surely involved in some sort of shady deal, I couldn't have named a single crime he had committed. In reality there was nothing.

During the next two weeks, a bench warrant was issued for Peel's arrest when he failed to show up for his scheduled court date. More information also came in from AT&T and the FBI. The feds caught a woman in New Haven who had tried to pass off more of the stolen AmEx checks. She signed them "Carol Peel." Coincidence? Still more checks surfaced at Bloomingdale's. These were signed "Theodore Collins" in a hand that looked like

Steven Peel's. AT&T then reported that the numbers found in Steven Peel's wallet had been traced to cards stolen from their owners in a series of gunpoint robberies. The victims had been shown mug books that included Peel's photo, but not one made a positive identification.

Under normal circumstances, I would have indicted Peel for possessing Collins's stolen credit cards, and if Peel ever resurfaced he would be sent straight to Supreme Court on high bail. But my suspicions about Collins formed parallel sets of legal problems that prevented me from going to the grand jury. Witnesses who testify before the grand jury in New York State receive automatic and complete immunity from any criminal charges relating to the case. The only way to prosecute a witness on the basis of what he or she says before the grand jury is to have the witness sign a formal waiver of immunity beforehand.

In Peel's case, the only provable felony was possession of a stolen credit card. The other events in the bookstore were all "only misdemeanors." Even the stolen telephone numbers, it turned out, probably didn't qualify as credit cards under the law. But to prove that Collins's credit cards were stolen required that Collins himself either appear before the grand jury or sign a sworn statement that Peel had no permission or authority to use the cards. In either case, Collins would be rendered immune to prosecution. Without Collins I had only misdemeanors against Peel. If Collins testified, he could never be prosecuted. It was a tidy, frustrating catch-22.

Collins eventually came in for his interview and repeated the same unbelievable story about discovering that his cards were missing. I let him know that his explanation made very little sense, but he must have realized that I had nothing on him. He stuck tenaciously to his version of the events, and eventually I sent him home.

For a while, Patton and I debated handing the matter over to the U.S. attorney. In federal court, a witness receives grand jury immunity only when agreed to beforehand by the government. Peel could be prosecuted feder-

ally for possessing traveler's checks stolen out of state—
creating a nexus with interstate commerce—and Collins
could be called to testify about his own signature and the
cards. We might then use Collins's federal grand jury testimony against him in a state prosecution. Or we could drop
the whole mess and cut our losses. We chose the latter
route, partly because of the U.S. attorney's lack of interest
in picking up a case against an absent defendant. When I
finally closed the investigation, I had a thick file folder and
an unsatisfied curiosity.

Patton, Jim Bronson (who had taken an interest in the
case), and I talked for hours about the Peel-Collins mystery. We all had different theories. Jim's was the most
exotic: Collins masterminded the theft of AmEx checks
and funneled them to the street through Peel, lending
Peel his own credit cards to help cash the checks. Patton
and I talked Jim out of that one. Why give your street man
your own ID? It's just asking for trouble. And why lie to
the DA about still having the cards?

My preferred scenario was a little less dramatic. I assumed that, for reasons never to be known, Collins racked
up debts to a third party—perhaps from gambling, drugs,
or extortion—and was forced to borrow relatively small
sums from a series of banks and to move into progressively
less expensive apartments. The unknown third party suggested that one way Collins could raise money was to sell
his credit cards. But Patton objected that stolen credit
cards sell for no more than $25 or $50 on the street, an
inconsequential sum to a lawyer, even of Collins's ilk. It
occurred to me, however, that the low street value of
cards stems from the likelihood of the owner reporting
their loss. In my case, Collins might have sold his cards to
Peel, or some other fence, with the agreement not to
contact the credit card company for a specified period.
Under these circumstances, a card's value might well be
in the thousands. This explained Collins's initial statement
that he had never lost the cards and therefore hadn't

reported them. Fearing that I could prove I had the real cards, Collins changed his story to fit the situation.

When I left the DA's office a year later, the warrant for Steven Peel's arrest was still outstanding. Because his case entered the Albany computers under an alias, it will probably be forever lost in a limbo of glitches and binary forests, never to be reconnected with the man himself, should he someday return to Criminal Court.

TWENTY

Supervisor

By February I had begun to hit my stride as a felony ADA. I attended Patton's weekly meetings and came to know all the members of the bureau. A different atmosphere prevailed among felony prosecutors. We worked more like solo practitioners than like a team of rookies. Our days were spent investigating crimes, interviewing witnesses, going to the grand jury, and trying cases, activities that kept us separate from one another. When we did convene, no one wanted to talk about crime—we all wanted a break. And because most of the cases we handled were unquestionably serious, the tension about who took a hard line and who was soft all but disappeared. Instead, it was baseball scores, poker debts, and more office gossip.

My file drawers had filled up with more than thirty felonies, and unlike in Criminal Court, where I was always digging through piles of cases I had perused only once, I knew each one intimately. There was Mitch Askew, a slick man-about-town who was attacked by a bodega owner in Spanish Harlem. The owner, who mistakenly thought Mitch had tried to pass off a counterfeit fifty, vaulted the counter and swung a hatchet-shaped meat cleaver at Mitch's neck. Mitch ducked and the blade sliced off a piece of scalp. He showed up for the grand jury presentation wearing an enormous turban of a bandage. Under his coat, he had a bottle of cheap Scotch. It was unopened, and he seemed sober, so I agreed to let him testify.

Another case involved the theft of two mink coats from a Manhattan refurbisher. The coats belonged to Barbara Bush, wife of the then vice president. Detectives found the missing furs, worth thousands of dollars apiece, at a notorious fence's warehouse. The thief, a former employee of the refurbisher, eventually confessed to selling the coats for a hundred dollars each and spending the money on a night's worth of crack.

My favorite defendant was Carl Ambers. Ambers had gone browsing in a children's clothing store in the West Village. When the other customers left, he went to the cashier, a petite Frenchwoman, and handed her a note reading: "I have a gun. Pass over the cash or get your ass shot. Now it's your move." She complied, and Ambers, a large Jamaican man, ran down the street clutching a wad of money and credit card receipts. The cashier gave chase, screaming, "Thief! Thief!" Steven Lee, a Chinese-American riding by on a bicycle, joined in. When they rounded the corner, a mounted cop started to gallop alongside Lee's bicycle. The motley band of pursuers saw Ambers in the distance as he disappeared into a three floor walk-up. Ambers ran to the top-floor landing and forced open a door. Inside, a woman in her underwear was microwaving a cup of coffee. "Get out!" she screamed. "I need your apartment to escape," he said, and climbed out a window onto the terrace of an adjoining row house. Unfortunately for Ambers, the terrace belonged to a high-profile member of the Guardian Angels. Through the combined force of Angels, mounted cop, bicycle-rider, woman in her underwear, and cashier, Ambers was captured.

I had a Fifth Avenue jewel thief; a bookkeeper who stole thousands of dollars from one employer after another, even while she was on probation for previous thefts; a drug dealer who worked over one of his runners with an aluminum baseball bat; and a number of garden-

variety robbers, burglars, chain-snatchers, and gun-possessors.

Over the last few months, I had also had some disappointments. Andrew Sussmann's case—he had been
beaten and robbed by a pack of kids in Times Square—
had ended abruptly when a judge offered both Sledge and
Jackson five years' probation if I would reduce the charge
to Robbery in the Third Degree. I discussed the matter
with John Patton, who reminded me that the case was
weak to begin with and the defendants still in their teens.
I was angry to see these two cocky, tough delinquents,
part of the wolf-pack phenomenon that had terrorized
the city, walk away from the crime with a slap on the
wrist. But a sure five years of probation, I explained to
Sussmann, was better than possibly losing at trial.

I had also been through a few felony jury trials—twelve
jurors and four alternates seated in clean, well-lit courtrooms. The first case seemed so strong, I was sure the
defendant would plead guilty when he heard the People
answer, "Ready for trial." Elmon Goins, eighteen years
old, had walked into a West Side brownstone, picked up
the owner's purse, and started to leave. The handyman,
who had left the front door open while taking some garbage bags out to the corner, returned and found Elmon
holding the purse in the vestibule. Mrs. Cora Handy, the
handyman's employer, came downstairs and telephoned
the police while he held the burglar.

At the stationhouse, Elmon gave his name as Luke
Jones. Under NYPD practice, whatever name a defendant
gives first remains his or her name throughout the proceedings. My case became *The People of the State of New
York v. Luke Jones.* (This practice, however, often yielded
absurd results. In a matter handled by a colleague, a Colombian man had been arrested for murder. Detectives at
the precinct began their interrogation by asking the man
his name, to which he spat back in a surly tone, *"Maricón"*
—a Spanish derogatory equivalent to "faggot." From that

moment forward the case was entitled *The People of the State of New York v. Marty Cohen.)*

In my burglary case, I offered Elmon a reduced charge with two to four years, but he insisted on a trial. After he testified in his own defense, claiming that he entered the brownstone looking for a job and happened to find the wallet lying on the floor, his fate was sealed. It didn't much help his credibility when I asked the young burglar whether his real name was not Luke Jones but rather Elmon Goins. The jury convicted in forty minutes and Elmon got four to eight years. His mother sat in the audience crying as the judge imposed sentence. Though I was proud of winning my first case in the majors, sending a teenager to prison was hardly something to rejoice about.

The next trial was even more of an unsettling success. A young man had driven his car up onto a sidewalk in midtown. When a police officer walked over to ask him to leave, the driver got out of the car and smashed the cop in the face with a twelve-inch steel flashlight. It took more than fifty stitches to close the gash. After the officer was knocked down by the blow, a crowd of people ran over and held the defendant.

Preparing the case for trial, I was delighted to find that everyone in the neighborhood wanted to cooperate. Among the witnesses who testified at trial were a young construction worker who had watched the crime from the start, a photographer who made his living taking pictures of tourists standing beside a life-size cardboard cutout of Ronald Reagan, and Daniel McKelvey, a twenty-year member of the Fire Department. After they all described the crime and pointed toward the defendant, the jury was enraged—they convicted after only two hours of deliberation.

But after the conviction, and over my bitter objections, the judge gave the defendant probation. Apparently ten years on the bench, listening to stories of murders, rapes, and mayhem, had so inured His Honor to violence that he felt a man who disfigured a cop for no reason deserved a break. When I telephoned the officer to give him the bad news, however, he wasn't surprised. "To be honest, Counselor," he said, "I'm surprised you didn't knock the case down to a misdemeanor in the first place."

One evening a senior ADA was out with the flu and I was assigned to supervise felony lobster in her stead. Every complaint written that night would bear my initials; I would have the final word on which cases to drop. If lineups, ballistics analyses, fingerprints, or crime scene investigations needed to be conducted, I would get on the phone and make the arrangements. I could bring recently arrested defendants up to my cubicle for interrogation, even before they had spoken to their attorneys. For eight hours I would be at the top of the bureaucratic ladder.

The shift began on a blustery, rain-frozen midnight. I arrived early and stopped briefly to talk with the court officers while I stomped the ice off my wingtips. I had slept only fitfully that afternoon before coming downtown, but excitement cut through my fatigue. Tonight I was going to be handling everything that came in, the heaviest crimes in the city other than homicides. I calculated about a six-hour lag between arrest and the officers' arrival at 100 Centre Street. Assuming no substantial backup, I would see crimes that took place starting about six o'clock that evening.

On the second floor outside ECAB the familiar sounds of police officers talking echoed in the hallways. The vestibule was full. In the supervisor's office—*my* office—an ADA from another bureau was finishing a write-up while two uniformed cops and a detective in a shirt and tie leaned against the walls. The felony basket held at least twenty cases. It was going to be a busy night.

The complaint room looked a little less run down than it had during my first shift, more than two years earlier. After mounting complaints from ADAs, a few improvements had been made to enhance the professional atmosphere and minimize the war zone mood. Doors now hung in the cubicle entryways, the disintegrating corkboard lining the dividers was painted a shiny beige (the ubiquitous color of the DA's office), and an intercom to the police waiting room rendered obsolete the practice of standing in the hallway and yelling. But there were still the same old bolted-down telephones on our desks and form complaints littering the floor.

After bidding my preceding supervisor good night, I began at the top of the felony pile: "Officer Marco Valens, please come to ECAB." Valens worked in the 24th Precinct, which covered part of the Upper West Side. The crime—Assault in the Second Degree—had happened just two blocks west of my own apartment building, near a construction site. It was a typical husband-and-wife dispute in which the violence had gone too far. Witnesses had seen the husband, Jesús Polanco, take a length of pipe, strike his wife over the head with it, and throw her into a construction pit. When she hit bottom, Mrs. Polanco's head struck an exposed sewage main. She arrived unconscious at Columbia-Presbyterian's emergency room.

Mr. Polanco, not surprisingly, had been drinking heavily, and when he understood that Valens wanted to arrest him, he fought back. Valens suffered a bruised hand in the scuffle, and consequently, wanted to charge an additional count of Assault 2 for intentionally injuring a police officer. "Let me see what you've got," I said, like a doctor asking to examine a patient. The officer held out a bruised hand. It was a little swollen and black and blue across the back, nothing requiring hospital care or bandaging. Apologetically, I explained to Valens that the injury was just not serious enough to support an assault charge: "I understand you got hurt, Officer, but cops are always getting cut and bruised on the job by drunks and vagrants, and we simply can't take every case to the grand jury."

"Listen, Mr. Supervisor," Valens said, reddening, "I'm out there risking my goddamn neck on the street, and there's laws that say it's illegal to cause physical injury to a police officer performing a lawful duty, and that's exactly what happened. Every time I come down to ECAB it's the same story: 'Sorry, Officer, you're not injured badly enough.' You're giving perps a license to beat the hell out of us, but if we touch them—'Oh, no, police brutality,' and the CCRB investigates the case.''

"Officer," I said, "I'm really sorry, and I appreciate what you guys must go through out there. But if we indict every person who injures a uniformed cop, the grand jury will be operating twenty-four hours a day. I'm sorry, but I won't charge Assault Two."

Valens left, grumbling. He had a legitimate complaint, but I was not about to charge a man with a felony for bruising an officer's hand. Forget the officer, I decided. Concentrate on Mrs. Polanco.

The next case was a double attempted murder. Its grisly facts reminded me of Special Projects. The defendant, Anthony Kibble, weighed over three hundred pounds and had known his victims, a pair of sisters named Latoia and Angela, for more than a year. After a few dates, Kibble had been romantically rejected by Latoia, but he continued calling her, obsessively. Latoia tried to let Anthony down easily, but whenever they spoke, Kibble kept repeating, "If I can't have you, nobody can." In desperation, Latoia turned to the police, but Kibble's threats were too vague to merit an arrest. It is an unfortunate reality of life in Manhattan that you have to wait until the burglar has a knife at your throat before the police bother to investigate.

The crime had been committed only eight hours before. Latoia had come home to the apartment she shared with her sister. Kibble was waiting for her outside in the hallway. They argued, and when Latoia tried to slip into the apartment he forced the door, went inside, and grabbed a knife from the kitchen. He yelled, "If I can't have you, nobody can!" and began jabbing her shoulder and arms with the knife as she ran through the apartment. He finally cornered Latoia and, holding her against the wall, tried to cut off her breast. She struggled free just before Kibble succeeded, and then she ran to the window. Kibble followed, grabbed her by the waist, and tried to throw her, bloody and screaming, to the sidewalk seven floors below. Neighbors across the street saw the terrible scene at the window and called police. At the same time, Latoia's sister, Angela, who had been sleeping in the next room, ran in and tried to pull the attacker off her sister. Kibble wheeled around and slashed at her chest. Instinctively, Angela grabbed the blade with both hands. The maddened attacker jerked the blade from her grip, slicing deeply into her joints.

Before Kibble could finish off either sister, police sirens cut through the noise. Kibble, now drenched in blood, ran down the stairs and into the street. It wasn't hard for the officers to locate a three-hundred-pound man in blood-stained clothes. Two police cruisers converged on a candy store, where they found Kibble hiding beneath a counter. When the officers tried to put him into the squad car, Kibble struggled furiously. One patrolman was thrown over a parked car into oncoming traffic that screeched to a halt. Three others wrestled Kibble, slippery with blood and sweat, to the ground, but he was so large and strong that it took two pairs of handcuffs to reach across his back. Even so, each cuff wouldn't close more than one notch around his massive wrists.

This was probably the most serious case of my felony career, and I discovered to my dismay that it contained a built-in handicap. The arresting officer, Joseph Peters, was among the slowest-witted cops I had ever dealt with. I tried to take into account that only a few hours earlier he had been wrestling with an enormous, crazed felon, but Peters had trouble answering even the most basic questions: "Did you recover the knife?" "Are the victims willing to testify?" "Are they back from the hospital?" At the end of the interview, I gave him a grand jury subpoena for each of the sisters. "Should I mail these to the girls?" he asked.

"Officer," I said, "first thing tomorrow morning, go to

the hospital and give one to each sister personally. We have only six days to indict this guy."

"Oh, yeah," he said. "I forgot."

As the night wore on, the rookies with their petty cases faded into the background. I was absorbed and excited by the enormity of the crimes piling up, one by one, in the felony basket.

Another case involved a man the police called "the black Arnold Schwarzenegger." He had gone into a Kentucky Fried Chicken and ordered dinner for his girlfriend. By the time the food arrived, the girl had left the restaurant and the huge, muscular man, now jilted, refused to pay the bill.

The fried chicken joint was run by two Indian men who bravely insisted that the defendant pay for the food. Without answering, he picked up a table and heaved it across the counter at the proprietors, who scattered for cover. One at a time, he then picked up the two large metal cash registers. One went through the plate glass storefront window and the other crashed onto the floor.

When the officers arrived they saw the debris and quailed at the sight of this mountain of rage. Surprisingly, though, he came along without any struggle. "I just wanted to get back at them," the defendant apologized, "but I broke the law. Take me in." As officers led him away, the employees claimed that he had also taken $1,500 from the registers before tossing them around the store. The cops searched the defendant but found only twelve dollars. I assumed that the employees saw the crime as a golden opportunity.

Next came a rape case. The cop, a quiet, slender man with a slightly effeminate manner, allayed my worries about abusive or crude questioning of the victim. Compared to the usual members of the force, he was a creampuff. But the facts were especially sordid. A young woman had somehow wound up, naked from the waist down and hallucinating on LSD, on the 103rd Street platform of the A train at midnight. The defendant tried to rape her on the open platform as the train pulled away from the station, but passengers on the subway heard the woman's screams, pulled the emergency brake cord, and ran out of the subway car in hot pursuit. As they approached, the defendant grabbed the woman and carried her up the stairs. The police heard yells from the mob and soon cornered the defendant in a stairwell. At the precinct he told a detective that "the woman was asking for it, running around half-naked." Later he admitted that he spent his days in Times Square exchanging crack for sex.

The victim, still hallucinating strongly, was rushed to a hospital, where she arrived in critical condition and was placed on a respirator. A nurse took a sample of fluid from her vagina with what is known as a Vitulo kit. She mentioned to the arresting officer that the victim's genitals "had a lot of mileage on them." I wondered what the defense attorney would make of that "medical opinion," if the case ever went to trial.

I drafted the complaint, double-checking the technical definitions and degrees of rape and sexual abuse. The front office would surely be watching this one. The write-up would go directly to the chief of the Sex Crimes Unit, another face of Big Brother checking to see whether I made a careless error, charged the right crimes, followed policy.

During the night the phone rang with strange requests. A desk sergeant reported that one of his men had shot a pit bull terrier in a basement suspected to be a crack den. "Why are you calling me?" I asked. "Counselor," he said, "there's a departmental policy to notify your office every time a weapon is discharged." I copied a few notes about the incident into a log book kept by the desk. Later, news reporters called for an official statement about an arrest that had yet to reach ECAB. "Call Mr. Morgenthau's press secretary in the morning," I replied. "I don't know anything about it." Later still, a man called and said, "Hi, this is André." "Can I help you?" I asked. "Yeah. What's going on with my case?" André couldn't even remember the defendant's or the ADA's name, so I told him to try again later.

Six A.M. I haven't taken more than a five-minute break, yet the felony basket still holds as many cases as when I came in at midnight. I have written up fifteen major crimes and barely kept pace. I start watching the clock, waiting for the eight o'clock shift to arrive. I am supposed to be able to handle heavy cases by now, but with a group of rookies worried about coke possession arrests running in and out of my cubicle, a stack of newly typed complaints demanding proofreading, an ever-growing pile of new cases in the felony basket, and listening hour after hour to the grim details of violent crimes heaped one upon another like a mountain of human carnage, I feel overwhelmed. The night has given birth to a host of bloody, depraved crimes. I have no idea why. I just want them to stop. So much aggression, tragedy, suffering, all my responsibility. The oppressive feeling hangs in the ECAB air like dust, stinging my eyes.

As I dial the hospital's number to see if Mrs. Polanco, the woman who had been thrown in the construction pit, is likely to die—"go out of the picture"—a few cops wearing black leather jackets and knee boots walk into my office and start thumbing through the misdemeanors. I shoot them an annoyed glare.

" 'Scuse us, Counselor," says one of the highway patrolmen. "Just checking to see how far back our cases are. You know, see if we have time to go out for a meal."

"Listen," I answer angrily, "just wait outside like everybody else."

A stack of misdemeanors still sits at one side of the desk waiting for a proofread and my signature. I glance at them and scrawl my initials. The felonies in the basket stare at me and cops are falling asleep outside, but for the moment my concentration is slipping too much to do another interview. Better to fall behind than make mistakes.

Two more cups of coffee and I'm back: "Officer Hovens,

please come to ECAB." Hovens had stopped at a West Side apartment building when he noticed a crowd of people holding someone who looked like a beggar. Members of the crowd had heard someone scream, "Stop, thief!" and had grabbed the defendant as he came running down the block. The defendant claimed he had been panhandling and been mistaken for the real criminal.

As Hovens tried to figure out what had happened, a doorman came down the street saying that a little old woman who used a walker had been robbed in her lobby a block and a half away. The frail, elderly victim was brought around to the scene. She unhesitatingly identified the beggar as the man who had come from behind her, put his arm around her neck, forced her to the ground, and taken her change purse, keys, and ten one-dollar bills. The defendant vehemently denied the charges and insisted this was a case of mistaken identity. He became less indignant when the officer removed ten crisp one-dollar bills from his pocket and the doorman found the old-woman's keys inside the lobby where he had been detained by the crowd.

Eight A.M. The day shift arrives. My first night as supervisor is over. Outside 100 Centre Street I emerge into a bright winter morning, a stack of xeroxed police forms tucked inside my worn Penal Code. I toy with the idea of not returning to the bureau and instead taking the subway home, but I need to speak with Sex Crimes about the rape and put in a few police officer subpoenas for the double attempted murder by the obese Anthony Kibble.

On the bulletin board in the reception area, yesterday's phone messages are thumbtacked below a cardboard square with my name on it. "Call Part 47 immediately. 2:15," says the topmost. "Too late." I smile to myself. "I wonder what could have been so important?" There are other messages: "P. O. Ojeda unable to appear on 2/24—R.D.O. [regular day off]"; "Cora Handy receiving threatening calls from Elmon Goins."

The Sex Crimes Unit arrives at nine and by nine-fifteen
I am heading toward the subway. Thousands of government employees flock toward Foley Square. I feel oddly
out of sync as I walk in the "wrong" direction, homeward,
against the waves of secretaries, lawyers, court officers,
and other miscellaneous functionaries, ready to resume
spinning the wheels of government. I must look oddly
wan and tired at an hour when most people walk briskly
to work, fueled by a cup of coffee.

Inside the subway, amid the people coming from
Brooklyn for work uptown, I spot a few drunks and a man
who opens a packet of cocaine. He lifts the powder to his
nose using a long, carefully trimmed nail on his little finger. If a cop had told me this story, I would have accused
him of dropsy.

"He's only a misdemeanant," I think, and try to imagine
his reaction if I told him what I do for a living.

Fighting off sleep, I remember a couple of times when I
had mentioned my job to strangers. Once I was having my
shoes shined at a one-man stand near Wall Street. "Man,"
said the grizzled proprietor as he put a final coat of polish
on my shoes, "you must work for one of them big corporations. I can tell."

"Nope," I said. "I'm in the DA's office."

"Serious? You seem kinda young for that job. You get to
carry guns?"

"You kidding?" I laughed. "Even if I could carry one, I
wouldn't. Someone might take it away from me and shoot
me."

"No way, sir," he said excitedly. "I mean, you just gotta
come into court and tell whatever story you want and the
judge'll believe you. You're the *Man*. You could shoot anybody you want and get away with it. The Man always
wins."

"Thanks for the shine," I said, and gave him a big tip.

The other time, I was jogging around the Central Park
reservoir. I had on a T-shirt that said NY COUNTY DA'S
OFFICE in large white letters on a blue background. As I

headed down a straightaway someone called from behind me, "Hey, you work for the DA?"

I stopped and yelled back, proudly, "Yes. I'm an ADA in Manhattan."

He pointed a finger and shouted, "Fuck you."

TWENTY-ONE

Copping Out

Every Tuesday was calendar day. It was the only task upstairs reminiscent of Criminal Court. Each of Bureau 20's indicted felony cases was funneled through a central arraignment court, Part 20, and from there to individual judges in satellite courts, who followed cases to their conclusion. As in Criminal Court, calendar involved shuffling stock memoranda and other legal arcana, but since there were fewer cases, more judges, more courtrooms, and more prosecutors, the workload was comparatively light and unreasonable delays weren't tolerated as easily.

In Part 20—the first stop for defendants after being indicted—Justice Hanson performs one function all day: arraigning felons. Five days a week, forty-eight weeks out of the year, and for God knows how many years, Hanson has presided over his front-line courtroom. The cases are serious: robbery, burglary, murder, rape, big-time larceny. Many of the defendants are hardened criminals, as familiar with 180.80 day, motion practice, suppression hearings, and habeas corpus as their lawyers are. Most are held on high bail.

Officially, court opens at nine-thirty, but Hanson, a habitually coffee-breaking sort, never takes the bench before ten. Even so, when I arrive at a quarter-to, a few defense lawyers are already poised in the front row of gallery seats, eager to get their cases called and move on to their next court appointment. As I begin to arrange a stack of manila folders known as indictment jackets across the prosecution table, the attorneys descend. "Is there an offer in Graves?" "Do you have your answer to my motions?" "Did the assistant leave a note about my client's cooperation with the DEA?"

Inside the jacket on Ronald Graves's case, the prosecutor in charge of the case leaves a note, written in DA shorthand:

On for Arr. F & S VDF and Ind.
Offer: C w/3-6. F & S PFS.

It means: "The case is scheduled for arraignment. File with the court and serve on defense counsel a copy of our Voluntary Disclosure Form (listing relevant witnesses, officers, dates, and places) and a copy of the indictment. We will agree to reduce the charge to a class C felony (the minimum sentence on which is three to six years) if the defendant will plead guilty. Because the defendant has a prior felony conviction, file a Predicate Felony Statement with the court."

I tell Graves's lawyer all he needs to know: "The offer's a C with three to six." He scribbles this on his own file and runs to a corrections officer, who can let him see his client. The officer opens a thick door set flush in the courtroom wall. I catch a glimpse of the hospital-green interior of the pens as the lawyer disappears inside. The door closes again, sealing off the world of bars and disinfectant smell from the high courtroom windows and leather chairs.

Another lawyer asks again about his client's cooperation with the Drug Enforcement Agency. There is no note in the jacket. Even in Supreme Court this is typical. "I'll make a call and let you know." As I cross the courtroom to use the DA phone, Justice Hanson, coffee in hand, strides in and climbs to the bench, implicitly bringing everyone to order. From my telephone across the room I call out,

"Good morning, Judge. If you'll excuse me, I have to make a call on a case."

Hanson and I have always been on good terms, so I can take these sorts of liberties. In fact, from the moment I first entered his courtroom carrying a governor's warrant as a member of Special Projects, Hanson treated me as if I had been coming through his courtroom for years. He almost certainly mistook me for someone else, but I was not about to disabuse him of a notion that worked so much to my benefit. Hanson has a strong sarcastic streak and, like most judges, is not above taking out his ill-tempered moods on whoever happens to be before him. For no good reason that I can discern, he still treats me as an equal, calling me up to the bench to hear his personal opinion on anything from DA policy to his son's graduation from law school.

Simultaneously hanging on the telephone, speaking over my shoulder to Hanson, and reading a note on a case is, by now, second nature; I don't even feel especially busy. Eventually the ADA I'm trying to reach answers the phone and gives me a rundown on the defendant's cooperation with the federal drug agents.

"Listen," I say to the defense lawyer who tags alongside me as I walk back to the prosecution table. "The investigation is still under way. We can't do anything with your man's case until we see how reliable his information turns out to be. Let's adjourn it a month."

"Mr. DA," says Hanson, now impatient that no business appears to be getting done, "let's go. Clerk, call the Blackwell case. I see Mr. Troy in the audience."

"Later," I say to the attorney and then I turn to face the court without waiting to hear his answer: it is just part of the daily give and take of minor rudeness in court. Brusqueness and a sort of thick-skinned machismo are the norm among judges and lawyers who spend their days dealing with felons.

The defendant, Eddie Blackwell, is already at the counsel table with Troy, his lawyer. Blackwell, a slender, middle-aged black man, wears a green polyester leisure suit and a shiny pink shirt. The clerk, who has worked with Hanson ever since His Honor took the bench in some prior decade, mechanically reads the charges: "Eddie Blackwell, you have been indicted by the Grand Jury of the County of New York for the crimes of Burglary in the Third Degree and Criminal Possession of Stolen Property in the Fourth Degree. How do you plead—guilty or not guilty?"

Blackwell looks over to his lawyer. "Say, 'Not guilty,' " whispers Troy.

"But, man, like, I thought I was gonna cop out today."

"Don't worry, just say, 'Not guilty.' "

"All right," says Blackwell. "Um . . . not guilty." The words do not come easily.

"Gentlemen," says Hanson, motioning with his hands, "step up."

At the bench we talk freely. I show Hanson the ADA's write-up, known as a "161." Unlike ECAB one-liners, 161s, which are prepared only for indicted cases, give fleshed-out descriptions of our cases. Hanson reads the document in a voice loud enough for Blackwell to overhear: *Arresting officer, plainclothes, sees D. and one other black male standing near a truck unloading dresses at 51st and 9th. The other unapprehended male goes into truck, removes an armful of dresses, and rejoins D. After a brief conversation they run away. Officer gives chase, catches D.; other perp. escapes. After arrest, D. stated: "I didn't go into the truck. I was just going to help him sell the stuff."*

"Mr. Blackwell, sir," says Hanson raising his eyes over Troy's shoulder, "you were just trying to help a friend out, is that right? You weren't actually doing anything wrong? Is that what your statement to the police means?"

"Well, Your Honor," stutters Blackwell, "I, uh, well, my friend went inside, you know, and I, uh . . ."

"Never mind, sir." Hanson cuts Blackwell off contemptuously and lowers his voice. "Mr. Troy, your client's got eleven misdemeanor convictions and one recent felony. In fact, it looks like he's still on probation for that case. He's only charged with a D felony. If he pleads today, I'll promise the minimum—two to four." Hanson slaps an open palm on the bench like a trader in an Arab market signifying, "It's a good deal, take it."

"Judge," says Troy, "from the People's write-up it sounds as if Mr. Blackwell was just standing around near the truck. It's a weak case. Two to four is too high. I think Mr. Blackwell will take an E with one and a half to three, but I'll have to ask him. Otherwise he'll go to trial." The bargaining has begun.

"Your Honor," I counter, "Blackwell was obviously a lookout. And this is a SLATS [Safe, Loft, and Truck Squad] case—they're some of the best cops in midtown. We'd win this one at trial. I can't come down to an E, not given Blackwell's record." I don't know a thing about the case, but my job is to sell it to the court. In fact, I suspect the defense lawyer may be right.

Hanson tells Troy to talk with his client. I wait at the bench. Even after two and a half years of haggling over jail sentences, bartering a sure guilty plea for a savings in prosecutorial time and effort still seems odd. Blackwell and his buddy were caught red-handed, and Blackwell confessed at the precinct. Minutes earlier I heard him tell his lawyer he expected to plead guilty. Yet now he and his counsel want to strike deals: coerce the court and the DA into giving him a light sentence by threatening to go to trial.

Troy steps back up. "Judge, Mr. Blackwell informs me that he's interested in one and a half to three but not two to four."

"Well," Hanson says to me, "one and a half to three or two to four—what's the big deal? Let him have it. I promise I'll make it up to you on the heavy cases."

Blackwell has regained his composure. With his worn polyester clothes and receding hairline he looks like the sort of man who would knock on your door and try to sell you a used vacuum cleaner. He would rip you off without a second thought, but he would never force the door and pull a knife. Every entry in his rap sheet is for larceny: no violence, no weapons.

I can end things now, ensuring that Blackwell does one and a half to three and gets another felony conviction on his rap sheet, or roll the dice for some other ADA and hold out for two to four. Maybe Blackwell will back down and take two to four. Maybe the SLATS cops will turn out to be terrible witnesses and blow the trial. Then there is the inconvenience to the owners of the property, who will have to testify, and the fact that a trial costs tax dollars. All in all, the plea bargainer's calculus seems to weigh in favor of giving in to Blackwell's deal, but still I dislike the idea that a cheap truck burglar is putting the squeeze on me.

Hanson motions for me to come closer. "Give him the E with one and a half to three," he says in a paternal tone. "I know the man's a career criminal, but you just don't have the goods on him. In a couple of years you'll get him on a better case. Those SLATS cops should have gotten his friend." Hanson smiles. I cave in. He's right: only six months' difference; what does it really mean to anyone?

"Okay, Judge. But don't expect this on every case."

"Mr. Blackwell," says Hanson in the vaguely mocking tone he reserves for defendants, "your lawyer tells me you want one and a half to three. Is that right?"

"Yes, Judge, but can I have some time to think about it— you know, talk to my probation officer?"

"No, sir, you cannot have some time to think about it," Hanson snaps. "The offer made by the People is an E with the minimum sentence: one and a half to three years in state prison. What's there to think about? Either you go to jail now or you can go to trial. Who knows? Maybe you'll win." Hanson looks over at me with a sarcastic smile. Blackwell, in his opinion, is wasting everybody's time. "If you didn't do it, don't plead guilty. But this is a one-time-only offer. Next time the case is on it'll be two to four. And if you go to trial and lose you could get the maximum—

three and a half to seven. So, what's your decision?" Hanson's pent-up anger, visible in the veins pressing out over his neat white shirt collar, makes me uneasy.

As we wait for Blackwell's response, the courtroom becomes a small stage, the defendant before the footlights, holding the attention of every person in the room, even the court officers. With a few words he can hand over years of his life or gamble for freedom, risking the remainder of his middle age—three and a half to seven years. Time stands still; silence spreads like a snowfall across the audience. Blackwell seems larger than life, a symbol more than a mere truck burglar. I sometimes share Hanson's disgust with career criminals, but this is more than offset by the pull of basic human compassion. The words "state prison" always sound sobering.

"Mr. Blackwell, sir," says Hanson, breaking the spell, "obviously you're not interested in the People's generous offer of one and a half to three. Let me save you some trouble. The offer is now withdrawn by the court. It's two to four now, and it will only go up from there."

"Wait a minute, Judge, please," says Blackwell, realizing there is no escaping Hanson's squeeze. "I want the deal. One and a half to three. Okay?"

"Your Honor," I interject, "the People are still willing to offer the defendant an E with one and a half to three."

In Supreme Court, the formal ritual of pleading guilty —called the allocution—is a more serious process than "downstairs." The judge must be satisfied that a defendant knowingly gives up his right to trial by jury, protection against coerced self-incrimination, calling witnesses, and forcing the DA to prove his guilt beyond a reasonable doubt. With old-timers like Blackwell, however, Hanson collapses the questions into one quick, run-on sentence, staring the defendant down as he speaks.

"Sir, you realize that by pleading guilty you are giving up your right to a trial by a jury, to call witnesses on your behalf, and to have the People prove the case against you beyond a reasonable doubt. You understand that?"

Blackwell, like many defendants, doesn't seem to take his rights seriously: "Judge, I plead guilty."

Hanson presses him: "Do you understand?"

"Sure."

"Now, in your own words, tell me what you did that makes you guilty of this crime."

"I don't know. I was there with my friend. He was taking dresses out of the truck."

"Mr. Blackwell," snaps Hanson, "that's not illegal. What was on your mind at the time?"

"Nothin', really. We was just there together."

"That's it!" Hanson's voice again fills with contempt, his veins stand out. "According to what you've told me, you're not guilty of anything. I won't accept your plea. Sir—"

"But Judge, I—"

"I won't accept it."

"Judge, listen. I was helping my friend steal the stuff, all right? I was going to help him sell it too. I want the deal, okay?"

"Enter the plea, Mr. Clerk."

Blackwell undergoes the transformation from accused man to prisoner. His presumption of innocence evaporates into the courtroom air. Two court officers appear behind Blackwell and hustle him back into the sickly green of the pens. In six weeks, following the Probation Department's report, Blackwell will be officially sentenced. As he walks across the courtroom, he thanks his lawyer.

He should have thanked me. A more zealous ADA might well have insisted on a D with two to four, milking a better disposition out of Blackwell when he got scared. But squeezing pleas out of defendants—even those who play the courtroom game like Blackwell—makes me sick at heart. I don't mind seeing a just sentence imposed, but why shouldn't Blackwell have a few minutes to think things over? Were I standing before the judge, I would want the same. Still, I think, the ADA on the case will receive his case jacket and read my note with satisfaction. A D would have been better, but accomplice cases like Blackwell's are hard to prove. The day is off to a good start.

The next three co-defendants—accused of selling fifteen pounds of cocaine—all refuse offers of ten to twenty years. If they lose at trial they risk life in prison, but a scandal involving the Transit Police has recently broken in the newspapers. For a few years, transit detectives in plainclothes have operated a series of decoy operations intended to lure robbers toward an undercover cop posing as a helpless bum. Some defendants claim to have been arrested without having done anything illegal. Independent witnesses corroborated the stories, and a pattern of corruption seems to be emerging. Although our office is investigating the perjury and false-arrest allegations, ADAs are losing all kinds of cases that hinge solely upon police officers' credibility, even those with officers outside Transit. I assume that the defendants' lawyers think they can play on the current skeptical climate. The presumption of innocence guarding defendants doesn't apply to police officers.

After the dealers' cases, Hanson calls an adjournment and I talk with the court officers. Up in Supreme Court officers act a little more dignified than their counterparts downstairs, but physically they still fit the cliché: overweight, cynical, kibitzing from the sidelines, and shamelessly spreading courtroom gossip. Judges and prosecutors tend to be on their good list: judges because they are professional assets, and ADAs because from the point of view of most court officers, we are on the right side of the law. Hanson likes me, so the court officers in Part 20 treat me especially well.

While Hanson chain-smokes and talks on the telephone, Dan, captain of the court officers, grumbles about my moving too slowly. "Listen," he tells me, "when Hanson says, 'Step up,' keep it short. I mean, what's to talk about? The skels are all guilty, so don't waste so much time over it. We all want to get out of here by three." Dan then demonstrates a new weapon he has just purchased, a slim metal rod attached to his key ring. He puts the rod against my wrist and presses it with his free hand. The pain is surprisingly intense. "It's good for keeping people in line," he says proudly. In the background I hear Hanson, still on the phone, talking about his daughter, who has just gotten into medical school.

By eleven-thirty Hanson is back on the bench and we hit the first major case of the day. The defendant, Ernest Timbers, has been indicted for a slew of heavy crimes: Rape 1, Sodomy 1, and Burglary 2. Timbers has three prior felony convictions, and since all are for rape he is a Mandatory Persistent Violent Felony Offender. On each charge he faces a minimum of ten to twenty-five and a maximum of life. The ADA has written a note insisting, "D. must get at least nine to eighteen."

Two court officers lead Timbers, still handcuffed, to the defense table. They remove the cuffs but remain close behind him. In court, no one is ever permitted to step between officers and defendants, and in Timbers's case the officers seem particularly intent on enforcing the rule. Timbers, however, does not appear to pose much of a threat. He is short and weak and slouches so much that I wonder if he might not be a bit demented.

The clerk reads the indictment. Timbers, in a barely audible voice, pleads not guilty.

At the bench I begin in a heat: "Your Honor, I want to say at the outset that there is no offer in this case and the People will go on the record to request nine to eighteen, even if the defendant pleads guilty today."

Hanson, amused by my zeal, tells me to simmer down and show him the 161. It reads: *The victim, a college student, came into her apartment building on a Thursday night. The defendant was in the vestibule and asked her for spare change. She gave him a quarter and turned to open the inside door. The defendant grabbed her from behind and stated, "Don't worry. All I want is your* money." He opened her purse, took all her cash, and then put his hand under her dress and touched her genitals. He then pushed the victim to the floor, where he raped her vaginally. He then forced her to perform oral sex on him and ejaculated onto her shirt. As the defendant dressed himself, he asked the victim her name. She gave him a false name but told him (correctly) that she lived on the fourth floor. As the defendant left, he told the victim that she should be in porno films.*

Hanson looks up and assesses the disheveled twenty-four-year-old defendant hemmed in by court officers. Still slouching, Timbers appears vaguely indifferent. I haven't seen many defendants as repugnant.

"He's an animal," says Hanson quietly but matter-of-factly. "He should just be killed. That would make things easier for everybody." There was a time when I would have been surprised to hear a justice of the Supreme Court express such injudicious sentiments, especially during a bench conference. Hanson, probably correctly, assumes Timbers is guilty, but just as probably incorrectly, he makes a show of his contempt. Caught in the middle, I keep a straight face, swallow a rebuke that springs to my lips, and push on.

"Judge," I tell him, "there's more."

"Oh," he says. "Let's see what else this pillar of the community spends his time doing." Part two of the write-up reads: *The following Sunday, the victim's apartment is broken into. The only item missing is a wallet containing her college ID. The same evening she receives a call from a man who identifies himself as Jim Peters. He says he has her things but will return them only in person. The victim sets up a meeting and shows up with two detectives in plainclothes. As the defendant crosses the street, he sees the detectives and runs. The detectives catch the defendant and find the victim's ID on him. D. says he was waiting to meet Jim Peters. The victim identifies D. as the man who raped her the previous week.*

"Isn't that nice?" Hanson remarks. "He came back to

visit her. Mr. DA, this case is a lock, and I can't see giving the man less than twenty-five years. Nine to eighteen seems low. Is there some problem you're not telling us about?"

As usual, I don't know any more than is in the write-up. ADAs never do, except in their own cases, yet judges and defense lawyers assume that prosecutors always hold something back and play cases like a hand of poker. It is as though judges and lawyers prove their own savvy by implying, "Of course, you guys never tell us the whole story." The fact is, we rarely know half as much as we would like to.

Improvising, I respond, "Judge, the impact on the victim has to be considered here. I mean, she's going to have to go through the stress of a trial. Nine to eighteen is a long time for any defendant."

Mary Madison, an experienced Legal Aid attorney sent to represent Timbers, has been watching quietly. Physically, she has kept a healthy distance from her client, and judging from her passive attitude, she appears to have little to say on his behalf. Legal Aid's job in Supreme Court is particularly tough: most defendants are unsympathetic characters who, unfortunately enough, deserve long sentences. Still, Mary says what she must; she is a good lawyer: "If I may, Judge, the minimum for Mr. Timbers is four and a half to nine. Are you saying that even if he pleads guilty this minute you won't consider the minimum?"

"Ms. Madison," says Hanson, "you heard the write-up. Your client is lucky the DA is recommending nine to eighteen. I wouldn't be inclined to go that low on what I've heard without their recommendation. Go talk it over with Mr. Timbers."

While Madison speaks with Timbers, Hanson and I stay at the bench. In a confidential tone, he says, "Mr. DA, you've got a conviction there. I hope he turns down the offer and gets what he deserves. Really, why did the ADA recommend nine to eighteen?"

Hanson's question triggers a memory, a scene from training, now almost three years behind me. A lecturer asked what we would do if a judge inquired about a pending case without defense counsel present. Ethically, such conversations, known as ex parte communications, are forbidden. Our lecturer therefore recommended that we politely sidestep the issue, but warned us to be ready, since judges always ask. I raised my hand, brimming with self-assurance and a little vitriol. "I don't think that's enough," I said. "I would say, 'Your Honor, without defense counsel present it would be a violation of ethics to go into the case. It could look like an ambush or giving an unfair advantage to the state.'" Though I was legally correct, I almost blush, recollecting my naiveté.

"Who knows, Judge?" I say to Hanson.

"Your Honor," calls Madison from the defense table, "my client has no interest in taking nine to eighteen. The rape, after all, is a one-witness ID. Mr. Timbers intends to go to trial."

"Very well, Ms. Madison." Hanson sends a contented glance in my direction. "Wheel it out."

The wheel, a spinning metal drum like a lottery wheel filled with court part numbers, is an integral part of the proceedings in Supreme Court. Any case not disposed of will be sent to a particular judge for hearings, motions, and trial. Under the law, judges have complete discretion in sentencing convicted defendants, within the minimum and maximum terms set by statute, and every judge's predilections are well known to experienced lawyers. The wheel was instituted to prevent "judge-shopping." Given the serious charges he faces, Ernest Timbers's best hope is to play the courthouse lottery. Like many decisions in Part 20, opting for the wheel is a gamble, and, given the life sentence Timbers faces, close to Russian roulette.

The clerk spins the drum, opens the side door, and pulls out a cardboard square. He reads, "Part 39, Justice Henry Callus." Madison rolls her eyes. Hanson beams. Callus is a tough judge—not the toughest, but he can be counted on to slam this perp.

"Part 39," Hanson repeats. "Sir, I wish you the best of luck before Justice Callus." Then, to me, he adds in a barely audible voice, "Henry will max him out, but really, the man should just be shot. He's an animal."

The last case of the day. An eighteen-year-old Hispanic boy, his eyes, big and brown, open wide in fear. His cheeks still have a youthful blush and his scrupulously clean clothes indicate a mother's care. It is his first arrest, a fact that emanates from him like an odor. After the clerk calls "José Martínez," I hear a murmur from the now almost empty audience. The family has come to see what will happen to their son. The father, in a dark suit and tie, looks dignified. The mother, sitting up straight as a pillar, fidgets with her gloved fingers. They look like kind, caring people.

It occurs to me how few families come to lend support to their relatives. Most people we indict have already been locked up a few times, and, really, why should a brother or sister bother over Carl or Tyrone or Suzie? They were always getting into trouble, and if they went to Riker's or Fishkill one more time, well, they had it coming. Don't expect your aunts and uncles to come crying to court to help you out.

With José Martínez it is obviously a different story, and I don't even need to read the folder to know that his is a drug case. His age, his ethnic background, and the fact that he is in on bail for a first-time felony offense are, to me, unmistakable signs, much as I resist falling prey to the overgeneralizations and prejudices that infect courtroom denizens.

I am right. The case comes from Special Narcotics, a division of the office devoted solely to felony drug cases. Across José's indictment jacket, stamped in large red letters, is the word CRACK. Special Narcotics has only one such stamp. Crack has become a major concern throughout the office, the city, and the country. The stamp also shows another, less political dimension of Special Narcotics—they are overwhelmed with new arrests. Their 161s are written in the kind of DA shorthand that trial divisions tolerate only for misdemeanors. But prosecuting felony drug sales—selling any amount of coke, heroin, or PCP— is a bulk business, written up, stamped, and indicted with the frequency of shoplifts.

José is distinguishable from other coke dealers coming through Part 20 only by his age and the presence of his family. They set the assembly-line narcotics prosecution into relief.

The write-up will have to be translated for Hanson. It reads:

UC B&B—Crack
UC does hand to hand; OP enters set.
2 vials for $20
PRMB and stash recovered.

Defense counsel and I crowd around Hanson's bench. "Your Honor," I explain, "This is an undercover buy-and-bust case. The undercover officer purchased two vials of crack from the defendant in exchange for twenty dollars of prerecorded buy money [PRBM]. Another officer in the observation post watched the sale through binoculars and entered the scene of the crime. The police searched the defendant and found the buy money as well as a stash of more vials of crack."

The charge is a B felony and carries a minimum of one to three and a maximum of eight and a third to twenty-five. If José pleads guilty, Hanson still must give him at least one to three years in state prison.

"Judge," says Bill Pappalardo, José's Legal Aid lawyer, "this is my client's first arrest. If the DA will come down to a D with probation, he'll plead. Otherwise, Judge, he has no choice but to fight the charges. He's never done time before, and look at him—he's a good-looking kid. They'll eat him alive upstate."

José's is a tough case. New York has a crack epidemic of crisis proportions, and if our office doesn't take a firm stand, all the undercover operations and beefed up drug laws will be rendered useless. Deterrence means a hard line, no exceptions.

José looks at Hanson and me from the defense table. He still goes to high school and lives happily with his parents. Why not show mercy? Demanding that José do one to three means sending him to graduate school in crime and violence, and rape in a jail cell, sealing off any hope of rehabilitation. With probation he will have a chance. But to the kids who will see José's freedom, days after being indicted for crack sale, as a free ride, leniency sends a bad message.

There is justice in the larger sense and in the individual case, and the two are not always compatible. The long-term social gains from DA toughness—which have been impressed upon me since I received Dave Ames's first memo during my rookie year—are too intangible to fuel my zeal. All the DA policies to the contrary, I can't resist showing mercy to a kid like José, looking up at me from the defense table.

Why do I wince at the prospect of sending a criminal to jail? My wife, Kate, and my friends outside work think my sympathy is only natural, but they can't know what it is like to deal with criminals day to day, listen to stories of rape and robbery ad infinitum, meet victims and examine their scars, and every day watch people reduced to tears by something you have done or said. I often wonder if compassion isn't a professional liability. There are days when I think I would gladly send Timbers, the recidivist rapist, to jail for a life sentence. Or would I? Perhaps I would rather somebody else did the dirty work. Plenty of other ADAs feel that they can't be hard enough on defendants—let them do it. At a party recently, somebody asked me, "What's it like in the DA's office? I bet it's fascinating." "It depends," I said, "on whether you like locking people up for a living."

I offer a D with probation. Today will be José's one break—a fact that Hanson knows better than anyone in the courtroom. We all step back to our posts to hear the allocution.

Allocutions by first-time offenders are especially serious, and it is crucial to move slowly and deliberately. Abstract legal principles probably sound meaningless to José after hours in handcuffs and days in the pens, but a felony conviction will permanently mar his life. The event must be treated with religious sanctity.

In a slow, clear voice Hanson asks José a litany of questions about the rights he surrenders by pleading guilty. One by one, José gives up his rights to trial by jury, cross-examination of the People's witnesses, and remaining silent. He understands that a guilty plea is the same as a conviction after trial. No one has coerced him. He has spoken to his lawyer. He knows that if convicted of a second felony he will be a Predicate Felony Offender.

"Mr. Martínez"—Hanson leans forward—"tell me in your own words what you did that makes you guilty of Criminal Sale of a Controlled Substance and Possession with Intent to Sell."

"I did it, Your Honor. I'm guilty."

"Yes, you're pleading guilty, but what did you do?"

"I sold to a cop, I think. At least that's what they told me. He looked like a regular guy to me."

"Was it coke you sold, or crack, or what?"

"Cracks."

"All right. And did you possess crack with intent to sell it?"

"Yes."

"How many vials?"

"I don't know."

"What do you mean you don't know?" Hansons's voice hardens. "Was it about ten, twenty, twenty-five?"

"Twenty-five."

"Are you sure it wasn't thirty?" Hanson queries sarcastically.

"Okay, thirty."

"Mr. DA, what do the police records indicate?"

"One hundred and fifty vials, Your Honor," I answer. I knew all along that José was trying to minimize his guilt for fear that probation would be withdrawn. He is just like Eddie Blackwell, or any number of defendants: willing to give up legal rights and accept a felony conviction with no more than a shrug, but terrified at the prospect of confessing to a crime before a judge. It must feel like tossing away a last shred of clothing.

"One hundred and fifty. Well, well," Hanson says. "Does that jog your memory, sir? One hundred and fifty vials of crack."

José hangs his head and mumbles, "Yes, sir. One hundred and fifty. At least, I know it was more than a hundred."

"What was that, sir?" asks Hanson, smoldering. "I want you to say it so your mother can hear you and so I can hear you. How many vials of crack?"

"One hundred and fifty, Your Honor. I swear I won't do it again. Please." José starts crying.

"And did you possess those drugs with the intent to sell them?" Hanson presses forward relentlessly, derisively, intent on scaring the hell out of José. It is a small price to pay for probation.

"No, sir." José is apparently confused.

"Oh, really? One hundred and fifty vials. What were you doing, then? Catering a friend's wedding?"

"No, no, Judge. I'm sorry. I didn't understand. Yeah, I planned to sell them, but the police took them away." Tears stream down his cheeks, but he stands erect, accepting Hanson's browbeating.

"Very well. Mr. Clerk, enter the plea."

This was plea-bargaining: a calculus of public policy, law, emotion, and humanity; defendants holding out for a better deal, calling the DA's bluff about the strength of a case, spinning the wheel in the hope of getting a lenient judge, reliving their crimes, handing over great chunks of their lives, dealing in years and decades. All the while, my colleagues and I standing by, trying to ensure that defendants are punished with sufficient severity. If defendants play along and agree to spare the state the effort and cost of a trial, we repay them in time. If they insist on their rights, we get tough. In every case, we called them as we saw them.

Friends outside of work used to ask me, in a suspicious manner, whether I plea-bargained my cases—as if plea-bargaining were somehow illegal or immoral, and the cause of the city's crime problem. The question was also asked with unease. Plea-bargains allow criminals to escape just punishment, and return recidivists to the streets all the more quickly. The very notion of the DA's office making deals with criminals suggests corruption: you don't make deals with criminals unless you are one yourself. Ironically, these were often the same friends who would call me, months or weeks later, asking, "I just got called for jury duty. Can you get me off?"

The threat of heavy sentences and the promise of one-time lenient offers must have coerced some innocent men and women into pleading guilty. But if every defendant—from prostitute to farebeater to murderer to extortionist—had insisted on going to trial, the wheels inside 100 Centre Street would have come to an enormous, grinding halt. Our deals helped keep the criminal justice system from falling apart. Like so many aspects of the justice system, plea-bargaining was a matter born not only of policy but of necessity.

TWENTY-TWO

The Dwarf

Once I had become more confident about presenting cases to the grand jury, I decided to try out some variations on the DA's textbook method. My test case was a simple purse-snatch. The defendant had come up behind a woman in the Port Authority Bus Terminal and tried to grab her purse. She struggled, the strap broke, and the defendant ran. When the victim came to my office for an interview, she rolled up her sleeve, exposing three nasty-looking scars surrounded by red and blue bruises in the crook of her elbow.

"I fought with him as hard as I could until the strap broke," she said proudly. "I guess these are friction burns."

Generally, we charged purse-snatchers with Grand Larceny in the Third Degree—stealing property from the person of another without the use of force. Here, however, there was not only force but physical injury. Adding force to a larceny elevates the crime to Robbery in the Third Degree; adding physical injury to the robbery increases the crime yet one step further, to Robbery in the Second Degree. Robbery and larceny can coexist happily in an indictment; they merely represent different legal analyses of the same crime. But office policy was to charge only the highest crime, in this case Robbery 2—no need to confuse juries with the building-blocks of criminal law.

Contrary to the received wisdom, I decided to indict for both Grand Larceny 3 and Robbery 2 (which by definition includes Robbery 3). If at trial some jurors felt that the defendant hadn't intended to injure the woman or to use any substantial force, the panel could compromise and convict only for Larceny, a lesser felony. It was certainly a bad idea—and one that might have posed legal problems on appeal—but Patton agreed to let me try it out.

Witnesses in tow, I went to the grand jury. Outside in the waiting room a colleague of mine, Fernando Márquez, sat next to a frail old woman whose arm was swathed in bandages. My victim, much younger and more vigorous than Márquez's, sat down beside the old woman, and the two began discussing their crimes. Coincidentally, both had been the victims of violent purse-snatches. In the old woman's case, however, the defendant had held the victim in a choke hold and pulled her purse so hard that she had severe cuts up and down her forearm. Given the more extreme violence, Fernando had done the proper thing and charged only Robbery 2. There was no question that this robber had intended to injure his victim. The victim in my case, however, was hurt only because she refused to let go of her purse.

Fernando and his victim went into the grand jury first, and seconds after he completed his presentation a buzzer sounded, indicating an indictment. In all little-old-lady robberies—unfortunately, a large class of crimes—I sensed that grand juries just couldn't wait to indict defendants, and would probably have been just as pleased to administer punishment themselves. Frail, elderly women may have bad eyesight and faulty memories, but the sympathy they elicit ensures them a place among a prosecutor's favorite witnesses.

My case went in right after Fernando's. Testimony went smoothly, and although Fernando had just instructed the panel on the robbery law, I read them both the Grand

Larceny and the Robbery statutes. Unknown to many grand jurors, a large percentage of cases fall within two or three interpretations as to which crimes actually were committed. In the privacy of our offices we decided which charges to submit to the grand jury and which to hold back. Only when it was to our advantage did we "remind" the jury that they could vote an indictment for a more or less serious felony, or reduce the case further still to a misdemeanor. But hearing two nearly identical purse-snatches submitted back to back with different charges tipped this panel off.

I went outside, expecting a swift vote. Instead, five minutes ached by. Herc, the waxed-headed grand jury warden, sniped, "All right, Heilbroner. It looks like you're in for some kind of trouble. I thought it was strange charging both larceny and robbery."

"It was the right thing to do," I said defensively, wishing that the jury would hurry up and indict the lousy purse snatcher. The jurors, I knew, were just trying to carry out their duty, but back at my office two other witnesses waited for their own 180.80 cases, and I was supposed to begin a trial the next morning.

Finally a double buzz sounded, indicating a question.

I went inside and said, "I understand the panel has a question."

"Yes," said a woman at the rear of the room. "We just heard a case exactly like yours, only the ADA didn't charge Grand Larceny. From what you said about the law it sounds like Grand Larceny fits the facts, but why didn't the other ADA charge it too?"

Not wanting to start a general discussion about charging crimes, and hoping to get back as soon as possible to the other cases waiting for me in my office, I answered peremptorily, "I really can't tell you why another ADA presented certain charges to you. All I can say is, you've heard the facts in my case and I read you the law. If the law fits the facts, I ask you to vote an indictment."

"Yes," continued the woman in the rear, "but which would be more serious, both charges or just Robbery?"

"Oh, come on," said a fellow juror. "He doesn't have to answer that."

"Well, I want to know anyway. That lady in the first case was hurt worse than the second one, and I want to be fair. Mr. DA, don't we have to do the same thing in every case? I mean, justice should be the same for every person, right?" That was a big subject.

"Ma'am," I said, sensing that I was about to be carried off by a runaway train, "it would be improper for me to discuss another ADA's case with you. Do you have any questions about my case and the law I read to you?"

Grumpily the woman answered, "No."

Moments after the door to the grand jury room swung shut I heard a single buzz: an indictment on both counts.

I was escorting my witness out the door and thanking her for coming downtown when another double buzz sounded. I looked over at Herc: there wasn't even a case before the panel. He went inside and reappeared a few seconds later, looking annoyed.

"What's up?" I felt an unnerving presentiment, the rumble of an approaching train.

"They want Márquez," Herc said.

"Did they say what for?"

"Additional charges," he replied, dialing the phone. "Well, Heilbroner, that's what you get trying something new and different. They said they want to add a count of Grand Larceny to Márquez's case."

Fernando came up from his office and went back in to face the now unfriendly panel. I sent my robbery victim home, but decided to stay around since I was responsible for setting the situation in motion. After about ten minutes, during which raised voices filtered through the heavy grand jury door, Fernando emerged sweating.

"Jesus," he said angrily. "What did you do to them? They asked which would be worse for the defendant, Larceny *and* Robbery or just plain Robbery? Before I could even get a word in edgewise they started arguing among themselves. The stenographer gave up transcribing halfway through the—"

A single buzzer sounded, interrupting Fernando's complaint, and Herc ventured inside the room.

"I can't believe it," he grumbled as he came out holding the grand jury slip. "They voted to keep the same charges Márquez originally submitted."

According to law, grand juries are administrators of justice, sharing many of the powers entrusted to the prosecution. They have discretion to reduce felony charges to misdemeanors, subpoena witnesses, draft letters, and even disregard the law entirely in order to dismiss a case in the interests of justice. The wording of indictments themselves reflects the grand jury's role as a part of the law enforcement machinery: "The Grand Jury of the County of New York, by this indictment, accuse the defendant of the crime of . . ."

But under the strict guidance of prosecutors, grand juries rarely exercise any powers other than indicting. During our ten-minute presentations inside the sealed rooms, we ran the show—balancing the schizophrenic roles of prosecutor, judge, and legal adviser. We kept damning facts from the jurors, recited certain portions of the law and not others, screened which questions could and could not be asked of witnesses. Even a little learning on the part of the jurors disrupted the orderly flow of cases, so we fed them as little as possible.

Of course, some grand jurors were indifferent, torn between reading newspapers and listening to the evidence. But most took the job seriously, especially at first, when the notion of indicting a person not even present in the room was still foreign. They sometimes asked hostile questions that betrayed suspicions about the fairness of the system, but their desire to know more about cases and legal technicalities seemed not only understandable but laudable. A judge had charged them with representing the public in the difficult decision of whether to bring felony charges, and the accused person was conspicuously absent during most proceedings. For the inexperienced, the act of indictment must have seemed contrary to basic principles of Anglo-American criminal justice.

Through our gentle prodding, and after voting on twenty cases a day for weeks on end, indictment almost inevitably degenerated into a rubber stamp for all but the most unusual matters. Jurors became inured to the subtleties of cases—which ADAs did their best to eliminate. Even the most independent-minded grand juries were eventually numbed into unquestioningly doing our bidding. Around the trial bureaus they were referred to as "seasoned juries."

My misgivings about the rapid-fire indictment process and the incestuous relationship between prosecutors and the grand jury surfaced full-blown in the aftermath of "the dwarf case." The case itself was hardly sensational: simple possession of a loaded pistol without a license, an E felony. The defendant was thirty-eight years old, had no prior convictions, and had been caught by an off-duty cop who spotted the gun inside his waistband. He admitted possessing the gun illegally but explained to the officer that he used it only to protect his friend, a dwarf whose deformity made him a regular victim of harassment, robbery, and abuse. The story sounded far-fetched, a typically unbelievable lie concocted in the desperate police-station atmosphere, but days after the defendant's arrest he arrived in Bureau 20, accompanied by his lawyer and cradling the dwarf in his arms.

Office policy regarding gun possession was to indict all cases, in the absence of truly extenuating circumstances. After some discussion between Nicholas Huff, who had the misfortune to pick up the case in ECAB, and members of the front office, it was decided that the grand jury should take the initiative and dismiss the matter. No one in Bureau 20 would have to buck policy, and if the defendant committed some new crime, our office could hold up its clean hands. The plan was typical. Huff was to present the facts in such a sympathetic light that the grand jury would wonder why the case had ever come before them. There wouldn't be a dry eye in the house. Then, just prior to leaving the jury room, Huff would "remind" the jury that they had the power to dismiss the charges—a reminder never given in run of the mill matters.

To help steer the panel in the right direction, Huff called the dwarf—much smaller than any dwarf I had ever seen, virtually a homunculus—as a witness. He corroborated every detail of the defendant's tale: they had been friends for fifteen years; he was the victim of continual abuse; his hands were too tiny to hold a pistol, so his friend used it to ward off troublemakers. The defendant himself testified that he had never been arrested before. A ballistics lab report showed that the gun, though operable, had never been fired. John Patton had no doubt that, under the circumstances, the grand jury would do the right thing and, at the very least, reduce the case to a misdemeanor.

Once the evidence was heard and the jury instructed, Huff, the defendant, his lawyer, and the dwarf waited anxiously for the vote. After an inordinately long period, a single buzzer sounded. The warden came out holding the slip indicating their vote: a felony.

For the next day, the grand jury's failure to dismiss the dwarf case hung in the air around Bureau 20. "Our" system hadn't responded as it was supposed to.

"It was insubordination, mutiny, I tell you," said Huff as we sat around the large conference table in Patton's office.

"What do you expect?" chimed in Lewis Sparks. "They're not a bunch of nuclear physicists."

"Yeah," said Jim Bronson. "I went before the same jury last week with a burglary case. I think one guy in the front row had had a lobotomy. No wonder they screwed up."

No one suggested that *we* had screwed up by doggedly following policy, and once more I felt a gulf separating me from the core of career prosecutors, the team players.

Despite our powers of discretion, the tendency among prosecutors was to go for the highest charges, pass off responsibility, protect ourselves and "our" system. The grand jury might have originally been established as a buffer between the public and an overzealous prosecution, but regardless of the rhetoric in its favor, we had rendered it no more effective than a rubber stamp.

We acted as if we had a right to an indictment in ten minutes, no questions asked, and we viewed the grand jury as a tool, not as an autonomous body demanding respect. The process bore an uncomfortable resemblance to my former Star Chamber notion: no judge, absolute secrecy, as little testimony as possible, jurors numbed into following our instructions and keeping their questions to a minimum. Some prosecutors insisted that the grand jury at least screened out cases too tenuous to win the support of even a well-trained jury: if a witness won't come downtown for a grand jury presentation, surely the matter shouldn't proceed further. But those cases were rare, and could be culled out by any number of simpler means. John Patton, as usual, had been right: after weeks of service any grand jury would indict a ham sandwich, and for whatever charges we thought appropriate.

TWENTY-THREE

K-9 and Mookie

For me, the lesson had begun two and a half years earlier with Andrew Straight's case. It was a frustrating strain that ran through the days and nights of every prosecutor, a fact of life more disturbing than rubber-stamp indictments, coercive plea-bargaining, or inflexible office policies: witnesses rarely tell the whole truth. Everyone suppressed something, even if only an embarrassing detail. Handling serious cases, however, we were no longer to be forgiven for our naiveté. John Patton pressed us all to interview our witnesses until they broke: "Threaten them with a polygraph test or tell them you'll indict them for perjury. Do whatever you have to until you're sure they're telling the truth."

At 6:00 A.M. one Saturday morning in December in front of Carey, a Spanish Harlem housing project, Police Officer Mark Mullins and his partner were on a routine patrol in their blue-and-white squad car. They cruised slowly down Second Avenue, at that hour alive with only a handful of people on their way to work or coming home after a long night on the town. Wind sucked between the towering red brick apartment buildings and blew across deserted concrete basketball courts, sweeping newspapers, whirlpooling soot. Red-and-green crack-vial caps lay crushed on the sidewalk like confetti.

"Hey, police!" called a tall, skinny black kid who came loping toward the car.

Officer Mullins, young and blond, leaned out the driver's side window. "Yo, Keith, what's up?" Mullins had patrolled Carey for a little over two years and knew most of the residents by name. This was Keith Holiday, "K-9" to his friends. He lived with his mother in Carey 26.

"Hey, you look terrible," Officer Mullins said as the young man came near. "What happened to you?"

"I just got robbed by this guy with a gun. He came up to me over there." Keith pointed to a park bench on the sidewalk. "Then he pulled some kinda automatic pistol. Man, he put it right to my chest and said, 'Give me my money.' I said, 'I don't owe you no money,' but he just stood there with the gun. So I showed him I didn't have but forty cents on me. Then he says, 'All right, give me your jacket and your watch,' so I gave them to him. Then he got back on his bike and rode off with my stuff."

Mullins took a description of the robber—a male Hispanic, forty years old, five-eight, on a black bicycle—and the jacket—a blue windbreaker with a letter P on the left breast. Keith climbed in the backseat of the cruiser and they began canvassing the neighborhood. Less than fifteen minutes later, Keith tapped Mullins on the shoulder and pointed to a man leaning up against a brick wall. He was wearing a blue windbreaker with a P and standing next to a black bicycle. Mullins pulled up onto the sidewalk next to the suspect and got out. His partner stayed by the car. Keith slunk down in the rear seat.

"Excuse me," asked Mullins. "Where did you get that jacket?" The man looked at his shoes, scraped the pavement with his shoe tips, and dug his hands into his pants pockets.

"Uh, I bought it off a Puerto Rican guy on the street a year ago."

"Pssst, Officer." Keith's disembodied voice emanated

from the rear of the cruiser. "Look inside; it's got my name under the 'P.'"

"Okay," said Mullins, "let's have a look." Mullins's partner nursed his revolver in its holster as the suspect removed the windbreaker. In embroidered letters, "Keith," spelled backwards, appeared against the fuzzy white lining.

Mullins arrested and searched the man. Neither gun nor watch were found. At the precinct, the prisoner gave his name as Herculano Quintana. He lived two blocks from where he was arrested and had been unemployed for over a year. He denied the crime and then asked for a lawyer.

Mullins sat in an orange plastic folding chair facing my ECAB desk. It had been a dull day for me, helping the rookies get through a pile of misdemeanor drug cases and waiting for felonies. Herculano Quintana's arrest was the best thing to come through all day. A "solid Rob 1 displayed": *displaying what appeared to be a pistol.* The facts of the crime and the bits of pedigree information complemented each other perfectly.

Mentally, I rehearsed my summation to the jury. A good prosecutor always begins a case thinking how it will play in public. The summation ends: *Quintana, out of work and presumably out of cash, robbed a neighborhood kid, a kid whose word the cops might not be inclined to believe. But Officer Mullins did listen to Keith. He gave him a chance. After the robbery, Quintana sped home, just three blocks away, on his bike. There he ditched the watch and the gun but smugly, proud of his crime, wore the jacket. Because he never suspected the jacket would tie him to the crime, he never bothered to look inside.* I open the jacket before the jury: "Keith." *Members of the jury, the evidence speaks for itself.*

The case is a lock, a rock-crusher.

* * *

Two days later, Officer Mullins and Keith Holiday came to
my office. In the interim, my papers had gone through
typing, arraignments, our computer system, and John Patton's office. They appeared in my mailbox, as usual:
folded, crumpled, torn, stapled, restapled, and bearing a
little note that read, "If witness credible, GJ." There was
my ECAB write-up, sloppy penmanship and all. A judge
set $5,000 bail, placing 180.80 day four days away.

At forty-one, Quintana had a long history of arrests,
thirteen in fact, all in Brooklyn and all for felony drug sale.
Twelve of the convictions, as opposed to the arrest
charges, were for misdemeanor drug possession—probably the result of plea bargains. On one of the most recent
arrests, the sale charge finally stuck and he received a
"split": six months in jail followed by four and a half years
probation. Since serving the half year, he had twice violated probation with two more misdemeanor drug convictions, but the Department of Probation, in its wisdom, had
not sought reincarceration.

Something, however, was missing. It is easy to discern a
pattern in a robber's, con man's, or junkie's rap sheet.
Burglars don't forge checks. Robbers might break into
cars, but wouldn't bother with the Spanish handkerchief
switch. Gunpoint robbery didn't fit comfortably into
Quintana's criminal résumé: no pattern of weapons use,
no theft, no violence. Still I convinced myself that since
firearms and drugs are common enough partners, the in-
congruity can be ignored.

Keith Holiday—K-9—nineteen years old, energetic and
clear-eyed, made an immediately favorable impression on
me. He showed up on time wearing clean clothes, fresh-
out-of-the-box high-top sneakers, and a well-trimmed flat-
top Afro. He stood a slender six-foot-one, "the same as
Isiah Thomas, my basketball hero," he said. Most important, he had no rap sheet, a fact that in itself acted like a
disinfectant. I had seen plenty of kids Keith's age, crack-
smoking hoodlums who traipsed in and out of Criminal
Court, already Mandatory Persistent Violent Felony Of-

fenders, eligible upon their next robbery conviction for a life sentence. Keith had somehow steered clear. If anyone deserved the benefits of the justice system, it was K-9.

But I had been burned before. Having to explain to John Patton, later, that a nineteen-year-old had pulled the wool over my eyes was a particularly unpalatable prospect. Duty and self-interest, therefore, required that I play the skeptic: bait and challenge the victim, then try to win back his confidence. The prosecutor-witness relationship, I had learned, is two-edged. A witness tells me what happened and I repeat the story, deliberately altering minor details, waiting to be corrected. In round two, I force the witness to go over and over a host of facts while I look for a slip-up. In round three, I try to win back trust. From my side of the table it is an obstacle course; from the witness's it must be perplexing and even embittering. Certain prosecutors repeated, with a cynical pride, an old maxim: "You're not supposed to win any friends at this job."

Keith left high school at sixteen to work with his uncle as an apprentice electrician. After that, he spent afternoons working at Job Corps. A year later, he received the blue windbreaker with his name embroidered on it, my potential People's Exhibit Number One, as a Christmas gift from the Corps.

"Keith," I asked, "where'd the P come from?"

"Bible-study group. They gave everyone in the group a P. It stands for Panthers, the name of our basketball team." His long, oval face beamed boyishly.

"Oh, come on," I said, sensing that he was putting on some good-boy routine. "You don't go to Bible-study group."

"Sure I do," he insisted. "All my buddies go."

"All right, Keith, tell me what chapters you've been studying lately."

"Well, we don't actually study much," he answered. "Mostly we play hoop. That's the main reason I go, anyways. But afterwards we, like, sit around while this lady reads us stuff from the Bible. Usually I just chill out and fall asleep on the floor. It's relaxing."

At least he hadn't said he was interested in the epistles of Paul.

"Okay, so you got the letter in Bible class, but what were you doing out at six in the morning? You had been up all night getting high, right? Isn't that why you couldn't go home?"

"No, I always come home at five or six in the morning. Ask my mom. I like it outside at night. I practice hoop, hangout with my girlfriend. That kinda stuff. It's the truth." His eyes held mine steadily.

"Keith"—I leaned over my desk, trying to appear and sound authoritarian—"nobody just hangs out all night without a reason. If you're on coke or crack, you know, it's not too easy to go to sleep. And let me warn you, if you lie inside the grand jury, I can indict you for perjury."

"I'm telling you, it wasn't like that. I used to get high, but I looked around and saw where my friends was at. It's not worth it."

For forty minutes I confronted, threatened, and offered less unbelievable alternatives, but through it all Keith clung to his story, down to the gray-blue color of the gun. After a few phone calls to Job Corps, Keith's mom, and the electrician uncle, I felt convinced that he was telling the truth and could begin to treat him more civilly.

Officer Mullins's overall demeanor added to the strength of the case. It was a personal attribute that, at the moment, I particularly appreciated. I had recently concluded a trial in which a shy fourteen-year-old girl burst into tears on the witness stand as she described how the defendant had thrown her against a wall and twisted her arm until she dropped a ten-dollar bill. The jury seemed ready to convict until the arresting officer, a slack-jawed, careless rookie, testified.

"Officer," I inquired, "do you see the man you arrested anywhere in the courtroom?"

"I think that's him over by the defense lawyer."

"Officer," I asked, "are you sure that's the man you arrested?"

"I think that's him, but I wouldn't bet my paycheck on it."

The jury that should have convicted in fifteen minutes deadlocked after thirty-six hours of deliberation. When I sheepishly returned to the courtroom to schedule a retrial, the court officers chorused, "Hey, Mr. ADA, would you bet your paycheck on the next trial?"

Mullins, however, was as true-blue as a storybook cop. His good looks only enhanced the eager, positive attitude and diligence that shone around him like a halo. "I tell you, sir," he said, "Keith is a good kid. I've never seen him in any kind of trouble. And I catch kids doing all kinds of nonsense—smoking crack in the corridors, drinking whiskey cocktails laced with LSD first thing in the morning, even screwing on the roof. All the time I've been at the Carey project, which is no piece of cake, Keith's been one kid I never worry about. When he came up to me that morning he was shaking like a leaf, just like someone had pointed a gun at him. If it makes any difference to you, I believe him."

It did. That morning we went to the Grand Jury and obtained an indictment against Quintana for Robbery in the First Degree:

THE GRAND JURY OF THE COUNTY OF NEW YORK, by this indictment, accuse the defendant of the crime of ROBBERY IN THE FIRST DEGREE AS AN ARMED FELONY, committed as follows:

The defendant, in the County of New York, on or about December 18, 1987, forcibly stole property from Keith Holiday, to wit, personal property, and in the commission of the crime and in the immediate flight therefrom, he displayed what appeared to be a firearm, to wit, a pistol.

"Rob 1 displayed" is a B felony and carries a mandatory jail term, even for first offenders. By virtue of an ingenious legal provision, the prosecution need not prove that the defendant displayed a real pistol, just something that *appeared to be* one. A finger in the pocket can suffice, as long as it reasonably appeared to the victim to be a firearm. The brilliance of the robbery law, however, lies in its coercive effect. If the defense can prove that the pistol was a fake, the crime drops to Robbery in the Second Degree, which carries a substantially lower sentence. But in order to use the defense, the defendant tacitly admits that some sort of robbery took place. The accused acquits himself of Rob 1 and confesses to Rob 2. Out of the frying pan . . .

Quintana, already on probation for felony drug sale, faced a minimum of four and a half to nine years. This was his first robbery case, so I offered him a C with three to six before Justice Hanson in Part 20. Given the strength of the People's case, I assumed Quintana would jump at the offer. But he didn't cop out. Instead, he hired a top-notch lawyer named Amos Harrigan and began a vigorous defense. They went to the wheel and drew Justice Bruce Davidson.

My faith in the case, nevertheless, remained intact. Defendants turned down lenient offers for any number of reasons. Sometimes they hoped their victims will lose interest, or that some catastrophic event, such as death or illness, will squelch the prosecution. If they can drag matters out sufficiently through filing motions, unexpected religious holidays (many defendants displayed a sudden interest in the Muslim faith, a creed that holds Tuesdays sacred), or being ill at convenient moments, the People's case inevitably suffers and sometimes disintegrates. Time, the ally of all defendants, weakens memory, generates confusion, and blunts animosity.

And so things went. Quintana's lawyer stalled for time shamelessly, sometimes appearing in court, sometimes not, never ready at hearings, and there was nothing I could do about it.

"I'm sorry, Mr. Quintana," said Justice Davidson, "but your lawyer is engaged in Federal Court. We will have to put your matter over another week."

"But Your Honor," complained Quintana, looking around the courtroom, bewildered, "I don't even know what's going on."

"Mr. Quintana, I'm sure your attorney will contact you. He's a gentleman, I can assure you. And the matter's out of my hands. If he's not here, we can't proceed. That's that." Davidson slapped his palm down on the bench. Quintana's anxiety about his seemingly delinquent lawyer was sufficiently common that no one felt any particular sympathy for him. He would just have to wait in prison or come up with $5,000 bail. It was a sorry old story. Quintana wouldn't have complained quite so bitterly had he known how much Harrigan's absence was working in his favor.

Three months after the case arrived in Justice Davidson's part, it ripened for trial. At four in the afternoon I telephoned Keith Holiday at home to let him know the court date. As usual, he was sleeping. His mother woke him up, and Keith, a little groggy, readily agreed to come see me the day before trial to prepare. Everything looked fine. I had two good witnesses and solid evidence: another conviction in the bag.

At first I thought Keith had just overslept. It was the day before trial and he was two hours late. But his phone, as never before, went unanswered. Witnesses had stood me up before, yet Keith had seemed so reliable and honest. Maybe he had been threatened.

When Officer Mullins arrived for his own rehearsal at eleven, Keith still hadn't called in. Mullins left at noon carrying a subpoena that ordered Keith to appear in Supreme Court at nine o'clock the following morning. I instructed Mullins to leave nothing to chance and to bring the recalcitrant witness in personally by eight-thirty.

At noon the following day Mullins knocked on my door. All morning I had paced my office in my freshly starched white shirt and pressed suit. Trial was set to begin that morning and I didn't have a single witness prepared. I didn't even know where they were. Not only was it embarrassing, but something had obviously gone seriously wrong.

"Mullins," I said when my office door opened, "where the hell have you been, and where is Keith? We're supposed to begin a trial today. And we're talking about a Predicate Felony offender, not some half-assed misdemeanant."

"Listen, sir, I'm sorry I'm so late, but I've been scouring Carey and nobody seems to know where K-9 is. I spoke to his mom and a bunch of the neighbors, but as far as I can tell he's in the wind. Anyhow, I left the subpoena at his house." I went over to Davidson's court part, rehearsing explanations en route.

When I first began trying cases in Supreme Court I encountered the usual gossipy talk about judges. One had been caught having sex with a law assistant in a bathroom; another had gotten into office through bribes. Usually I discounted the stories as the usual rumor-mongering. Justice Bruce Davidson, who was balding and wore a goatee with a handlebar mustache, was reputed to be somewhat mad. "Daffy Davidson," people said. Ha ha ha.

In Davidson's case, however, the rumors turned out to be true. Recently I had appeared before His Honor in one of my heaviest cases, a gun-toting career criminal I had indicted for four separate robberies. The defendant, a thirty-five-year-old black man, agreed to cop out in exchange for the minimum sentence, eight to life. The sentence was hard time by any measure, and not a matter to be treated lightly. As the prisoner stood before Justice Davidson and recited the catalogue of his misdeeds, His Honor motioned for me to approach the bench. Staring through the thick magnifying lenses of his eyeglasses, Davidson said, "Mr. DA, let me ask you a question, man to man."

"Okay, Judge," I said, listening with half an ear to the defendant's confession in the background. *"I pointed a gun at the couple and said, 'Gimme your—'"*

"Mr. DA, do you love me?"

"Excuse me, Judge?"

"Do you love me?"

"Well, Your Honor, I certainly enjoy being in your courtroom." In the background: *"I took their money and left them—"*

"No, no, Mr. DA." Davidson pressed on, seriously seeking an answer. "Do you love me?"

"Judge," I repeated, "I really do enjoy being in your courtroom."

"Well," he said holding out his hand, "I love you." We shook on it. A white judge and white prosecutor. In the background, the defendant completed his allocution. I shuddered to imagine how it must have appeared to a black man about to begin a life sentence.

Since that encounter, I knew Davidson could be relied upon to cut me slack, even if at the expense of some importunate antics. After he showed me pictures of his baby daughter, I told His Honor that Keith Holiday, my key witness, couldn't be located. Davidson gave me two weeks. Amos Harrigan, Quintana's lawyer, fulminated about lackadaisical prosecutors, but I saw in his eyes a glimmer of hope: there might be a hole in the DA's case.

Again I sent Mullins out on Keith's trail, and in the meantime I reran my evanescent witness's rap sheet. I doubted that anything would come of it, but being arrested was a common cause of a witness's disappearance. The rap sheet that came back from the Investigations Bureau confirmed my most distressing suspicions: K-9 had been arrested for selling cocaine just two weeks after the Quintana robbery, and worse, after being indicted, he jumped bail. A warrant had been ordered for his arrest. My star witness had fallen from the sky.

I called a prosecutor in Special Narcotics, who told me that Keith had sold two vials of crack to an undercover agent on 120th Street and Second Avenue—just a block away from the scene of the Quintana robbery. The narcotics prosecutor said he believed that the warrant squad had "executed" Keith's warrant and placed him in the Riker's Island Men's House of Detention, wing C-76. The outlook for Keith was decidedly grim, and as his almost certain conviction loomed up, it cast a shadow over my "solid Rob 1 displayed."

So much for the Bible-studying, clean-cut witness who had overcome a potentially damaging upbringing in the projects. His whole story must have been one giant fabrication, custom made for me. Why hadn't I heeded my suspicions about kids from the projects being outside at six A.M. and thrown Keith Holiday out of my office?

Nevertheless, there remained the indictment, voted by a New York County grand jury. I couldn't dismiss the matter simply because Keith's arrest had lifted the veil from my eyes—not, at least, without trying to answer a number of questions. Had Keith been involved in a drug deal with Quintana? Did a robbery take place anyway? Even if the case did involve a drug sale, a robbery remains a robbery, whether motivated by a bad deal or simple greed. Quintana wasn't entitled to a free ride because he robbed a fellow dealer—if that is what happened.

One thing was certain: K-9 had to be found. The computers at Riker's Island were down, so I again called Keith's home, hoping his mother would know something of his whereabouts. Mothers may love their children, but from what I had seen in court, they will almost always hand them over to the law.

"Hello," mumbled a familiar male voice.

"Keith," I said, restraining my anger, "you were supposed to come to my office yesterday to prepare for the trial today. What happened?"

"Yeah, well, I knew I should've come," he said slowly and deliberately, like someone recovering from a bad hangover, "and I was meaning to call you. Like, um, I got arrested for selling and I didn't want to get into worse trouble with you all."

"That's okay, Keith," I said, harboring thoughts of a perjury indictment, "but you still have to come downtown. Your drug case has no effect on our trial. You're the main witness against Quintana, and I need you." Keith agreed, and even tossed out a few more apologies into the bargain, but in spite of his protestations he never came back to see me—at least, not voluntarily.

Over the next four weeks Mullins dropped off six more subpoenas during unannounced visits to Keith's house, but Keith was obviously laying low. Things had gotten out of hand, and all the while Quintana continued to sit behind bars. Every time I saw Quintana's name approaching on my calendar I tried to think of new ways to explain to "the judge who loved me" why the entire Manhattan district attorney's office still remained powerless to bring a nineteen-year-old witness to court. I showed Judge Davidson copies of all the subpoenas and described how, whenever Officer Mullins went to haul Keith to court, Keith mysteriously vanished. And still Quintana waited.

Before joining the DA's office I had promised myself that above all, I would never take a case to trial if I had any doubt about the defendant's guilt. At the time it seemed an easy enough standard to abide by. But during the past few weeks I realized that the Quintana case would probably force me to put my personal ethics to the test. The defendant faced a minimum of four and a half to nine years in jail, all on the word of a crack dealer who had lied to a gullible prosecutor. Sending him to prison on K-9's say-so would be unthinkable. I went to see John Patton about dismissing the Quintana indictment, a procedure technically referred to as a Dismissal on Recommendation of the People, DOR for short—a prosecutorial "abandon ship."

Patton flatly refused. "Take it to trial," he said. "You could win it." He was disingenuous, fulfilling his duty as bureau chief, and he saw that I knew it. Twisting in his seat, he even looked physically uncomfortable.

"Come on, John," I argued. "Keith was selling crack just blocks away from the robbery. He lied to me about drugs and he doesn't want to come to court, so why are we wasting our time over the case? I'm wondering if he didn't frame Quintana. And if *I* have doubts, a jury will never be convinced. The moment Keith takes the stand it will be obvious that he's a liar. And I don't exactly savor the idea of taking an innocent man to trial. Suppose he gets convicted? Davidson could send him to jail for eight and a third to twenty-five!"

"You won't have to do that," John said. Apparently I had said the requisite incantatory words: taking an innocent man to trial. "But you didn't have any doubts about the case before you went to the grand jury. Just because your witness is giving you a hard time and got arrested doesn't mean he's lying. This is just not a DOR situation. Quintana still lied about the kid's jacket. And for all you know, Keith told you the truth about the robbery. Come on, try the case."

If Quintana had gone to trial before Keith's arrest I would very likely have convicted him and sent him to jail for years. Fate had intervened on Quintana's behalf, yet Patton refused to let me do what quite obviously should be done—dismiss the indictment.

Around this time, a friend of my family complained to me at a dinner party about her experience during jury duty. She said she had wound up on a "stupid" robbery case: "One street person had punched another wino and then taken a dollar out of his hand. What a waste of time and money! It made me really angry. Who lets cases get that far?"

I left Patton's office determined to set my mind at rest about Keith and, with luck, get rid of the case.

At six the next morning, Officer Mullins, acting at my

behest, once again returned to Carey. This time we were lucky. Mullins pulled Keith out of bed and brought him downtown in a squad car. I arrived at the office at nine to find Keith facedown on my desk in a dead sleep, oblivious of the handcuffs binding his wrists behind his back. Mullins dozed in a chair in the corner. This is the DA's life, I thought: another day of coffee and browbeating.

Our first stop that morning was Justice Davidson's courtroom. As Mullins, Keith, and I walked across the street, we garnered inquisitive stares from passersby. Where are that officer and the man in the suit taking the nice-looking boy in handcuffs? Even court officers looked our way and grunted. I explained to Keith that since he had refused to cooperate, I was going to have him housed in the city jail under a Material Witness order. Arresting my own witness was a desperate measure, but this was indeed a desperate situation.

Judge Davidson postponed starting a trial in order to deal with Keith. He excused the jury, told the lawyers to wait in the audience, and ordered Quintana brought up from the holding cells. Reading over my motion papers, he muttered some of the key phrases aloud: "Six subpoenas . . . repeated telephone calls unanswered . . . failure to testify in court when required. . . ." He looked the loose-limbed teenager up and down, searching for the right approach.

"Now, listen, young fella." Davidson's eyes expanded to the rims of his thick glasses as his voice rose. "You're playing a man's game. A man's game." He struck the bench with his fist. "So you see, the DA over there and I, we've got to treat you like a man, not a kid. Do you understand?" God, I thought, Davidson really is a loon. His Honor went on without waiting for an answer. "If you're telling the truth, you've got nothing to fear." He smiled as his rage metamorphosed inexplicably into beneficence. "But you didn't come to court when you were told—you didn't come at all—so you've got to stay in a place where the DA can put his finger on you at a moment's notice." Davidson snapped his fingers in the air: back to rage. "And I intend to keep you there under the state's Material Witness order until I feel you're ready to play by the rules. Maybe I'll let you out tomorrow. I don't know. Charlie"—he called to a court officer—"take him."

Meanwhile, Quintana sat at the defense table with a look of satisfaction spread across his face. He had spent four months in Riker's Island Prison on this kid's word.

"Sir," Davidson said to him, "I am going to release you without bail. However, you must"—again he pounded his fist—"return to court for trial. Do you give me your word as a gentleman?" Davidson had a knack for appearing absurd. Even Quintana seemed taken aback.

"I promise, Judge."

"Good," Davidson concluded. "And you know something? I believe you. Don't you believe him, Willie?" he asked his clerk.

"Sure, Your Honor, anything you say."

Mullins and I left the courtroom bewildered. The case had been turned inside out, although the situation was partly of my own making. My star witness sat behind bars, while at the same time Quintana and I waited side by side for the elevator.

I let Keith mull things over for a night in the Tombs and in the meantime convinced John Patton to interview him the following morning. The next day, Davidson signed an order releasing Keith in my custody. As Keith and I walked across the street, I explained that my bureau chief wanted a word with him. Playing a sort of Mutt and Jeff routine, I tried to soften Keith up, bought him a hot dog, and warned him about my boss, the tough guy. I looked forward to watching a twenty-year DA interrogate this crack-dealing, lying troublemaker and get to the bottom of things.

I should have known better. For one repetition-filled hour, Patton fruitlessly rehashed every point I had already explored. There were no brilliant tours de force, just the same dogged, methodical approach I had learned in training. To my further displeasure, Patton even left with a favorable opinion of the witness. "You know," he told me as we exchanged a few whispered words outside my office, "he's a nice ki . Li able. Just keep at him." Patton headed back down the hallway.

Keith and I sat alone back in my office. It was nearly noon; the cool spring air blew in across my sooty window sill, and a parallelogram of sunlight lit up the floor. Keith looked sickly from eating Corrections' bologna sandwiches and sleeping on a prison bunk. He sat quietly, either sorting out the tangled shreds of his conscience or daydreaming; I couldn't be sure which. It didn't matter anyhow. This teenage crack dealer had the DA's office pleading with him to put an end to an absurd chain of events. For the moment, he had us all under his control. I felt like slamming K-9 up against the wall—anything to get the truth out of him.

This wasn't the first time a witness had lied to me, but somewhere among the innumerable days buying time before Justice Davidson, learning how intransigent our office could be, and watching Quintana's desperate face, I felt the first real stirrings of having had *enough*. Enough of crack dealers; enough of men and women robbed, beaten, burgled, raped, conned, abused, cut, shot, threatened, lied to, and lying back; enough of throwing people in jail; enough of seeing crime-scene photos; enough of watching as blind justice tapped slowly forward. The cops' cynical humor, which had once seemed so seductive, now grated. It was a defense against walking out the door and conceding defeat in the face of a system that is too cumbersome, a reality too uncertain. Only five more months and my three-year commitment to the office—a gentleman's agreement made by all ADAs that we would stay on at least three years—would be up. I could leave with a clean slate. I began counting the weeks.

But the Quintana fiasco was not about to disappear in a swift fade to black.

"Keith," I said, "I know what's on your mind and why

you won't tell me the truth. You testified about the case one way in the grand jury and now you think we'll go after you for perjury. Am I right?"

"Yeah, you bet you're right." For the first time since our interview months ago, his features showed some life. "Man, I just wish I could disappear and stay disappeared. I told you the basic truth the first time, but, like, there *is* some other stuff."

"All right, Keith, listen. If you level with me, I promise we won't charge you with perjury. I mean, you might think I'm lying, but if I wanted to charge you with perjury I could probably do it anyway. If you just tell me the truth we'll give you complete immunity. This is your one chance."

"Okay," said Keith. "Let me tell you the whole deal." I listened, expressionless, afraid that a sudden move or show of satisfaction might scare away the truth before I even glimpsed its outlines. "I wasn't there alone. My friend Mookie was with me. Mook and me, we was up all night. Anyways, we sold some crack to the guy who robbed me. But we sold it to him maybe two weeks before. You know, it was no big thing. He gave me twenty bucks and I gave him two cracks. And it weren't beat or nothin'.

"Well, that night—the night I got robbed—I saw the same guy riding around on his bicycle, and Mookie and me was hangin' out, but we didn't sell him nothin'. At least I didn't. But he said, 'Give me my money.' I told him, 'I don't owe you no money,' but maybe he thought I was someone else. Anyway, when the guy came over to me, Mookie was backing away like he saw the whole thing coming. We even laughed about it later. Mook was sayin' how scared I looked."

"Keith," I asked, "why didn't you tell me before that Mookie saw the whole thing? He's a witness who can help you out."

"Well, you know, Mook's got warrants out for robbery and other shit. I tried to find him a couple of times, but he's chillin' somewhere. Maybe he got arrested again. But that's the whole truth. I just didn't want to admit I sold drugs to the guy because I thought I'd get into trouble."

"It couldn't be much worse than now, could it Keith?" I asked.

"Nope. Like I was saying, I wish I could just disappear. Besides the guy's back out now and he knows where I hang out. I hope he doesn't shoot me."

"Listen, your best hope is to help us find Mookie. If he backs up your story, we can still go to trial and lock the guy up."

That afternoon the bureau secretary told me Judge Davidson wanted to see me "forthwith." The Quintana case had all but exhausted my credit balance of goodwill, so I skulked back across the street, fearful that he might finally subject me to the tongue-lashing a less patient, or crazy, jurist would have administered weeks ago.

"Mr. Prosecutor," he said, "has the witness shown a better attitude since his night as a guest of the state?"

"Your Honor, the witness is more cooperative. But the People have encountered a new, unforeseen difficulty." I always lapsed into high formality to sugar-coat an irksome request. "We have discovered the identity of a potential witness, an eyewitness to the entire event, or so the People have been led to believe. We require two weeks to locate that person, at which time we will answer ready for trial, with or without the new witness."

Davidson turned to Amos Harrigan, seeking support to lambaste me for delaying the trial yet again. Harrigan, however, took the opportunity to appear flexible. He even tipped me off about his defense. "Your Honor," he said, "I have no reason to question the prosecutor's good faith. In addition, with my client out of jail and better able to assist me in preparing for trial, I welcome a delay. Mr. Quintana was framed, and he will be vindicated. On the night in question he purchased bogus drugs from the elusive Mr. Holiday. When he returned to get his money back, the People's witness said he had spent the money. My client insisted on keeping the jacket as collateral until he was repaid. I am only too happy to let the DA chase after his chimerical witnesses."

"Mr. Prosecutor," said Davidson, "you should appreciate the indulgence shown to you in this courtroom by both Mr. Harrigan and myself. You have been before me often enough to understand that I never"—he struck the bench with his fist—"never tolerate any monkey business, no monkey business whatsoever. Two weeks for trial."

During the next two weeks I received regular reports from Officer Mullins and Keith on their efforts to locate Mookie, whose real name turned out to be James Williams and who lived near Keith in Carey. Keith had been right about Mookie's outstanding warrants. According to his rap sheet, Mookie, seventeen years old, had had three narcotics arrests and currently faced two robbery indictments. He had jumped bail on all of his cases. But as the Quintana trial drew nearer and our efforts to pin down my mystery witness's whereabouts proved fruitless, I began to fear that Mookie, if not a chimera, might be another of K-9's ruses. He was out there somewhere, and if I found him before trial I could resolve matters one way or another. As things stood at the moment, however, the indictment against Quintana should be shelved. "Better to let a guilty man go free than to convict the innocent," goes the old saying.

If we had gone to trial months ago, Quintana's defense would have crumpled under the weight of the original Keith Holiday, a clean kid with no police record, someone who had sidestepped drug addiction, violence, and crime. To impugn the good faith of this exemplar with a ridiculous story about a drug deal and a jacket as collateral amounted to an insult. How dare a felon like Quintana, with a list of convictions as long as your arm, assassinate the character of a decent kid just to save his own skin? It would have made a convincing summation.

Now, in the wake of Keith's crack-sale arrest, bail-jump, and disregard of government subpoenas, Quintana's "insult" had the ring of truth. I had promised never to try a case about which I had doubts. But the office, that monolith with its chiseled-in-stone policies, continued to pronounce, "Take it to trial."

On the morning of trial I was ready. Keith and Mullins were in my office on time, Keith in handcuffs, just in case. When we arrived in Supreme Court and I arranged my files on the counsel table, Davidson seemed in a headlong rush. "Mr. Harrigan informs me," said His Honor with uncharacteristic focus, "that his client wishes to waive a jury and have the case tried before me. I am delighted to accommodate his request. Delighted. As you know, I always make every effort to oblige counsel. Is the state ready to proceed?"

I stood up. My eyes lingered on the neatly typed indictment, my pages of notes, list of police forms, photos of the jacket, Keith's rap sheet. Ready. A mindless G-man. I wanted to slip out of my skin, let my body mechanically carry out the repugnant task of trying a defendant without moral conviction. It's virtually a crime, totally unethical. There is Quintana, next to his lawyer. He looks nervous. Who wouldn't be?

I stood up and looked Davidson, the loon, straight in the eye. The experience of two and a half years in the DA's office, a year in federal court, three years of law school was now all rendered pathetically useless by a simple lie. "Yes, Your Honor. The People are ready to proceed." Damned.

"Mr. Prosecutor, we will commence trial in one hour." Once more Davidson's fist slammed down on the bench.

Hope springs eternal, especially when hope is all you have left. In my remaining moments, my final hour, I telephoned Riker's Island Prison. At least Davidson couldn't accuse me of laziness. A young woman with a heavy southern drawl responded, "James Williams? Let me see. Yes, here he is. He was arrested last week."

"Last week? Are you sure? I called every day but was told you had no record of him."

"Mr. Williams is in the *Women's* House of Detention:

the Men's House is all full up. That's probably why we couldn't locate the body."

A new star had risen out of oblivion. I was ecstatic. Mookie and I would meet, and the mysteries of the Quintana robbery would unfold. If Mookie shrugged his shoulders and said he had never seen K-9 robbed, I would have enough information to dismiss the indictment with the blessing of the DA elite. If his story corroborated Keith's, Quintana's conviction was assured.

I delivered my opening statement, which proceeded with a good deal more alacrity than I would have anticipated only an hour earlier, and Judge Davidson signed an Order to Produce, commanding the corrections bureaucracy to bring "said James Williams forthwith to New York Supreme Court."

Putting my best witness forward, I let Mullins testify first. The case proceeded especially slowly, since Davidson wanted to transcribe every word into his logbook. His practice would have been sensible, even laudable, had there not been a stenographer seated next to him doing precisely the same task at three times the speed. "Excuse me, sir," he said to Officer Mullins, "but you'll have to repeat that entire statement. I told you before, I want to get down every word, everything. Am I making myself clear?"

Through it all, Mark Mullins was a model cop: accurate, diligent, and unimpeachable. When he reached the moment of unfurling the jacket, I saw Davidson's magnified eyes expand to otherworldly dimensions. Quintana lowered his head. People's Exhibit Number One.

Trying to see the case afresh from Davidson's perspective, I felt a renewed flush of confidence. Things had begun exactly as I had imagined they would, six months ago in ECAB. "No cross-examination, Your Honor," said Harrigan.

But I was only delaying the inevitable. "The People call Keith Holiday"—the new Keith Holiday, the crack-selling, subpoena-scoffing liar from Spanish Harlem who once sold drugs to the man he says robbed him. The whole story came out: selling a couple of "jumbos" to Quintana weeks before with Mookie, being up till six in the morning to play basketball and see his girlfriend; the Bible study class and the Panthers; Quintana riding up on his bicycle, pointing a gun, and demanding "his money"; selling crack to an undercover officer weeks later, the bench warrants, the subpoenas, the Material Witness order. I hoped that if Keith at least fessed up to his catalogue of recently acquired horribles he might sway Davidson with his candor.

Harrigan's cross-examination raised more questions than it answered. He spent most of his energy asking about Mookie, the mysterious witness whom I had fished out of some cell in the Women's House. Harrigan obviously saw Mookie as the last obstacle standing between his client and the front door.

"You say your friend Mookie was backing away when my client came up to you. Is that right?"

"Yeah."

"And he was there after my client rode away on his bicycle?"

"Uh-huh."

"And he was there when Officer Mullins spoke to you?"

"Nope. Mook took off when I ran after the police car."

"But Mookie stood nearby while you were allegedly being robbed?"

"You bet. He was even laughing about it the next day, saying how scared I looked."

"If you saw Mookie the next day, why didn't you tell the district attorney's office about him?"

" 'Cause, like, Mook's got warrants and he was afraid he'd get locked up."

The next morning, Mookie, wearing handcuffs and flanked by two corrections officers, was brought to the jurors' deliberating room behind Davidson's court part. "Mr. DA," Davidson said, "go speak to your witness. Take all the time you want. I'm delighted your efforts proved successful. Delighted."

My star witness turned out to be a little tarnished and worn. Dirty, red-eyed, and full of slow-moving malice, Mookie looked like a stray dog. He was on his way to becoming a real "skel." But ratty-looking though he was, Mookie was my last hope.

I introduced myself and tried to explain that although he faced two indictments from ADAs who worked just down the hall from me, I was not an enemy. Mookie stared back, his eyes a blank. I repeated my little introduction, intended to put him at ease, but talking to Mookie was like shouting into a deep well. My voice echoed as it sunk further and further into the empty darkness.

"Officers," I said, using an ancient DA ploy I had learned from television, "take the cuffs off. He's not going to give us any trouble." As he rubbed his wrists, Mookie's mood seemed to brighten.

"Mookie, listen to me. Do you know a kid from the projects named K-9?"

He looked around the room warily and then, without moving his lips, said, "Uh-huh."

"Do you remember hanging out with K-9 in December in front of Carey, early in the morning?" Again Mookie looked uncertainly around the jury room. It must have seemed sumptuous compared to the cells at the Women's House.

"Whaddya mean?"

"Okay, Mookie, here's the situation," I said, hoping that a crack habit hadn't destroyed all his brain cells. "Keith says he got robbed and that you were there. If you *were* there, tell me what you saw. It could make a big difference to this case and to Keith as well. He might be in a lot of trouble if I find out he lied to me. And I promise I'll tell the DAs in your other cases about your cooperation here."

"Is that it?" As he looked up at me, the haze lifted.

"You bet. Just tell me what happened to K-9." Another pause. It wasn't difficult to imagine what gears were turning in Mookie's head.

"Look," he began, "we was hangin' in front of Carey

and this kid comes up to K-9 on a bicycle, points an automatic at his stomach, and takes his jacket. I was right next to him. Then the cops came and I rode around in the backseat of the cruiser for a while. Only, I split before they found the guy. You know, they dropped me off, 'cause I didn't like being inside no cruiser. But, like, later that day I saw K-9 and he said they got the sucker."

"Wait a minute, Mookie. About how old was the kid who pointed the gun at K-9?"

"You know, young-like, maybe twenty-two."

"And you're sure you rode around in the police car?"

"Of course I'm sure. We looked along the avenue till I said, 'Lemme out.' Then I went home. That's what happened."

I had been confused enough about the case going into the jury room, but now my mind reeled. In a few sentences Mookie both corroborated Keith's story and totally discredited himself. Had they both concocted the robbery story back in December, and Mookie had gotten it confused in the meantime? But then Keith would have mentioned Mookie as a witness right from the start. Mookie had ridden in his share of squad cars; maybe he had this incident confused with some other ride . . .

More than ever I wanted to dismiss the indictment. I had no idea in the world whether Quintana had robbed K-9, but at this point the edge of my resolve had been worn away by the steady stream of lies, disappointments, and false leads in the case. To hell with my personal opinion; let the mad Justice Davidson sort things out.

Mookie testified that morning, but with two convicted crack-sellers accusing another crack-seller of robbery, and with inconsistent stories, the case became a farce. Quintana also took the stand and gave Davidson his own version of the events. He claimed that Keith had sold him bad drugs earlier in the evening. When he returned to complain about the "product" Keith said that he had already spent the money, so they struck a deal. "Give me your jacket as collateral," Quintana said. "I'll hold it until you get me my money." Neither of the stories—mine nor the defendant's—made much sense. But I had the burden of proof. After the last of Quintana's testimony, Davidson retired to his chambers to assess the evidence. Five minutes later he returned. Out of habit I felt nervous, though I knew the verdict.

ADAs at Bureau 20 sympathized with me, but no one, not even Jim Bronson, suggested that I had done anything wrong. Taking an innocent man to trial was a professional liability. "I remember so-and-so's case," people mused. "My witnesses were probably lying, but I had to take him to trial. Of course, he got off." I refused to take solace as readily. We were supposed to be administering justice, not following bureaucratic policies.

As I headed home that evening a woman stopped me on the street and asked for a dollar. I had seen her on the corner bumming change from people for the last two weeks. "My car broke down," she said, "and I need some money to get back to Brooklyn."

"What year is your car?" I asked.

"Uh, eighty-three," she said uneasily.

"What color?"

She paused. "Blue."

"Two-door or four-door?"

"Uh . . . four."

"License number?" I spat back.

"It's 4-2-6—" She paused, now sensing my caustic manner. "Listen, I don't have to take this shit."

"Fine," I said. "I don't have to give you a dollar."

As she stalked off I felt a pang of regret for taking a sardonic pleasure in cross-examining an unfortunate beggar. I should have walked past her and said no, but I was sick and tired of being lied to. Since starting work I had tried to use my discretion wisely, to do justice. But to be just, I had learned, you have to know the facts, and in the DA's office facts were a rarity. The true, the honestly mistaken, and the deliberately false stories of witnesses blurred indistinguishably into one another. I was doing the best I could under the circumstances, but the circumstances continued to wear me down.

TWENTY-FOUR

Abated by Death

In June I received a telephone call letting me know that Kenneth Chimes was dead.

Chimes's case was not particularly serious, and the news, at first, was not particularly stirring. Other defendants of mine had died before: one had stolen a car and in a drunken spree raced through town mowing down pedestrians, until he smashed head on into a brick wall; another had overdosed. Chimes's case, in fact, was one of those matters that sat gathering dust in my file drawer. He was overwhelmingly guilty but refused to cop out, so his lawyer dragged the case out for months trying to avoid the inevitable.

Last November, two officers in a marked police car had been on patrol in Harlem at two in the morning when they turned onto a small side street and noticed Chimes. He glanced up, turned on his heel, and headed off in the opposite direction, hugging the sides of buildings. The officers followed. As one cop drove alongside, his partner in the passenger seat spotted the outline of a pistol in Chimes's outside jacket pocket. He got out, put his hand over the outline, felt the gun, and within moments had Chimes spread-eagled against the wall.

In one pocket the officer found a 9mm automatic pistol with a clip that held eleven live rounds of ammunition. In the other pocket were twelve more bullets and a gravity knife. Gravity knives—hybrids of switchblades and stilettos—are illegal, deemed "per se weapons." Chimes was cuffed, booked, and taken downtown. At the precinct he surrendered a small bag of marijuana to the desk sergeant.

In ECAB it was just another unlicensed-gun case—Criminal Possession of a Weapon in the Third Degree. Boring, repetitive: every prosecutor had his or her share of CPW 3s, along with slashings, muggings, robberies, and murders. They took five minutes to indict and almost never went to trial. But it was our job to care about gun cases, and we showed our concern with a policy requiring all handgun possessors to plead to the crime, a Class E felony. No plea-bargains, no deals: a hard line. People without criminal records were promised probation, but they had to "eat" the felony, taking the step from solid citizen to convicted felon. The gun policy, which had caused such a furor in the dwarf case, was enforced as rigorously as that against dismissing indictments. There were, of course, exceptions, but they were few. So even though Chimes was twenty-six, had no criminal record, and was gainfully employed, I took the case to the grand jury.

The day after I filed the indictment, Chimes's attorney, Ron Bonamo, telephoned me. Every defense lawyer called ADAs looking for misdemeanor offers on first-offense gun cases, hoping theirs would fall within some undefined exception to the general rule of plea to the charge. Some zealous advocates hammered away at us on the telephone as relentlessly as they did at arraignment judges, whining, cajoling, wheedling—anything to get their clients a break. Bonamo first went for the solid-citizen argument.

"Chimes is a security guard in Brooklyn and carries the weapons only for protection," he said. "The guy is really a decent person. Look, we've worked AR-1 together, so you know I wouldn't ask for a break if he were a sleazeball."

"Listen, Ron, what about all those extra bullets in his

other pocket? And the gravity knife? One wrong move and an innocent bystander could have ended up dead."

"I know. That's the weak part of the case. But Chimes still deserves a break. I mean it."

"I'm sorry, Ron," I said, "but you'll have to do better than that."

Bonamo's next line of attack was better. "My client wants to leave his dead-end job as a security guard and become an electrician. He's taken all the necessary courses and is just at the end of his apprenticeship. I've got the paperwork to back it up. But electricians have to be bonded in order to receive their license, and no bonding company will insure my man with a fresh felony weapons conviction. You're stopping him from becoming a productive citizen. If it were just the felony I'd tell him to live with it, but this is too harsh."

Bonamo had a point. It was one thing to insist that Chimes get the same treatment as any other person in Manhattan. But when an "even-handed" policy frustrates someone from honestly improving his lot, justice, not policy, should win out. I agreed to order a pre-pleading investigation report on Chimes.

Six weeks later the report came in. A court agent had interviewed the defendant at his 145th Street apartment, where he lived with his father. According to the report, both Chimeses, junior and senior, were uncooperative to the point of belligerence, even though they knew why the investigator had come. Kenneth Chimes downplayed the seriousness of the crime and said he thought the arrest and search were unconstitutional. Neither father nor son displayed any remorse or a sense that Kenneth had made a mistake. From Chimes's point of view, it couldn't have been more harmful. I had no choice but to insist that he take a felony.

The DA policy of demanding felony pleas on weapons charges was too deeply embedded, and I couldn't ignore the gravity knife and extra bullets—certainly not without a good investigative report to back me up.

Bonamo called me after the report came in. "I don't know what happened out there," he said, "but it doesn't sound like they got along. Anyway, I still want you to consider a misdemeanor. He needs this new job, and he's put so much time into preparation. There's a city full of burglars, robbers, and dope-dealers out there. Do you really want your pound of flesh out of Chimes? You're ruining his one chance."

"I'm sorry, Ron," I said sounding like a politician on the campaign trail, "but I have an obligation to all the other people on the street next to the Chimeses of the world, people who might get shot."

"Yeah," he said sourly, "but they didn't get shot, did they?"

The case was set down for hearing and trial.

At the suppression hearing, a month later, there was one issue at stake: whether the officers had illegally stopped and searched Chimes. If they had, the gun would be suppressed, and, of necessity, the People would be forced to dismiss the indictment.

My only witness was the arresting officer, a sandy-haired, street-wise young cop named Chris McCabe. He was one of those officers who had an unsettling vigilante streak—a cowboy. McCabe took the stand and gave his name, rank, and shield and command numbers. He summarized his training and experience: six months at the academy, two and a half years in the field.

"Officer," I asked, "directing your attention to the night in question, please explain to His Honor the circumstances leading up to the arrest."

"Okay. Judge, my partner and I were on patrol in a marked RMP on One-Ten and Saint Nicholas Boulevard; we call it Sector Adam. At approximately zero-two-hundred hours, we turned a corner from Saint Nick onto One-Ten and I saw the defendant coming up the street. Maybe five seconds after we made the turn, the defendant turned around and started walking away and kind of hugging up to the wall. When he passed under a streetlight, I noticed the outline of a 9mm automatic in his right-hand jacket pocket. I know 9mm's because I have one at home.

"At that moment I signaled my partner to stop. I exited the vehicle, and since the suspect was armed, I asked him if he had dropped something, just to distract him. When he turned to look at the ground, I put my hand over the outline of the gun. After I determined it to be a real weapon, I removed it and found it had a full clip. At that point I placed the individual under arrest."

I reached over to my table and pulled Chimes's silver 9mm pistol out of my trial folder. The court officers snapped to attention at the sight of the weapon dangling from between my thumb and forefinger. His Honor leaned back cautiously.

"Officer McCabe, I'm showing you People's Exhibit Number One for identification. Do you recognize it? If so, tell the Court what it is and how you recognize it."

"Sure I recognize it. It's the gun I recovered from the defendant. Here's my initials I scratched into it right after I made the arrest."

McCabe was an experienced cop. He knew what to say, what judges and prosecutors wanted to hear: it was all routine, as smooth and slick as a good con man's patter. Before going to the grand jury I had grilled him about the search—how he could see the outline of a gun through the jacket at night, and so on—but McCabe had an answer for every question. After he had re-enacted the scene for the third time, I agreed to indict the case. Now, in court, it was Bonamo's turn to see if he could do any better than I had done, months before in my office.

He began with a surprise. Holding a blue nylon jacket in his hand, Bonamo asked portentously, "Officer, do you recognize this jacket?"

"Well, Counselor, it looks like the jacket the defendant was wearing the night I arrested him."

"Your Honor, I'm showing the jacket to the assistant district attorney and asking him to stipulate that it is the same jacket shown in Mr. Chimes's booking photograph, a photo taken the night of the arrest. I am prepared to produce witnesses who will testify that this is in fact the same jacket, but to save time I hope the DA will agree to stipulate."

It looked like the same jacket, worn through on one shoulder, a small tear in the lapel. I thought, What the hell? "The People stipulate that this is the jacket worn by the defendant the night of his arrest."

Bonamo put it on. It hung on him like a luffing sail.

"Mr. Prosecutor," he said, "may I see the weapon recovered from Mr. Chimes?" I handed him the gun, which he put into the right outside pocket. It disappeared into the folds without a trace.

"Officer McCabe," said Bonamo, "can you tell, even in this well-lit courtroom and at this close proximity, whether I have a gun—or anything else, for that matter—inside either jacket pocket?"

McCabe looked over at me for prompting. I shrugged my shoulders: it was his own credibility on the line. What did he expect me to do? "Honestly, Counselor, I can't see a thing inside. But I'm telling you I saw a gun that night."

"No further questions." Chimes smiled at me, content.

The one lesson I had finally assimilated after twenty trials and dozens of hearings was not to panic. I ignored His Honor's eyes staring me down and Chimes's mocking expression.

"Your Honor," I said, rising to my feet. "I ask that the defendant put on the jacket." I had no idea what would happen, but it was worth a try. "Mr. Chimes," said the judge, "please do as the assistant DA requests." Chimes's mockery curdled into fear as he pulled on the jacket. He looked down at the pocket still containing the gun. Nothing.

"Mr. Chimes," I asked, "would you please zipper the jacket closed?" He fastened the clasp at the bottom and slowly raised the zipper. He was fatter than he had appeared sitting at the counsel table, fat enough for his pot belly to press the gun's outline through the thin nylon shell.

"Now I can see it easily," McCabe spouted out. "I can even see that it's upside down." I walked over and gingerly removed the gun from Chimes's pocket. It was upside down.

Trial was scheduled for July. Then, one day in the interim, Bonamo called me with the news that Chimes was dead.

"How did he die?" I asked.

"Well, his father came to my office to let me know. He was pretty shaken up, but I understand Chimes walked out of his building and got his neck caught in some construction scaffolding. Something like that. Anyway, that kind of wraps things up."

In civil lawsuits, where money is involved, a judgment against a person survives their death and can be enforced against the deceased's estate. Criminal cases die with the defendant; a copy of the death certificate is filed in court and the matter is "abated by death." I filled out a subpoena requesting the certificate and sent it off. Though it was a selfish feeling, I was relieved at not having to take poor Mr. Chimes to trial, cross-examine him, and argue to a jury that this hard-working individual with a clean record should now be branded a felon.

Eventually, a letter from the Department of Health arrived in my mailbox. The certificate was in proper order —signed, sealed, and dated. Under "Cause of Death" it read, "Asphyxiation due to hanging. Suicide."

It was impossible to miss the significance of the prosecution I had so diligently pursued in Chimes's life and death. Before being arrested he was ready to embark on a new career as an electrician, hoping to better his lot. Maybe he would move out of the apartment he shared with his father and get married. Now, with the felony conviction before him, those dreams were crushed. The inflexible ADA, that serious young man at the hearing who had the power to dismiss charges with just a few words, seemed bent on squeezing every drop of blood from his case. Policy—what did it matter to Chimes compared to a new life? Why hadn't I relented? If Chimes had just sucked in his stomach at the hearing . . .

Not that I blamed myself for Chimes's suicide. There were myriad other forces invisible to me that must have pushed him over the brink of despair. Still, almost in memoriam, I had to pause to consider the powerful effect my decisions had on others' lives. It was vaguely sickening to know that day after day my energies were directed at meting out punishment, pursuing lawbreakers like a harpy. I comforted myself, as on other occasions: my job was defending victims, not just prosecuting criminals. But in Chimes's case the victim was too abstract an entity to afford me much ease.

After three years inside 100 Centre Street, stories that had once excited my imagination—robberies, assaults, murders, rapes—had begun to depress me. In court, in ECAB, in my office, I watched the fabric of the lives of both victims and defendants fray and unravel. Caring about victims was part of the job; it gave all the legal work a sense of purpose. But sympathy for defendants was an insidious shortcoming that had to be fought: it had no place in the prosecutorial mentality. To stay on much longer meant maintaining a blindered belief in the rectitude of our work, wanting to punish defendants, believing that our policies were all to the good: becoming the very sort of prosecutor I had always disliked and distrusted. It was time to leave.

TWENTY-FIVE

Time Served

Three months had passed since I left the DA's office. One evening, the night of the first snowfall that winter, a friend called asking for help: "Seth's wife got arrested downtown; they need a criminal lawyer. I figured since you used to work for the DA you could do something for her." Ten minutes later Seth called.

"God," he said breathlessly. "I don't know where to begin. Sarah didn't come home and then I got a call from the Ninth Precinct. I was told by a sergeant that she was arrested for buying drugs, I think pot, from a Rasta in Washington Square Park. But buying drugs on the street —it's just not in our family's vocabulary. Can you help me out?"

Though it was eleven at night, and taking the case meant driving through the snow like a country doctor on an errand of mercy, I agreed to do what I could. After calling the arraignment court, One Police Plaza, the Ninth Precinct, and the police room at the DA's office, I found that Sarah had already been taken to the pens. I put on the court clothes that had hung unworn in my closet since September and drove downtown. Across Tribeca the bulkhead of Criminal Court loomed out of the darkness, snow cutting diagonally across its regular, vertically fenestrated face. Inside, the gray-green hallway stretched toward arraignment court; two familiar court officers waved me past the police barricades and newly instituted metal detectors (apparently the officers hadn't noticed my absence); and the nightly groups of pimps, prostitutes, junkies, and defense lawyers milled about near the lists of cases taped to the wall. Upstairs in ECAB, I assumed, rookies were scribbling the same form complaints and climbing over more sleeping cops.

Sarah could have been shunted off to one of the secondary holding areas nearby and rendered almost impossible to find, but fortunately she was in the building. The arraignment court clerk filled out a slip of paper identifying me as Sarah's lawyer, and I headed toward one of the mysterious, rank-smelling tunnels where I had watched Legal Aid lawyers go to interview their clients, an area off limits to prosecutors. This would be my first trip inside the pens.

A corrections officer left me sitting in a hallway used for legal interviews while she went to get "the prisoner." Around a corner I glimpsed one of the holding cells—yellow-green tile, steel bars, defendants crammed shoulder to shoulder: the predictable squalor. I barely knew Sarah; we had met once over dinner a year ago. While waiting, I tried to recall her face: delicate, brown-eyed, a little French-looking, and very pretty.

The corrections officer returned with a wan, stringy-haired woman. "David, I'm so glad to see you," she said as she sat down next to me on the bench. "I didn't know who it would be when the officer said, 'Your lawyer's here.' "

"Sarah?" I asked, surprised that she recognized me so quickly.

She looked at the floor. "I guess I look pretty awful. I've been losing a lot of weight recently and I got sick twice in the pens. I couldn't keep my food down. But they've got me in a cell with a bunch of whores who've been really nice to me. They even tried to convince me to work the streets with them," she laughed. Her laugh became a hack and she doubled over. She was right: she looked awful. I was speaking to Sarah's shadow.

"Seth sent me down here. He's panicked about you, but I'll tell him you're doing all right."

"Can't he come see me?" Sarah asked.

"No, only lawyers. Now, listen, sometime tomorrow evening you're going to be arraigned by a judge, and you'll have to plead either guilty or not guilty. If you want, I'll represent you at the arraignment. If not, I understand."

Sarah nodded. "You can do it."

"Okay," I went on. "Tell me how you got arrested."

"They got me," she said. "I don't think there's much more to say."

"Seth told me you were busted for buying marijuana from a Rasta. Is that what happened?"

"No," she whispered, looking down at her feet. "It was smack. Three bags. I was buying from my regular dealer and the cops got us all—me, this other girl, and Carlos, my supplier. I've been going through withdrawal for the last three hours. I hope I can stand up when we go to court." She started to cry. "Seth doesn't know."

We talked about the arrest and the search, but there seemed to be no defense: Sarah would end up with a conviction on her record. With luck, I explained, she could plead to Disorderly Conduct and get Time Served. As I left, Sarah said, "Tell Seth I love him."

The following evening Seth and I came back to court for the arraignment. Nearly thirty hours had passed since Sarah's arrest, and Seth had worked himself into a frenzy of worry. We arrived at Centre Street five hours early, not knowing exactly when Sarah might be "produced," and as we paced outside AR-1, Seth ranted about suing the city for the delay and for keeping him from seeing his own wife.

Eventually I went inside to see the ADA about striking a deal. The arraignment courtroom had the same busy police-station look I remembered, the same smell of sweaty bodies, everything awash in a sea of brown floors, walls, tables, and pews.

I walked up to the rail behind a young woman working the prosecution table and introduced myself as Sarah's lawyer. After a minute of conversation it was obvious that she was a rookie on one of her first solo nights. I gave her the usual pitch: this is the defendant's first arrest, she's married to a respectable person, she wants to kick her habit, she has a regular job. Having listened to so many defense attorneys over the last three years, I fell right into the role. With a little prodding, she agreed to a Dis Con with time served.

The arraignment itself lasted about one minute. Sarah, deathly pale and unsteady on her feet, stood before the judge and admitted to being "disorderly." As promised, she got Time Served, and she stumbled out of court into Seth's embrace. God only knows how she became addicted to heroin without her husband knowing.

Had I been the prosecutor, her case would quickly have been lost among the hundreds of matters crossing my table in a night's work, but from the defense side I felt the pangs of Sarah's addiction, sensed her fear as she looked up at the judge: *Busted for heroin. My God, what are they going to do to me?* As I left 100 Centre Street that night, I recalled John Patton's comment from my rookie year: "They're only misdemeanors."

Whether out of circumspection or lack of interest, no one at the office ever asked why I wanted to leave, or rather, resign, as leaving was called. It was different from applying, when I had had to articulate my reasons. I simply walked into John Patton's office and announced my intentions. John seemed a little surprised but hardly taken aback. From early on I had sensed that I was temperamentally unsuited for the job, and no doubt it showed. After K-9's trial and Chimes's suicide I had been counting the weeks until September, the end of my informal three-year commitment. Assistants came and went—three years, five years; only a handful made a career of prosecuting. My departure was business as usual, nothing more. The following week I sent a memo to Mr. Morgenthau thanking him for the opportunity to serve. Five months later, Mr. Morgenthau sent me a kind letter thanking me for services rendered.

That final summer, however, still held a few surprises. One night, supervising ECAB, I spotted Sammy Magno's name on a misdemeanor cocaine-possession arrest. At my request, the arresting officer brought Sammy upstairs in handcuffs. His eyes swelled to the size of saucers when he saw me. I reported his arrest to Smokey and the Mental Hygiene authorities. Three weeks later Sammy stopped me on the street and gave me a calling card: HAVE GUN, WILL TRAVEL.

Another night, Kate and I drove into Manhattan via the Triborough Bridge. As we looked for our favorite pizza parlor in Spanish Harlem, I noticed a tall figure lurching through the dark crowds with an unmistakable gait. I drove around the block, and sure enough, it was K-9.

The two sisters attacked by Anthony Kibble came in and insisted on dropping charges.

Mitch Askew—who had lost a piece of scalp during a hatchet attack—had disappeared without a trace.

There were more convictions and a few acquittals.

In every neighborhood I recognized crime landmarks: the site of Andrew Sussmann's mugging, a woman's pursesnatch, the hand-hack case, pros corners, drug corners. I could have drawn a crime-watcher's map of Manhattan.

At the office, a new class of rookies arrived, bringing their electric enthusiasm to the job of holding back the flood of misdemeanors. An ever higher proportion of their cases involved drugs. The crack crisis was in full swing. With a sense of déjà vu I heard the newcomers' disappointed remarks about not carrying guns.

Jim Bronson, since our promotion to felonies, had thrown himself into work with ferocious intensity. He had a perfect win record, and his courtroom ability was already something of a legend. But our friendship had fallen by the wayside long ago, a casualty of our differing attitudes toward the job.

Roaming the halls during my last days, reassigning my remaining indictments, shaking hands, gossiping one last time with Ida, opening a few farewell gifts, I paid particular attention to the senior members of Bureau 20, career ADAs who had devoted their lives to indicting robbers, burglars, and gun-possessors along with high-level murderers and rapists. A few were tense, cynical sorts who seemed to revel in putting low-lifes "where they belong." But most stayed with the job, it appeared, because they believed sincerely that they were serving the public, protecting the city from wrongdoers. They loved prosecuting in an unquestioning way that I never could. It was doing God's work, they said, half jokingly.

I suppose the power we wielded over other people's lives made us feel as if we were the executors of morality. A word from us and a person goes free; another word and he is whisked away to the pens by court officers. We were judges of sorts, but also advocates—roles that were in some sense incompatible. And we had been handed power at an age when we were not likely to understand how to use it wisely. I still heard too much "lock up the sleaze" talk from rookies, and not enough worry over race relations, poverty, or rehabilitation. But at the same time, I had to admire those ADAs with enough stamina to face the pressures and frustrations year after year. They deserved respect for trying, in the face of an infinitely complex reality, to do justice.

There had been times when I wanted to slam the door behind me, but this was different. Somewhere, sometime the excitement and allure of the profession had drained away; my energetic enthusiasm had burned up. I had learned my trade: tried trials, interviewed roomfuls of witnesses and squadrons of police officers, listened to judges excoriate or laude me, watched victims storm out of my office and heard others call back months later to thank me for my diligence and kindness. The power I wielded bolstered me and weighed me down.

And in every direction innumerable aspects of the justice system cried out for reform: police misconduct, defense attorneys' delays, meaningless paperwork, the rubber-stamp grand jury, rigid strictures on sentencing, incarceration of psychiatric patients, insufficient numbers of judges and courtrooms, to name just a few of the more egregious problems. "The crisis in the courts," itself the result of too many cases, was also the product of broader social injustices: the inequitable distribution of wealth, the legacy of racism, bleak opportunities for minorities and the poor. None of these were any less a problem for my having spent three years as an agent of the system.

Looking back, however, I saw a few areas that could be readily improved: rookies should be encouraged to dismiss more of the marginal misdemeanor cases, so that serious matters can receive the attention they deserve; legalizing prostitution and marijuana, even though politically unpopular, would also help eliminate thousands more petty cases each year, cases that neither judges nor prosecutors take seriously, in any event.

The artificial misdemeanor-felony distinction should be reformed. Technical felons like Kenneth Chimes fall into a web of policies and limitations simply because their crimes are designated as felonies. And the current sentencing restrictions yield many absurd results: you may punch fifty strangers in the face, loosening teeth, blackening eyes, and bloodying noses, yet because the crimes are misdemeanors you cannot receive more than one year for each successive assault; by contrast, a petty thief who steals credit cards from purses left unattended by their owners—E felonies—faces a minimum of fifteen to twenty-five years and a maximum of life for his third offense.

The grand jury should be abolished, a change that would flow naturally from getting rid of the misdemeanor-felony categories. From what I saw, the grand jury accomplished little of substance other than to do the bidding of the state, yet it absorbed the time of thousands of citizens who might otherwise be freed to sit on ordinary juries. For the purpose of indictment, a single judge could just as easily pass on the merits of the prosecution's case.

Police officers should be fined every time they illegally search, question, or arrest a defendant. After a few offenses, they should be prosecuted. This might help cut back the dropsy syndrome—at least more than suppressing evidence in the few cases taken to hearings and won. Similarly, lawyers, both prosecutors and defenders, should be disciplined for the misrepresentations and countless undue delays that jam the wheels of justice. And judges, too, should be held more accountable for their abusive and callous behavior on the bench. Everyone stands when they enter the room. Silence reigns when they pound a fist. Defendants say, "Thank you, Your Honor," when judges send them to jail for "only" five to ten. Power has its effects and needs a counterbalance.

But prosecuting did not lend itself easily to analysis or reform. Keeping pace and some degree of perspective took all my energy. I left One Hogan Place with a sigh but without regrets.

On my last day, the members of Bureau 20 assembled at Forlini's for a long, drunken farewell luncheon chaired by John Patton. Arnold Weinberg had joined a West Coast law firm; Nancy White had left to work for the Environmental Protection Agency in Colorado; I went off to write. The rest of my colleagues stayed on to try heavier cases, eventually go out on homicide call, maybe make deputy bureau chief. My former officemate Annette Holt continued happily in Appeals; Scott Pryor returned to the office after finally passing the bar exam. There was much cheering and well-wishing all around.

Kate joined me that afternoon as I cleared out my desk, handed in my district attorney's identification card, and